THE CHURCHES AND MONASTERIES OF THE ṬUR ʻABDIN

THE CHURCHES AND MONASTERIES OF THE ṬUR 'ABDIN

GERTRUDE BELL

With an introduction and notes
by Marlia Mundell Mango

The Pindar Press
London 1982

Published by The Pindar Press
66 Lyncroft Gardens
London NW6 1JY

British Library Cataloguing in Publication Data

Bell, Gertrude
The churches and monasteries of the Tur 'Abdin
1. Church architecture–Tur 'Abdin
1. Title 2. Mango, Marlia Mundell
726'.5'09566 NA5861

ISBN 0-907132-08-1

Printed in Great Britain by Staples Printers
The Stanhope Press, Rochester, Kent

CONTENTS

PREFACE

Gertrude Lowthian Bell, the well-known explorer and archaeologist, began her extensive travels in the Near East in 1892. On two of her journeys, those of 1909 and 1911, she surveyed and photographed the monuments of the Ṭur 'Abdin in Turkish Mesopotamia. Hers remains the fullest published study on the subject, and preserves the only detailed record of some of the monuments which have been destroyed since her time (the two churches at Mayafarqin, Mar Cosmas at Diyarbakır, Mar Malka near Midyat and Mar Tahmazgerd at Kerkuk in Iraq). The two studies reprinted here are supplemented by the account of her travels of 1909 given in *Amurath to Amurath* (London, 1911), her unpublished journals and photographs now kept at the University of Newcastle upon Tyne, and her notebooks in the Royal Geographical Society in London. While most of her notes and plans of these monuments went into her published work, many photographs remained unpublished. Some of these are included here, 128 in all, while others, particularly those of the medieval Islamic monuments of northern Mesopotamia, await proper study. The title of her second work on the Ṭur 'Abdin was enlarged to include "Neighbouring Districts", with principal reference to the Christian monuments of northern Mesopotamia. Her travels there and in the Ṭur 'Abdin coincided with those of the German archaeologist Conrad Preusser, who apparently had prior claim to publish Deir Za'faran, Dara and Nisibis. A selection of her photographs of these sites as well as some from Osrhoëne (Urfa, Viranşehir and the Tektek Mountains) have been included here in order to present a fuller record of her work and the architectural context of the monuments of the Ṭur 'Abdin.

The contents of the book are as follows. The two studies by Gertrude Bell appear together at the beginning of the volume. Their text has, for technical reasons, been reset rather than reproduced photographically. Consequently, the photographs which were originally within the text of the first study have been withdrawn and placed at the end of the book together with those of the second study and the previously unpublished photographs. This reorganization has allowed for a greater integration of the illustrations which are now arranged by individual monument. The photographs have been divided into two groups—those of antique cities and those of the villages, monasteries and forts. The reasons for this distinction are made evident in the Introduction to the book. Within the two groups, the photographs are arranged alphabetically by site. Photographs published here for the first time are indicated by asterisks in the List of Illustrations. In resetting the text, the original spellings of proper names, sometimes inconsistent between the two studies, have been left.

The plans and most drawings have been left within the text. Gertrude Bell's footnotes, however, have been removed from the bottom of the page and inserted into the text in parentheses. The footnote numbers, which now appear in the text, refer to my annotations which are placed after the second article. These notes primarily indicate subsequent publications and cross reference between the two studies published here; some commentary is also included. The other alteration to the original text has been the translation, from German, of the captions to the illustrations of the first study.

Following the notes is a Catalogue of Sites which serves two purposes. One is to supply information about sites and monuments of which Gertrude Bell did not herself publish her photographs, but which are included in this book. For descriptions of this material I have relied chiefly, when possible, on her journals and notebooks. The second purpose of this Catalogue is to provide an alphabetized reference to all of the sites studied in this book. The entries in this Catalogue give the relevant text pages and illustrations for each monument; a bibliography; building dates by inscriptions and texts; changes to the monument since 1911, where known; and a short summary of work published hitherto on it. In the cases where Gertrude Bell has discussed a particular monument in both her studies, I have repeated the principal points within this summary. Within the Catalogue are a number of additional plans, two of which are newly published here from Gertrude Bell's notebooks. For the Catalogue entries I have given alternative versions of place and proper names, the present Turkish names being italicised. The principal place name, in most cases, is that used by Gertrude Bell in her text. I thank Sebastian Brock for his help in making a final selection of names. I apologize, however, for whatever inconsistencies in spelling remain, as for instance between the text of the Gertrude Bell studies and the captions to the figures. The volume concludes with a Short Glossary, a List of Dated Monuments, an Administrative List of Provinces, a Map and the Illustrations.

The previously unpublished photographs and excerpts from Gertrude Bell's journals are reproduced by permission of the University of Newcastle upon Tyne, which holds the copyright for this material. Further notes and plans made by Bell are published here by permission of the Royal Geographical Society, London. I should like to extend my thanks in the first instance to Professor R.M. Harrison and Mr. Stephen Hill of the University of Newcastle upon Tyne, to Dr. S. Brock of the University of Oxford and to my husband, Professor Cyril Mango, for their encouragement and help. For assistance on various points connected with this study, I should also like to thank Dr. J. Allan, Mr. G. House, Abbé J. Leroy, Dr. W.H. Plommer, Mrs. L. Roberts, Professor J.B. Segal, Mr. T. Sinclair, Mr. M. Vickers and Mr. M. Whitby.

MARLIA MUNDELL MANGO
February 1979

THE ṬUR 'ABDIN: AN INTRODUCTION

Geography and History

The Ṭur 'Abdin, literally "the mountain of the servants (of God)"– "the Mount Athos of the east" as it has been called – may be compared to another holy mountain, that of Sinai, in the continuous use of its shrines over nearly a millennium and a half, in spite of Muslim rule during most of this period. The survival of its Christian communities may be explained in part by its self-contained and elevated situation away from the major cross-roads of northern Mesopotamia. This latter area I am loosely interpreting as the Roman land lying between the Tigris and Euphrates rivers, an area somewhat smaller than the al Jazira of the Arab geographers. Towards the north (map p. 185), our area of principal concern in this book, this land mass is dominated by the volcanic Karaca Dağ and a basalt plateau which has Diyarbakır near its centre. To the southwest of this the limestone region between Urfa and Viranşehir is intersected from north to south by the low hills of the Tektek Dağ; to the southeast stretch the limestone hills of Mardin, and beyond them to the east the stony plateau of the Ṭur 'Abdin (also called Mount Masius or Izla), which at its eastern extremity is composed of basalt and on its southern edge falls steeply into the Mesopotamian plain below. The entire area is watered by seasonal rivers which flow north into the Tigris and south into the Khabur and then the Euphrates rivers. The Ṭur 'Abdin lies along the eastern flank of the triangle formed by the ancient cities of Amida, Edessa and Nisibis. Its perimeter is formed on the north and east by the Tigris and on the west and south by a line running south to Mardin Dağ and then east to Cezre. The cities ringed around its edges are Hasan Keyf, Mardin, Dara, Nisibis and Cezre; Diyarbakır is ca. 40 km northwest and Mayafarqin is 40 km north.

For nearly one thousand years, between its conquest by Alexander and the arrival of the Arabs, northern Mesopotamia was part of the frontier area between the Graeco-Roman and Persian worlds. It was inhabited by Arameans, Arabs, Kurds, Jews, and colonists from Macedonia, and dominated by the eastern and western empires in turn. Under the Seleucids it formed a bridge between their eastern and western capitals on the Tigris and Orontes respectively. This dynasty is associated with the foundation of Edessa and Nisibis, both called Antioch, but these cities, as well as Mardin, Harran and Batnae, were undoubtedly more ancient. The Parthians took control of the region in B.C. 140 and the Romans in A.D. 165. In A.D. 363 the emperor Jovian ceded Nisibis to Persia and the frontier between the two empires was redrawn. This new frontier has a direct bearing on our subject because it would have placed the Ṭur 'Abdin in either Persian (according to Honigmann) or Roman (according to Dillemann) territory. The *limes* as traced by Dillemann is that indicated on the map below (p. 185), and it places most of the Ṭur 'Abdin in Roman territory, a fact also stated in an account of the history of the monastery of Mar Gabriel (Nau, "Notice", 51) which Dillemann was unable to consult (p. 229 note 1). What is left outside the *limes* is the eastern edge of the Ṭur 'Abdin along the Tigris and the lower fringe of the plateau, where lay the Nestorian monasteries subject to Nisibis.[1]

The organization of the ecclesiastical administration of most of northern Mesopotamia according to the *Notitia Antiochena* of A.D. 570 is given below (p. 159). Whether it corresponded exactly to the civic provinces at that time is unclear (Jones, *LRE*, III, 294 note 8). Before A.D. 363, the province of Mesopotamia, with its capital at Amida, included both Nisibis and the territory of South Mesopotamia which encompassed the Ṭur 'Abdin. Following Jovian's treaty, Nisibis became the main city of the Persian province of Beth 'Arabaye. When hostilities between Persia and Byzantium were renewed in the late fifth century, the emperor Anastasius sought to replace the lost strategic advantage of Nisibis by constructing, between 505 and 507, the city of Dara, which became the residence of the Dux of Mesopotamia (507–532, 540–573), the military headquarters of the Byzantine army in the East (527–532) and a bishopric (from 507). By 553 it is known as a metropolitan bishopric, and it has been suggested that this elevation took place between 514 and 518. The *Notitia Antiochena* of 570 lists as the suffragan bishoprics of Dara, "Theodosiopolis (= Resh'aina), Turabdion, and Mnasoubion or (?) Banasymeon" (Honigman, *BZ*, 75, 83 f.). "Turabdion" would seem to refer to the Ṭur 'Abdin and it was also the name (tou rhabdiou) of a *limes* fort at present identified with Qal'at Ḥatem Ṭay (p. 145). The Mar Gabriel monastery (which had Symeon as a titular saint from the fifth century) has been identified as the fort of Banasymeon, and it is therefore interesting to note a bishopric of the same name. There is some evidence presented below (p.111f.) that Ḥaḥ too may have been a bishopric at this period.

The repeated military conflicts between the Romans and Persians spanned the sixth and early seventh centuries and coincided with the religious persecutions, which began in earnest in the early sixth. When in the fifth century the Nestorian (i.e. the East Syrian) and Monophysite (i.e. the Syrian Orthodox) churches split off from the Byzantine Orthodox church (called subsequently in the east the Melkite – or king's – church) the former generally found adherents on the Persian side of the frontier and the latter on the Roman. While the first group was safely held outside the empire, a situation eventually prescribed by an imperial treaty in A.D. 562, the second group was relentlessly persecuted. The Monophysites had briefly enjoyed legitimacy under Anastasius, but after the death of that emperor in 518, Severus, the Monophysite Patriarch of Antioch, and his entire hierarchy were forced into exile. The subsequent hardships suffered by the Monophysites of northern Mesopotamia were recorded by John of Ephesus, originally a monk of Amida, and the history of the Mar Gabriel monastery relates the invasion of that monastery by patriarchal troops and the exile of the monks to Singar and elsewhere. In the mid-sixth century the Monophysite Christians of Syria and northern Mesopotamia were provided with a reorganized church called "Jacobite" in honour of Jacob Baradaeus, who was responsible for many of its ordinations. Both Persian and Byzantine rulers continued to interfere in ecclesiastical affairs by replacing one set of bishops by another. In 629 Heraclius, fresh from his conquest of the Persians, threw out the Monophysite bishops installed by Chosroes II in favour of Melkites. Within ten years the Arabs had taken Mesopotamia and declared that the cathedral churches were to remain in hands of the current incumbents, who were in most cases Heraclius' Melkites. This state of affairs led eventually to a period of building activity, when a number of Jacobite bishops sought to provide themselves with cathedral churches.

Building Conditions Before and After 640

For the first time in nearly a thousand years the frontier beside which the Ṭur 'Abdin lay was removed by the Arab conquest. The frontier had been the arena for a variety of political and military operations, which had a direct bearing on the building activities there. Conditions for Chrisitian building changed after 640: not only were Byzantine subsidies cut off, but the new Muslim rulers sometimes, as might be expected, played an obstructing role. Before the conquest the tactical sophistication deployed by the Persian enemy had required that Byzantine military architecture on the eastern frontier be inventive as well as solidly constructed. Furthermore, a succession of floods and earthquakes in the sixth century left a number of cities in need of large-scale restorations. The construction work sponsored by Anastasius on the eastern frontier – his foundation of Dara has just been mentioned – is less well known than that of Justinian, which was very well publicised by the historian Procopius; in the latter's *Buildings* one finds a lengthy description of the refortification of Dara, of which he had first-hand knowledge. In the area covered by the present book, Procopius catalogued building activity at: Dara, Amida (Diyarbakır), Rhabdios (Qal'at Hatem Tay ?), Sauras (Savur), Theodosiopolis (Resh'aina), Constantina (Tella, Viranşehir), Cepha (Hasan Keyf), Margdis (Mardin), Banasymeon (Mar Gabriel ?), Sinas (Fafi), Edessa (Urfa), Carrhae (Harran), Batnae (Sarug) (Book II); and Martyropolis (Mayafarqin) (Book III). The ecclesiastical arm of the Byzantine government was also responsible for many building projects. By the fifth century the church had grown rich and powerful, and many resources were concentrated in the hands of the bishops, who undertook secular (see e.g. p. 154) as well as church construction. The possibility of a Melkite "episcopal architecture" in the Patriarchate of Antioch has been proposed by Kleinbauer, who has examined as a group the fifth- to sixth-century aisled tetraconch churches which stand from Amida to Bosra. Monophysites were the recipients of imperial largesse from Anastasius (491-518) and Theodora (527-548). Monasteries also grew in size, number and importance, particularly for Monophysites in times of persecution. John of Ephesus gives some idea of the magnitude of monastic communities in Amida, and also describes how monks exiled from that city as well as Edessa built monasteries "around Dara", which may refer in part to the Ṭur 'Abdin. The monks exiled from Mar Gabriel also built new monasteries. Anastasius is credited with building at Mar Gabriel, and Justinian restored a number of monasteries in Mesopotamia named by Procopius (those of Delphrachis, Zebinus, Theodotus, Sarmathe, Cyrenus, Begadaeus and two of John).

The Arab conquest cut off Byzantine patronage in northern Mesopotamia. In general the fortunes of the Mesopotamian Christians fluctuated according to the policies of individual Islamic rulers. A principal area of concern was the building of churches. A document called the Covenant of 'Omar, which contains the Christian promise "not to build a church, convent, hermitage or cell, nor repair those that are dilapidated", has been shown to be later than 'Omar I (634-644) and may instead be associated with 'Omar II (717-720). The covenant contradicts the spirit of early treaties made by the Umayyads with cities like Homs, in which they promised to "give them security for their persons, property, the city wall, the churches and the mill". During the first one hundred and fifty years [2] of Islamic rule only the brief reign of 'Omar II witnessed opposition to church building and not until A.H. 239 (A.D. 853) did Mutawakkil put into law for the first time such a ban. But this law was not consistently enforced, and Tritton in his survey of Christian building activity traces the changing pattern of encouragement and obstruction by both state authorities and mobs. In addition to the opportunity to build, Christians had sufficient financial resources, though not on the same scale as in the sixth century, Christian bureaucrats continued to hold high office under the Arabs, as did Athanasius bar Gumaye of Edessa, an extremely rich merchant, an office-holder in Egypt and a treasurer to 'Abd el 'Aziz, who is known to have built in ca. 700 several churches including a magnificent one dedicated to the Mother of God in his native city. From the seventh century on, Jacobite merchants of Tagrit in Iraq were responsible for the patronage of churches and manuscripts in many quarters from Malatya and Harran to Egypt. The eponymous Mar Gabriel (593-667), abbot and bishop of the monastery near Qarṭamin, was granted in 639 a charter by the Caliph 'Omar which allowed him to build churches and monasteries and gave him power from the "Ṭur 'Abdin as far as Babel." The prosperity of this monastery was undoubtedly increased by the donations of property mady to it by Symeon d-Zayte, formerly a monk there, who became bishop of Harran (700-734). He built and restored a number of churches in his native Ḥabsenas, at Nisibis, and elsewhere, planted large olive groves (hence his name) and constructed mills and villages in the Ṭur 'Abdin (see pp. 109 and 137). As mentioned above, the Arab decision to leave cathedral churches in the hands of Melkites in 640, led some Jacobite bishops to build new churches. The list of dated monuments on p. 162 below illustrates the continuation of construction after 640 and some of the churches surveyed by Gertrude Bell date from that period.

The Monuments

There are two broad problems concerning the monuments of northern Mesopotamia and especially of the Ṭur 'Abdin: 1) their dates (in general whether they were built before or after the Arab conquest); and 2) the architectural types (for the Ṭur 'Abdin this has been discussed in terms of either Persian or Syrian influences).

Dating

Inscriptions and published historical sources have until now provided only limited information, as may be seen from the preliminary list of dated monuments on pp. 161f. Though far from complete, this list conveys the impression that until the Arab conquest most of our knowledge is confined to the cities – Nisibis, Amida, Edessa, etc. – rather than the Ṭur 'Abdin and that this trend is reversed somewhat after 640. This imbalance may be due, in part, to an insufficient effort to collect inscriptions. So far the Ṭur 'Abdin has yielded no dated building inscription before 640, but the fact that three from the subsequent period (691, 740, 751) have only recently been discovered gives some hope of future finds. As noted below, continued work on the local written records should sift out the legendary from the more reliable, and produce much useful information. For monuments securely dated before the Arab conquest one must, therefore, turn to the neighbouring cities. Of particular importance in this respect are the remains at Dara, which was the metropolitan bishopric exercising authority over the Ṭur 'Abdin and which preserves remnants of building activity documented to 505-7 and *ca.* 530. Indeed, legendary accounts ascribe to the architects "Theodosius and Theodore, sons of Shufani", the building of both Dara in 505-7 (Bar Hebraeus, Appendix, p. xxiii) and the main church at Mar Gabriel in 512 (Nau, "Notice", 22).

While buildings securely dated to the period before the Arab conquest in the Ṭur 'Abdin are scarce or non-existant, a number can be assigned to the Umayyad and Abbasid periods (pp. 162f.) and these may be of great value to architectural historians.

Gertrude Bell was the first to pose the question of dates after the Arab conquest for some of the major Ṭur 'Abdin churches (pp. 82f. below). Herzfeld repeated this possibility, and suggested that the primary value of the monuments of the Ṭur 'Abdin may lie in their links with Islamic architecture rather than as the forerunners of global Christian architecture as postulated by Strzygowski. The churches of the seventh and eighth centuries may well provide instructive comparisons with the late Umayyad mosque at Harran (750) and may also help somewhat to fill the gap, pointed out by Creswell, which exists in Persian architecture between Qasr-i-Shirin (590-628) and the Baghdad Gate at Raqqah (772).

Least explored in the Ṭur 'Abdin are churches built entirely in the style of the later medieval Islamic architecture of northern Mesopotamia. The churches published here are mostly earlier buildings endlessly restored and altered, and sometimes rebuilt; among the most disturbed monuments in this book are those at Arnas and Kefr Zeh. The field of Oriental Christian architecture in the medieval period is one that, except perhaps in Iraq, has been little explored. Northern Mesopotamia, with its numerous dated Islamic constructions at Mardin, Hasan Keyf, Mayafarqin, Diyarbakır, and Dunaysir, preserves a wealth of comparable material for such a study. The fifty-odd churches built and rebuilt in the twelfth century by the bishop of Mardin, for example, may prove a rewarding area of research.

Architectural Types

The second problem concerning the monuments considered here, that of architectural type, has perhaps been more clearly formulated for the Ṭur 'Abdin than for northern Mesopotamia in general. The latter has been somewhat neglected as an area of systematic research. Krautheimer lumped it together with the Ṭur 'Abdin and demoted it from "province" to "borderland" where "popular forces cling to isolationist folk ways." Some steps have been taken to correct this distortion, notably by Deichmann, Peschlow and C. Mango, but much work remains to be done, particularly in the field. Ideally, both the military and ecclesiastical architecture should be studied together. As noted above, the local rock was limestone in many places (Urfa, Nisibis, Mardin, Ṭur 'Abdin, etc.) and basalt in others (Diyarbakır, Cezre); a mixture of both was used at Viranşehir; extensive quarries are found at Dara. Clay was available (see note 30 on bricks), as was wood (poplar, oak) in some areas. The masonry is ashlar (single-faced and double-faced with rubble core) with some brick and rough stone work. The roofing was of timber (basilica at Mayafarqin) and masonry (St. Sophia, Edessa). Circuit walls still stand at Dara, Diyarbakır, Mayafarqin, Urfa and Viranşehir; bridges are illustrated here at Dara, Nisibis, and Urfa; there are various large cisterns (e.g. Dara) and *horrea* (Viranşehir and Dara).

The city churches of northern Mesopotamia are not well known. The cathedral at Nisibis (313–20) leaves behind only its baptistery (359) converted later into a church (713-758). At least one of the Diyarbakır churches (el 'Adhra) had a centralized plan, as did that of the domed St. Sophia at Edessa (*ca.* 525). The large circular building with an octagonal interior, which stands outside Viranşehir was probably a church. Dara preserves parts of basilical-shaped and centralized (?) structures. Mar Cosmas at Diyarbakır may have been originally a basilica, while the only certain example of a basilica was at Mayafarqin, which also had a centralized church. Excavations at Harran have partially uncovered a basilical church of uncertain date. The only medieval churches published from these cities are that in the citadel at Diyarbakır, the north church at

Nisibis, and possibly, the el 'Adhra at Mayafarqin.

Thanks to Gertrude Bell, the churches of the Ṭur 'Abdin have been better recorded, studied and classified than those of the cities, even if there is much room for revision and enlargement of this work. The basic classification is quite simple: 1) churches which are long from east to west; and 2) those which are broad from north to south. Both are nearly always barrel-vaulted. Bell (p. 56 and note 152) called the first type "parochial" and the second "monastic" because in most cases their function seemed to coincide with their form. The "parochial" type is represented here by at least twenty churches and chapels and is of longitudinal plan with the entrance on the south, outside of which there is often an oratory called a *beth ṣlotha* (see p. x). The nave has a brick barrel-vault which rests upon arcades built flush against the north and south walls of the church. This architecture has been interpreted in a variety of ways. In the cases of Arnas and Kefr Zeh, Bell hesitated as to whether the arcades and vaults were original or added. In Mar Sovo at Ḥaḥ she decided they were later and that the church was originally single-naved without arcades and had a wooden roof. She designated this the prototype of the other "parochial" churches, but made the important distinction that at Arnas and Kefr Zeh the churches were designed with vaults and arcades.

This assessment was taken at face value by Reuther and Monneret de Villard, who both related the Ṭur 'Abdin churches to barrel-vaulted Sassanian churches, particularly those excavated at Ctesiphon and Hira. Another school of thought links the "parochial" churches to Syria. Guyer deduced that the churches at Arnas and Kefr Zeh as well as Mar Sovo were originally timber-roofed hall churches, a hypothesis recently repeated by Deichmann and Peschlow who have suggested a possible prototype in just such a church at Kale-i Zerzevan between Mardin and Diyarbakır, and, of course, in northern Syria. The timber-roofed basilica at Mayafarqin testifies to the penetration of that Syrian church type north of the Ṭur 'Abdin and what was said to be a replica copy of Basilica B at Rusafa, with ashlar masonry and timber roof, was imported ca. 550 by a Monophysite bishop into Singar just south of the Tur 'Abdin. It is extremely interesting to note in the present context that the latter church still preserves the evidence of its conversion at an unknown period from timber roof to masonry barrel-vault (see p. 125).

The problem presented in the "parochial" churches by the original nave windows now blocked by the later barrel vaults, e.g., at Mar Philoxenus and Kefr Zeh, is best resolved in theory by reconstructing either a timber roof or a very steep barrel vault; but the former seems the more likely possibility. The present arcades (e.g. Fig. 34) of the "parochial" church naves serve to reduce the span to be vaulted. This principle could apply equally to timber roofs, particularly as small oak is the type of wood available around Midyat. The church at Kale-i Zerzevan, which has been proposed as a prototype of the "parochial" church of the Ṭur 'Abdin, has no arcades, but its timber roof covered a nave only 6 m. across. The naves of Arnas, Kefr Zeh and Mar Philoxenus, however, measure ca. 8.50 to 9 m across from wall to wall and their present arcades reduce the width to an average of 6 m. While some of the present arcades are clearly later additions, there is evidence that the south arcade at Arnas, for example, may be contemporary with the apse and therefore original. The roofing span between this arcade and a reconstructed north arcade may be calculated as *ca.* 7 m. Wood long enough to span the central nave (w. 10.90 m.) of the Mayafarqin basilica was obviously available for this expensive church and the same may have been true of Mar Sovo at Ḥaḥ (w. 11.26 m.), which may have been a cathedral church and which apparently does not preserve evidence of early responds for lateral arcades (p. 112). A need for economy in ordinary village churches may explain their internal arcades. The local wood, oak, may have yielded building lumber in lengths comparable to the 6-7 m. roof span of these church naves: the cheapest timbers listed in Diocletian's price edict were oak and ash, at 250 denarii for lengths of 7 yards. Oak is, however, very heavy and the arcades may have provided better support for the cross beams than the series of wall brackets usually found in basilicas. The wooden roof at Mar Dodo collapsed in 1474 because "they had placed no pillars under it" (see p. 100). The arcades supporting a timber roof in a small building at Ḥaḥ (p. 113) may reflect an established building practise borrowed from larger edifices since the width of this chamber is a mere 3.17 m. I would tentatively suggest as a working hypothesis that the "parochial" village churches were modelled on the wooden-roofed cathedral (?) of Mar Sovo, but were adapted with internal arcades to the demands of a short, cheap and heavy timber. At a later period these churches were remodelled with larger arcades bearing low barrel-vaults.

The chronology of the "parochial" churches needs to be reviewed. Mar Sovo would seem, on the basis of its sculpture, to be of the early sixth century. The other buildings either lack dates – e.g., Kefr Zeh, Mar Ibrahim, Mar Yoḥannan, and Mar Philoxenus at Midyat – or are known to have been built or rebuilt at a late period – e.g., Mar Dodo (1199, 1474), Mar Awgen (1271), and Kefr Beh (1465). The vault at Arnas dates in part to 1591/2. There are, however, a number of related monuments of the eighth century– i.e. Mar Symeon (700-734) at Ḥabsenas, the north church (713-757) of Mar Ya'qub at Nisibis, and, perhaps, Mar Addai (772 ?) at Heshterek, as well as parts of the church at Kefr Beh. These churches, which are all included here, merit closer examination and comparison with the better-known "parochial" churches.

The second type of church, the "monastic", is represented here by seven examples. It is nearly square in plan with a nave at its widest from north to south, three separate chambers to the east, and a narthex to the west. Low, heavy arcades, reminiscent of *arcisolia*, are flush against the north, south, and west walls, and from the west and east walls springs a barrel vault. There is (with one exception) no oratory (*beth ṣlotha*) outside. Two buildings of this type have been dated: the main church at Mar Gabriel to 512 by a written source, and Surp Hagop, at Kaishum west of the Euphrates, to 813-845 by inscription. The el 'Adhra at Ḥaḥ (which is not known to have been a monastery) presents a variation of this barrel vaulted type by converting the lateral curtain walls into squinch-supported semi-domes under an octagonal dome on a drum. Most writing on the "monastic" church has centered on problems of dating (e.g. Guyer, Baumstark) or the question of prototypes (e.g. Guyer, Herzfeld, Monneret de Villard) which may range from ancient Near Eastern *bit hilani* (as per Bell) to Nabatean temples in Sinai. The transverse nave and separated sanctuary of the "monastic" church resemble somewhat certain sixth-century monastic buildings of northern Syria, especially near Apamea. These have been identified by Tchalenko (I, 178–182) as composed of a broad (north to south) communal room with a single square oratory projecting from the east. Deichmann and Peschlow noted the similarities between these Syrian buildings and Mar Ya'qub south of Urfa (before 521) which also has a separate east chamber. These authors see in the architecture of Edessa, as reflected in this latter monastery, a plausible point of contact between the monastic oratories of northern Syria and "monastic" churches of northern Mesopotamia. The Syrian buildings, however, are timber roofed, and those of Mesopotamia barrel vaulted; furthermore, the sanctuary of the "monastic" church is tripartite.

One church in the Ṭur 'Abdin that does not fall easily into either major category is that of Deir Za'faran. Although it resembles in its triconch elevation the el 'Adhra at Ḥaḥ, the latter, of course, is nearly square in plan (exclusive of the narthex). The Deir Za'faran church, however, has three apses in plan and is massively constructed with walls

2.35 m. thick. The hypothesis has been presented elsewhere that it was originally constructed to bear a dome and that its model may have been the St. Sophia church in Edessa (rebuilt *ca.* 525) which had a masonry dome on squinches. The Deir Za'faran church is also of the sixth century, judging by its sculpture.

In the courtyard of what are called the "parochial" churches of the Ṭur 'Abdin (as well as the "monastic" church at Deir Ṣaliba) often stand apsed exedras which are called *beth ṣlotha*, i.e. "house of prayer", oratories where, at least in modern times, service is celebrated in summer. All the examples recorded here are built of stone in the same fashion: an open, free-standing apse inscribed on three sides in a square. The façade is defined by vertical frames at the outer edges (Pls. 105, 185) which may have originally continued along the top. The archivolt is often profiled and rests on capitals and columns or on the cornice from which the apse conch springs. There is usually a large cross carved in the conch (Pls. 126, 185), as in a number of Ṭur 'Abdin church apses (Pl. 158). The earliest dated example in this book of a *beth ṣlotha* may be that at Heshterek (A.D. 772, see p. 118, Pl. 151) whose interior walls bear thirty commemorative inscriptions and under whose floor there may be burials indicating perhaps a funerary function in addition to that of holding summer services. Commemorative inscriptions are found in other *beth ṣlotha*. In this connection it is interesting to note the similiarities between the latter and some tomb façades at Dara (Pl. 8): framed façades, and arched openings with columns and capitals. The *beth ṣlotha* of the Ṭur 'Abdin differs in form, placement and function from the oratories of Syrian monasteries (see above), but their consistent placement to the south of the church is in common with the development of the south martyrial chapels in northern Syria (Lassus, *Sanctuaires*, 161-180).

As concerns the decoration of the northern Mesopotamian churches, the one surviving example of a typical, richly-ornamented Early Christian church is that at Mar Gabriel which still retains on its sanctuary walls and vault mosaics of good quality, illustrating a vine trellis, crosses and two non-figural compositions, as well as a marble opus-sectile pavement. It seems probable that the lower walls were revetted in marble. There is evidence for further wall mosaics in the church. The total absence from the church of architectural sculpture, which is the principal extant form of decoration of the other churches of this book, sets the Mar Gabriel church apart. Further evidence of external intervention may be the mosaic inscription which is the only one in Greek thus far known in the villages and monasteries of the Ṭur 'Abdin. The wealth of its mosaics and marbles has understandably been attributed to imperial patronage, that of Anastasius in 512. The larger city churches must have had comparable embellishments, partially preserved in Mar Cosmas, Diyarbakir, and attested in the case of St. Sophia at Edessa.

Remains of marble sculpture at Diyarbakir and Mayafarqin are illustrated here (Pls. 19, 22, 48, 50), but most of the extant church architectural sculpture is in limestone. The buildings of northern Mesopotamia, including the Ṭur 'Abdin, are noted for their late-antique style mouldings. Exterior doorways usually have profiled door frames and relieving arches which could be described as omega-shaped (Pl. 246). Other external decoration includes engaged pilasters (Pl. 133), arcades (ibid.), niches (Pls. 190–193) and inhabited compositions (Pls. 154, 189). Interior mouldings are elaborately ornamented and sometimes continuous (Pls. 79, 194–197). Continuous mouldings (in one case ornamented) are also found on a few exteriors (Pls. 74–76, 151, 188). The ornaments include some variations on the standard repertory in the form of darts as diagonal arrows, dentils as crenellations (or in the Ṭur 'Abdin, dentils in double alternating rows) and split palmettes, as well as a pulvinated frieze carved with a vine scroll often originating from an amphora. These scrolls take basically two forms – an undulating vine with alternating grapes and leaves, and a crossed vine with oval loops enclosing grapes and leaves. The first type is found mostly on monuments that are probably sixth-century (see p. 134) in both city (e.g. Deir Za'faran, Pls. 194–197) and village (Ḥaḥ, Pl. 122), and is continued in a debased form in the Theotokos church at Ḥaḥ of A.D. 740 (Pl. 147). The second type also decorates monuments of both city (Nisibis, A.D. 359, Pl. 79) and village (Ṣalaḥ, on pilasters instead of cornice, Fig. 28). This second type is continued in a reduced, schematized form at el 'Adhra at Ḥaḥ (Pl. 140), Arnas (Pl. 101) and Deir Ṣaliba (Pl. 187). The most complete extant monuments with extensive interior ornamentation are Mar Ya'qub at Nisibis and Deir Za'faran. A large body of the same type of sculpture has also been found at Rusafa below the Euphrates.

Most capitals are acanthus (both cut and uncut) and are often garlanded (e.g. Pls. 20, 246:see Kautzsch, 215–221). Examples of the acanthus capital extend in our area from the second or third century (citadel capitals, Urfa) to the sixth (e.g. Deir Za'faran) and beyond (el 'Adhra, Ḥaḥ, Pl. 143). The persistence of such capitals into the sixth century and later is considered a regional peculiarity since by the 520's capitals in Constantinople and elsewhere were adorned with increasingly abstract patterns while the old classical repertory was abandoned. At least three main-stream Byzantine capital types or examples of carving style are noted in this book. One type is found at Dara (Pl. 7) and Diyarbakır (Pl. 19), while the other two types are on the Persian side of the frontier, in the orbit of Nisibis: at Mar Ibrahim ("Theodosian" leaves: Pl. 220) and Mar Awgen (two-zone basket capital: pp. 3f). To this third type are probably related the basket cornice bosses (Pls. 194, 196–7) at Deir Za'faran and what are probably later plaited capitals (Pls. 66, 67a, 83: see Kautzsch, 231f.). Some of the sculpture at Mayafarqin is related to Byzantine as well as to Ayyubid and Armenian carving of the medieval period (Pls. 51–53, 63, 65).

An outstanding feature of sculpture in the Ṭur 'Abdin are the large crosses carved in relief in the apse conch of both churches and *beth ṣlotha* (see above). The earliest extant example may be that in Mar Sovo at Ḥaḥ, probably of the early sixth century (Pl. 121). Similar crosses are known in Thrace, Lycia and Cappadocia (Mundell, "Decoration", 66 note 79).

MARLIA MUNDELL MANGO
February 1979

1. Because this fringe area is represented in this book by only a small number of monuments, the focus of the introduction is upon the Byzantine and Monophysite aspects of the frontier region, whereas a fuller treatment would do equal justice to the Sassanian and Nestorian.

2. See also Fattal, 34–36, 174–203.

THE CHURCHES AND MONASTERIES OF THE TUR 'ABDIN

It was almost by chance that I took my way from Mosul to Diarbekr through the Djebel Tur 'Abdin. I had intended to explore a piece of the country that lies to the north of the Tigris between Hassan Keif and Diarbekr, thinking that while that district was comparatively unknown, the Tur 'Abdin had been thoroughly examined by Pognon and others and contained little of further interest. But when I set eyes upon the buildings of which I here give plans and photographs, I determined that no time must be lost in making some small record of these wonderful specimens of early Christian architecture. Nowhere in the world does there exist a group of early Christian shrines more remarkable than that which lies about Midyat, and few monastic establishments can rival in interest the great houses of Mar Augen and Mar Gabriel. I take it that Amida and Nisibis should be regarded as the sources whence emanated that culture of which the evidences are to be seen scattered through the Tur 'Abdin. Nisibis I have not yet visited; the church of St. James needs careful study and would no doubt throw further light on the problems presented by the buildings in the mountains. Moreover there are several other sites known to me which will furnish additional, and I hope abundant, evidence. Mean time I embrace the opportunity of publishing, under the auspices of Max van Berchem and Professor Strzygowski, the material already collected, without waiting to complete it by a second journey into northern Mesopotamia, which I have in contemplation. Half a loaf, in matters archaeological, is very much better than no bread, and more work is wasted by being stored up in note books until it can be perfected than ever finds its way into the light of day.

When I left Mosul, I turned first to the east and visited the monasteries that lie along the foot of the Kurdish mountains. The existing buildings, both in this district and in Mosul, are not very ancient, though I believe them to preserve an old and important artistic tradition, the tradition of that eastern Christian world which was included in the Sassanian empire. This view is held by the modern incumbents of church and deir. I was sitting one morning in the high-placed religious house of Rabban Hormuzd, listening to the prior as he developed for me the history of Asiatic monasticism. "Here", said he, "and all round Mosul, the monks belonged to the Persian church; but when you get into the Tur 'Abdin you will find that it belonged to Rum." He had stated the problem perfectly correctly; the Tur 'Abdin belongs to Rum, that is to say its civilisation was a part of the wide-spread culture of the Hellenistic East. The architecture of the Mosul district, in structure and in decoration, is unadulterated Persian, but the northern limits of the Mesopotamian plain, and the mountains beyond, were ruled by those mighty influences, part Greek, part Asiatic, which were probably the most powerful and the most productive of all the forces that were brought to bear upon the ancient world. I do not care whether they be illustrated by pagan or by Christian monuments, by the temples of Comana or the churches of Khakh; both, as the prior would say, belong to Rum, both are chapters in the unbroken sequence of Hellenistic Asia. It is this history, the vital importance of which is gradually being recognised, which has now to be pieced together. The architectural material for it is abundant, so abundant, and often so difficult of access, that the archaeologist may well quail before the labour that lies ahead. But the reward is commensurate with the labour; it is that which comes to every student, however slender his equipment of learning, whose eyes are riveted on a period of great artistic development: a keen delight in the creative power of mankind, a deep appreciation of artistic achievement, of the growth of one beautiful form out of another, each bearing with it the memory of all that has been and the promise of all that is to come.

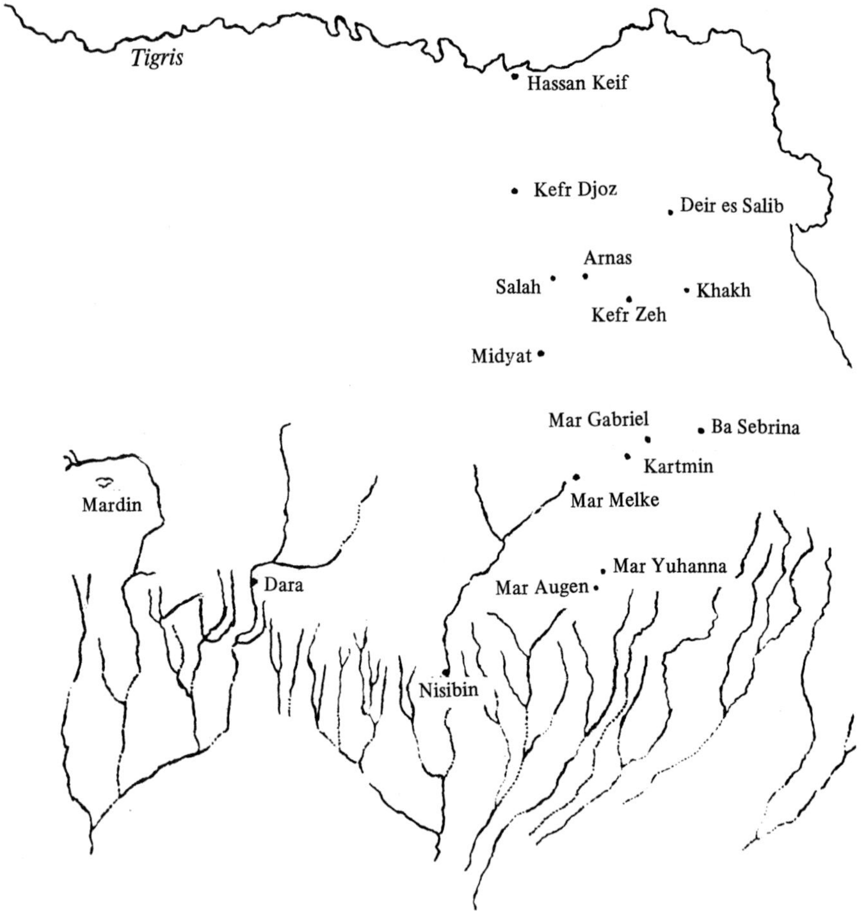

Fig. 1. Map of Ṭur 'Abdin

Mar Augen [1]

By far the most striking monastery which I visited in the Tur 'Abdin is that of St. Eugenius. It clings to the south face of the mountains, but a few hundred feet from their highest point, and is approached from above by a rocky path; the whole great Mesopotamian plain lies spread out before it, with the Djebel Sindjar lifting a long crest across the wide expanse. The monastery is half hewn out of the rock itself (Pls. 199-200). The face of the cliff is honeycombed with cells and the few monks who still inhabit these wild solitudes are lodged in the caves of their earliest forerunners[2]. They claim for the foundation the title of mother house of all the Tur 'Abdin. Their patron saint, Mar Augen[3], was a disciple of St. Anthony of Egypt and transplanted the first monastic traditions from the deserts that border the Nile to the rugged heights above Nisibis. (This is the local tradition; I give it for what it is worth: in all the ancient monasteries of the Tūr 'Abdin there is the same traditional connection with Egypt.) The monks are persuaded that the church with the group of monastic buildings round it are the handwork of the founder and date from the third century.

The monastery was visited by Pognon and is mentioned by him in a short note. *(Inscriptions de la Mésopotamie,* p. 109: see Moltke, *Briefe aus dem Orient).* He observes that the present occupants, the Jacobites, have probably not been in possession for more than a hundred years, while there is reason to believe that the Nestorians held it as late as 1505[4]. He found one inscription of the early period, dated in the 12th century[5]. He believes that the church and monastic buildings had fallen into complete ruin after the Nestorians were driven out and that the existing structure was raised by the Jacobites. It consists of a church, flanked on the S. side by a cloistered court; to the E. of the court is a large burial chamber with a crypt; still further to the S. is another court, not cloistered, with a chapel at the eastern end and behind the chapel a small cell. There are two wells within the building, one in a dark chamber to the N. of the church, and another between the two courts. The whole complex lies on a narrow platform at the foot of formidable cliffs and forms a kind of citadel in the heart of a system of monastic fortifications in which long lines of wall, now ruined, helped out the natural defences supplied by steep rock and mountain side (Pl.199). The only entrance is through a modern porch to the W., which leads into a narrow vaulted chamber[6]. A door in the E. wall of this chamber opens into the cloistered court (Fig.2)[6a]. The court has been in great part rebuilt, but it preserves traces of old work. They can best be seen on the S. side where a series of five arches (the arch at the W. end has been filled up) rest upon slender masonry piers (Pl.203). The western arch retains an old column and another can be observed built into a pier in the N.W. corner (Pl. 201). In both cases the column is crowned by a much battered Corinthian capital (Pl.202)[6b]. On the N. side of the cloister a door leads into the long vaulted nave of the church. It is very dark, being lighted only by exceedingly small windows high up in the S. wall. At the E. end lies the sanctuary, raised by a couple of steps above the nave. On either side of the great arch of the sanctuary are two capitals which are of the highest interest. They belong to a well-known type of basket capital and bear a strong resemblance to two capitals in the central mihrab of the Mosque of Ibn Tulun in Cairo[7]. (See too Strzygowski, *Catalogue du Musée du Caire, Koptische Kunst,* p. 71.) It was unfortunately almost impossible to get a satisfactory photograph, but I do not doubt that we have here relics of the earliest church and I am inclined to think that they are in situ (Pl.204). The prior informed me that the arch above them, which had been removed in recent years, had been carved with leaves and flowers; it was probably a finely moulded arch of the late 4th or early 5th century, to which date there would be no difficulty in assigning the capitals[8]. The altar was covered by a domed brick canopy resting on two columns and two engaged columns. There were pitch dark chambers on either side which communicated both with the nave and with the sanctuary.

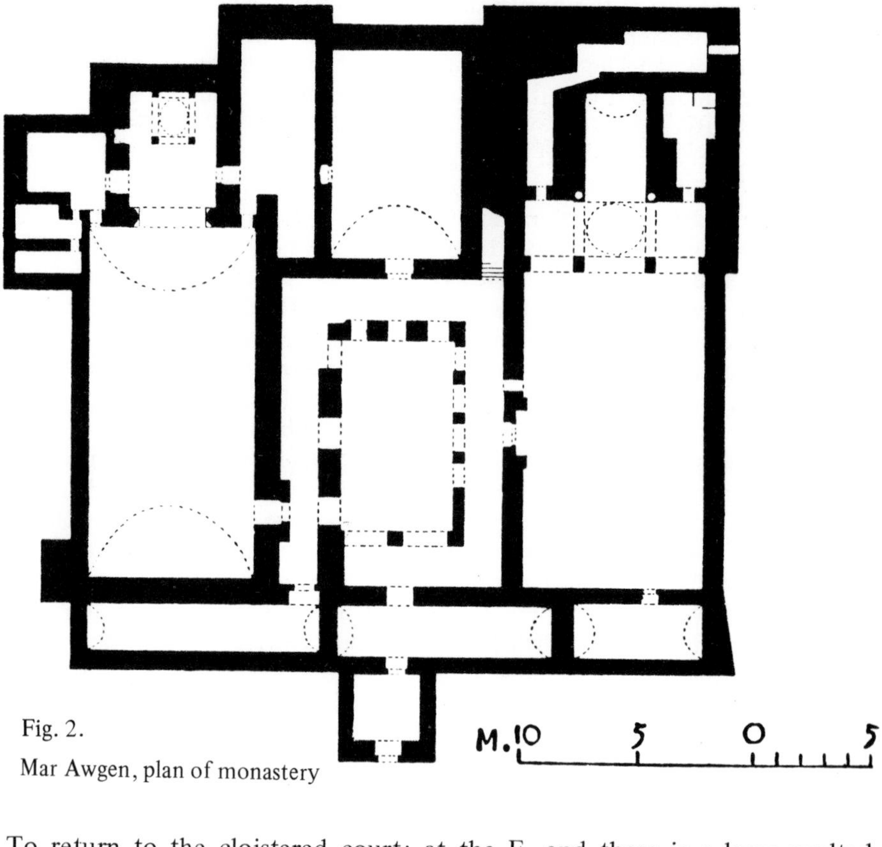

Fig. 2.
Mar Awgen, plan of monastery

To return to the cloistered court: at the E. end there is a large vaulted chamber which contains the tombs of Mar Augen's disciples[9]. A door in the N. wall leads into a tiny crypt where Mar Augen himself is buried, together with his sister and another member of his family[10]. On the S. side of the cloister a door leads into the open court which is bounded on the S. side by a low wall. The hill drops away steeply here so that there is no need for a high boundary wall to the S. At the E. end of the court there are three brick arches (Pl.205). Behind the central arch lies a small square chamber covered by a brick dome set on brick pendentives (Pl.206). (I should like to call attention to the importance of these bricks placed near the corner producing the pendentive, for the history of the stalactite; see *Amida,* p. 182: the brick canopy over the altar in the big church, which I could not photograph on account of the obscurity of the apse, was of much the same character.) On the E. side this dome is carried by columns bearing capitals much broken but evidently taken from an earlier, if not from the earliest building. Further to the E. is a vaulted oblong chamber containing an altar in the thickness of the wall; behind the chapel, there is a cell lighted by a window to the S.

I believe that we have in the present structure of Mar Augen much more of the original foundation than Pognon thought possible. The reparations, which are of several different dates, seem to have been carried out mainly along the original lines and my impression is, not only that the monastery preserves in its disposition the plan of a very ancient building, but that a considerable part of the masonry may well belong to the earliest period[11].

Mar Yuhanna[12].

The monastery of Mar Yuhanna, founded by a disciple of Mar Augen[13], lies upon the steep hillside some two miles to the E. of the mother house [14]. It is not nearly so interesting architecturally (Fig. 3). The church consists of a narthex, a very long narrow nave and a rectangular choir. The exterior is entirely unadorned (Pl. 223). The narthex is covered by a fine brick dome set on squinches (Pl. 225). The nave is vaulted with a mixture of brick and stone. The sanctuary is raised above the nave and separated from it by a screen. Mar Yuhanna and his mother are buried in niches in the N. and S. wall near the eastern end of the nave. The high narrow door between nave and narthex presents a curious feature (Pl. 224). It is covered by a brick arch, slightly pointed and this arch is set back on either side of the door exactly in the manner of which Ctesiphon furnishes the best known examples. In the great palace of Kheiḍar, which I found in the desert W. of Kerbela and intend shortly to

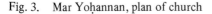

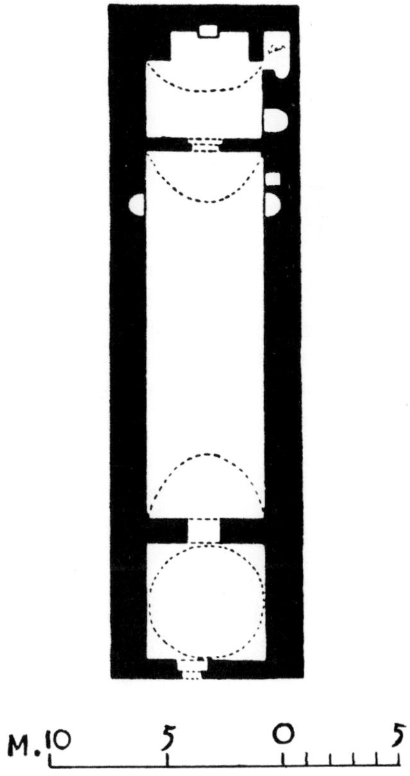

Fig. 3. Mar Yoḥannan, plan of church

publish, every door is treated in this way[15]. Kheiḍar was certainly built by Persian workmen, but the scheme of its doorways is older than Sassanian times; it appears in the N. door of Nebuchadnezzar's palace at Babylon.

Mar Gabriel. (Deir El 'Umar)[16].

The monastery of St. Gabriel of Kartmin is perhaps the most famous Jacobite establishment in Asia; it almost passes belief that this exceptionally important site should never have been carefully studied. Pognon devotes a few pages to it (op. cit., p. 39 et seq.) and gives a rough sketch plan made without measurements. Parry also gives a plan which is scarcely more illuminating than that of Pognon (*Six Months in a Syrian Monastery,* p. 334). I have attempted to give some idea not only of two of the churches (there is a third small chapel on an upper floor), but also of the great complex of monastic buildings in which they lie (Fig. 5; Pls. 211–3). It must, however, be borne in mind that the monastery represented in my plan is little more than half of the original building. The ground to the W. of it is covered with ruins (Pl. 207), among which I was assured are the foundations of a fourth church dedicated to Mar Shim'un. The tomb of the Egyptian monks, of which I give a plan (Fig. 4) stands in this group of ruins[17], and still further to the W. there is a square tower which popular legend connects with the Egyptian princess[18] who played a romantic part in the story of the foundation (Parry, op. cit., p. 215). S. of the great church of Mar Gabriel there are vast substructures which extend for a considerable distance (Pls.207,215-6); masses of ruined walls can be seen to the E. and if I remember rightly to the N. also. Another point to be observed is that (with the exception of the two churches, the long passage that leads from one to the other, the domed octagon with the hall used as a kitchen to the W. of it, and the passage leading from the main entrance to the atrium of Mar Gabriel) all the buildings on the ground floor are merely substructures, the lodgings of the bishop and monks being upon the first floor. These substructures are entirely unlighted and were intended to be used only as stables, cattle byres and store-houses. To such purposes they are still applied. Though they are of little architectural importance, I would have tried to get some more accurate plan of them but for the horrible state of filth in which I found them. I leave it to a braver explorer to face the legions of fleas that people them; there were certain doorways through which even the nun who escorted me would not pass.

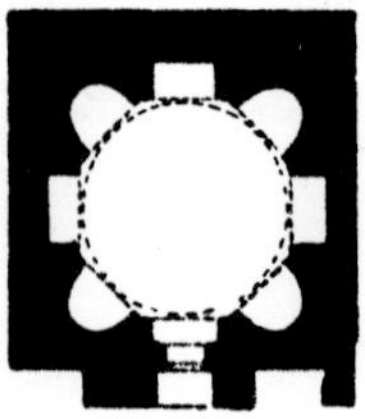

Fig. 4.

Mar Gabriel, plan of tomb of Egyptian Monks

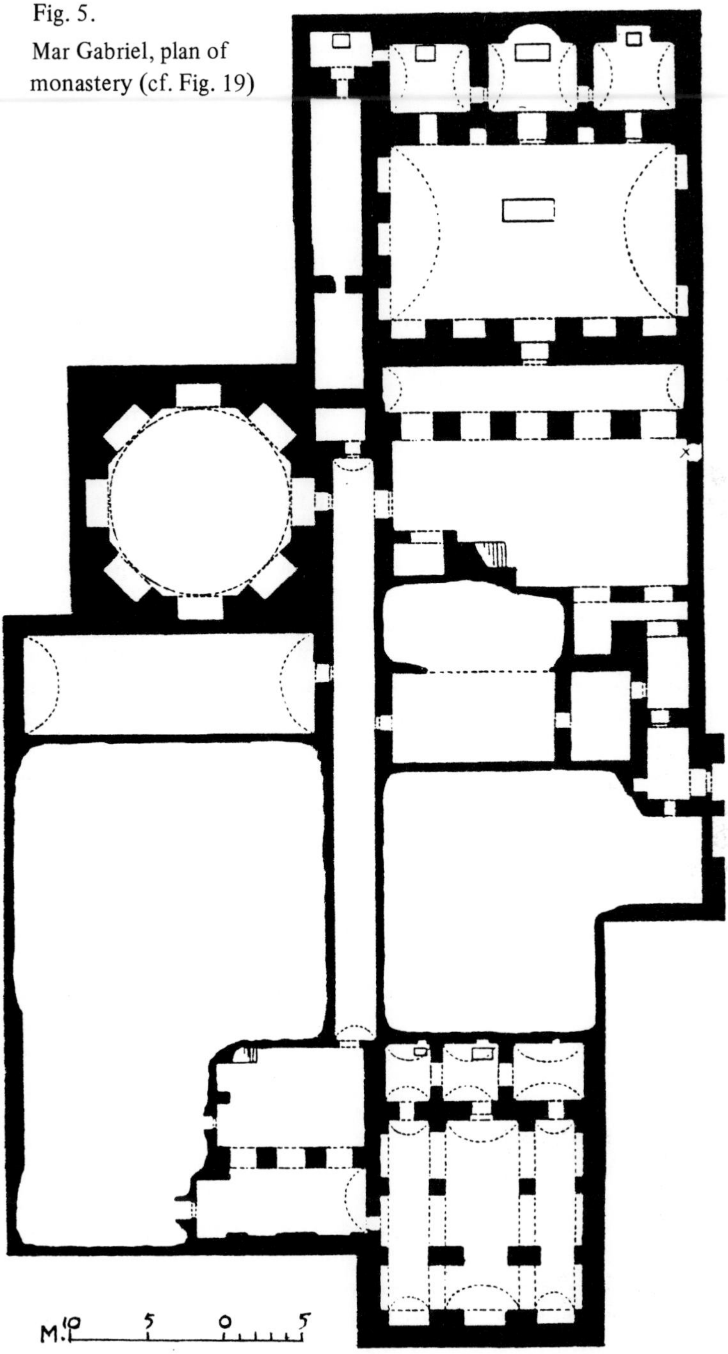

Fig. 5.
Mar Gabriel, plan of monastery (cf. Fig. 19)

The monastery is said to have been founded in the reign of Arcadius and rebuilt under Anastasius[19]. As Pognon observes, there is no reason to doubt that the great church[20] is a relic of the late 5th or early 6th century and I conjecture that it preserves the plan of a yet earlier church. It consists of a narthex and nave, three sanctuaries and three burial chambers. The narthex lies to the W. and is covered by the vast tiled gable roof that extends over the whole church (Pls. 211–214) . In a life of St. Gabriel, quoted by Pognon, it is stated that a similar gallery once ran round the other three sides of the atrium, but of this there is now no trace[21]. From the narthex a single door opens into the nave, which is a large barrel vaulted hall (Pls.217-8), 10.70 metres from E. to W. and 18.25 metres from N. to S. A nave lying with its greatest length from N. to S. is not found only in the church of Mar Gabriel. Mar Yakub at Salah offers another example at least as early, if not earlier, than Mar Gabriel; the church in the monastery of Mar Melko, difficult to date on account of the rude character of its architecture, is a third instance, and Mar Ibrahim at Midyat, now entirely rebuilt, but upon the old plan, a fourth[21a]. We have therefore a type which was familiar in the district at an early date, and used apparently as frequently as that of the nave set with its greatest length from E. to W. which occurs in churches of the same period. It is perhaps not superfluous to observe that the two schemes, the hall lying broadways and the hall lying lengthways, are both known to ancient Mesopotamian architecture. The broadways-lying chamber is Babylonian, the lengthways Assyrian, though possibly borrowed from architectural creations outside Mesopotamia[22]. Even the Assyrian builders retained the broadways-lying hall in their palaces (Andrae, *Anu-Adad-Tempel,* p.83). The nave is very insufficiently lighted by small windows in the S. wall. A great stone slab stands near the middle of the church (Pl. 218) ; on it is an inscription of the 8th century (Pognon, p. 42). Three doors lead into the three barrel vaulted sanctuaries, each of which contains an altar. The S. sanctuary has a rectangular niche to the E. built in the thickness of the wall; the central sanctuary, in which is the main altar, has a curved apse, also hollowed out of the thickness of the wall. Except in the three other churches of the type to which Mar Gabriel belongs, the main altar is not concealed from the worshippers in the nave. In all other examples in the Tur ʻAbdin there is either a light screen of columns and architrave between nave and sanctuary, or if there is a wall it is palpably a later addition. (On the differences between the two types of sanctuary see Pognon, p. 91, note 2. He suggests that the closed sanctuary may indicate a monastic church, the open a parish church.) Even the screen is in one case much later than the rest of the church. On the floor of the central sanctuary there is a mosaic pavement of big stones[23], but the chief beauty is the mosaic on the vault. This needs careful study with proper appliances, as the chamber is very dark and the mosaic much blackened by smoke. By burning a few pieces of magnesium wire, which I happened to have with me, I managed to get a partial view of it. In the centre is a large cross laid upon a gold ground, while the space on either side is covered by S-shaped vine scrolls, intertwined so as to form circles, each circle being filled with a decorative motive. Tradition says that the whole church was once adorned with mosaics[24] but that all except this small portion in the sanctuary were destroyed by Timur Leng. The cross on the semi-dome of the apse over the altar is a familiar object in the Djebel Tur 'Abdin[25]; generally, however, it is carved in relief on the stones. A small door leads from the northern sanctuary into a burial chamber, very dimly lighted and containing an altar[26]. To the W. there are two more burial chambers, totally dark and approached by a door so small that it is only just possible to squeeze through it.

The second church, dedicated to the Virgin[27], lies at the W. end of the monastery. It occupies the big rectangular block of buildings which appears between two courts. This church is in a bad state of repair; it is dark, damp and full of fleas. A long vaulted passage leads from the atrium of Mar Gabriel to the small court lying to the N. of El Aḍra. There is a vaulted arcade in the W. side of this court and from the S. end of the arcade a door leads into the church. In ground plan it has the appearance of a cross-in-square, but there is no dome over the centre of the cross. The church is roofed like a basilica with three parallel barrel vaults over the nave and aisles. (This type is frequently found in and near Mosul.) Three irregularly shaped sanctuaries lie to the E. I have no means of dating El Aḍra, which is entirely without decoration, but the monks do not believe it to be as old as Mar Gabriel and I should say that they were certainly right. On the N. side of the arcade a door leads into a crypt full of graves.

The third church, dedicated to forty martyrs[28], is also approached from the inner court. A stair at the N. E. corner of the court leads up to it. It consists of two barrel vaulted chambers, a narthex and nave, set with their greatest length from N. to S., and three sanctuaries to the E (Fig. 20). It may belong to about the same period as the church of the Virgin.

Almost opposite the door that leads into the atrium of Mar Gabriel, there is another door in the N. wall of the passage opening into a large octagonal chamber[29]. This very remarkable building is, I need scarcely say, full of filth and but dimly lighted. In each of the eight sides there is a large rectangular arched niche and above the arches rises a splendid shallow brick dome. The dome is entirely invisible from the outside; the building presents on the exterior the appearance of a square block with a flat roof (Pl. 212). Among the ruins W. of the monastery and in other churches of the Tur 'Abdin I have frequently found brick used together with stone. In every case when I have been able to take measurements of the bricks they have proved to be thin square tiles, 0.41 x 0.41 x 0.3[30]. Pl.209 shows the character of these bricks. The arches here represented were in a ruined chamber to the W. of the monastery; it was pointed out to me as the chapel of Mar Shim'un. I do not doubt that the bricks used in the octagonal chamber are similar to these[31].

Pognon, in speaking of the stone block in the centre of the church of Mar Gabriel, alludes to its having been placed originally under a great dome resting on eight arches which was situated near the kitchen. He goes on to state that this dome has now disappeared. But it has not disappeared; on the contrary it exists in an excellent state of repair, indeed the interior looks as if the builder had just put his finishing touches upon it. I have mentioned that the dome is very shallow; it reminded me forcibly of the magnificent flattened domes and vaults which I have seen in Mohammadan work of the best period, for example in the great medresseh at Baghdad which is now used as a custom house (de Beylie, *Prome et Samarra* , p.33; but he mentions only the inscription)[32] . For the lack of any but architectural evidence I should be inclined to date the octagon of Deir el'Umar in the 13th century [33].

To the W. of it lies the kitchen, a long vaulted hall. I have not represented in the plan the arcades that are placed against the E. and W. walls. They are constructed in the same manner as the arched niches in the nave of Mar Gabriel, the object in both cases being the same, namely to increase the interior space of the apartment without increasing the span of the vault. The kitchen was inhabited by hordes of ferocious fleas and in my hurry to escape from them I forgot to measure the details and will not now put them in from memory.

Finally there remains to be noticed the tomb of the Egyptian monks to the W. of the monastery (Pl.208). It is a small octagonal domed chamber, square on the outside. The niches in the eight sides are alternately rectangular and curved and each niche is filled with a tomb of no artistic pretensions . The dome is flattened, like the dome of the big octagon.

Mar Yakub, Salah[34] .

Of the exquisite church of Mar Yakub at Salah there exists a small sketch plan by Parry (op. cit., p. 332: his observations on the architecture of the church are more than usually wide of the mark). Pognon visited Salah twice and has published eleven memorial inscriptions which he found in the narthex, where they still stand (op. cit., p. 62 et seq.). They are dated in the 10th and 11th centuries. He found another inscription among the ruins of the bishop's palace N. of the church (Pl. 241), dated in the 14th century when the monastery of St. James was one of the most important in the Tur 'Abdin. The church lies outside the village. Of the monastic buildings little or nothing remains; there are some modern structures to the W. and S., and to the N. and E. masses of ruin[35] . Some of these ruins are of excellent solid masonry. Pognon believed that these buildings belonged mainly to the 14th century. There are no longer any monks at Mar Yakub (1909); the church is unused and the windows are all blocked up[36] .

The church (Fig. 6) as Pognon observes, closely resembles Mar Gabriel in plan and is at least as ancient – I should not be surprised if it were as old as the first foundation of Mar Gabriel in the reign of Arcadius. As at Mar Gabriel, the narthex was probably part of a cloister which ran all round the church. I may observe that Mar Ibrahim at Midyat had also once been provided with this open narthex; perhaps there too it was part of a cloister. Mar Augen is the only monastery where the cloister is still preserved, though even there it has evidently suffered much rebuilding. At Mar Yakub, atrium and cloister have disappeared, but the arcades of the W. side of the narthex are still visible, though three have been walled up and one has been filled with a door (Pl.233). The narthex is barrel vaulted, the upper part of the vault being of brick. This brickwork is treated in a way very characteristic of the Tur 'Abdin. It is divided into three square compartments,

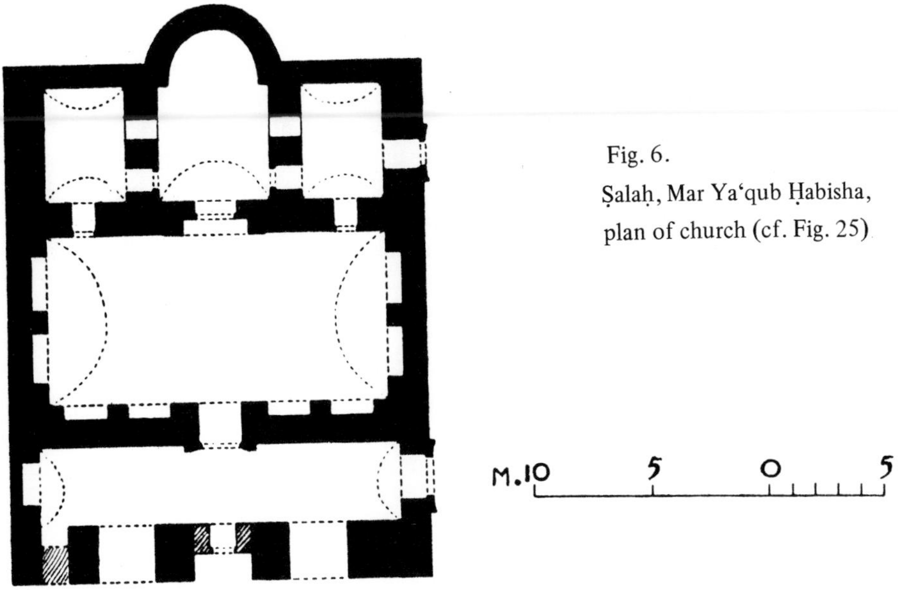

Fig. 6.
Ṣalaḥ, Mar Ya'qub Ḥabisha, plan of church (cf. Fig. 25)

each separated from the other by bands of nine courses of brick which give the appearance of a rib. The squares are edged with an ornamental band made of semi-circular tiles. The photograph (Pl.242) gives a better idea of the system than any description. There is a door at the S. end of the narthex, and a fine moulded door leads into the nave (Pl.243). All the windows having been blocked up it was extremely difficult to photograph the interior of narthex and nave, for there was no light except that which came in through the W. door. The nave lies with its greatest length from N. to S. as at Mar Gabriel, and shows the same arched niches in the N. (Pl. 245), S. (Fig.26) and W. walls. There was a splendid moulding all round the nave under the vault. The high barrel vault consisted of six courses of stone on either side while the upper part was of brick, divided into three square compartments like the narthex and even more elaborately treated (Pl. 244). Round each of the squares ran a broad border composed of two bands of the curved tile-work that appears in Pl.242 and between them a band of bricks set in a herring-bone, each of these separated from the other by two courses of plain brickwork. Three doors led into the three sanctuaries. The central door was singularly beautiful (Pl.246)[37] The lintel and jambs were boldly moulded, the mouldings resembling those on the narthex door; on either side stood two pilasters carrying a moulded string-course, which ran at this level all round the nave. Over the lintel of the door the string-course curved up into a horse-shoed arch, and the tympanum between arch and lintel bore traces of fresco. (Parry states that there is an inscription over this door recording that the church was built in 1109. Pognon does not mention it, I did not see it, and it does not appear in the photograph. Moreover the church was built long before 1109.) Of the pilasters I wish that I had a clearer photograph[38], for they are without rival in the Tur ʻAbdin. The decoration upon them is divided into bands(Figs. 7, 28; Pl. 246). The outermost band is plain; the next is composed of beautiful rinceaux, deeply undercut; within the rinceaux is a band of moulding and the centre of the pilaster is occupied by an upright band of carving showing small birds in relief, set one above the other. Some notion of this may be gathered from the appended sketch. The carved bands were worked on an inlay of darker stone. The capitals borne by these pilasters were of uncut acanthus with a rope or garland thrown over the corners and caught up in the centre of each face of the abacus, and a band of small dentils below the acanthus leaves.

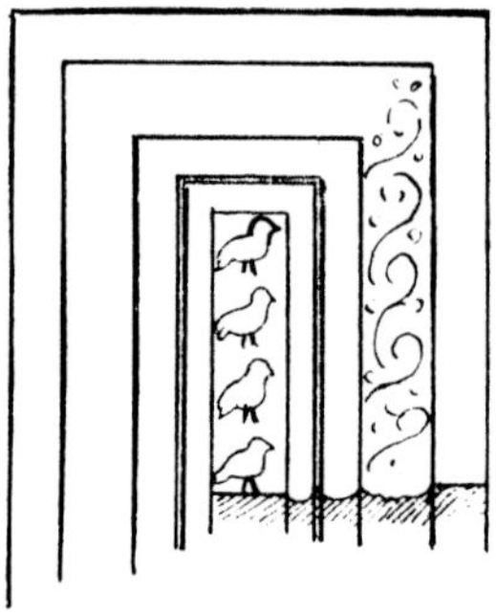

Fig. 7.
Ṣalaḥ, Mar Yaʻqub Ḥabisha,
sketch of ornament on sanctuary door
(cf. Fig. 28)

The three sanctuaries communicated with one another both by a door and by a window; all three were barrel vaulted, the top of the vault being made of a square of bricks. At the E. end of the central sanctuary there was an apse covered by a semi-dome (Pl. 248) . A door was placed in the S. side of the S. sanctuary.

It was only on the outside that I could see what had been the nature of the windows. They were narrow lancets covered by a moulding which was prolonged horizontally on either side of the arch (Pl.240). A dentil appeared on this moulding as on the other outer mouldings of the church. Pl.238 shows the E. end with gable roofs over the barrel vaults of the sanctuaries. These roofs originally ended with the moulding; the parts above are later additions. Pl.239 gives the N. sanctuary gable in detail, and the great cyma moulding which is used all over the exterior of the church. Beneath the cyma there is a small dentil which can be seen in the photograph though it is somewhat in shadow. This bold cornice is found on all the churches of the Tur ʻAbdin, but it is nowhere used so freely as at Salah, nor do I remember to have seen the dentil elsewhere; it may, however, exist, for it is difficult to distinguish when the cornice occurs only at a considerable height from the ground. The N. side of the church is comparatively plain, being broken only by the cyma below and round the gable of the nave vault, and by a big lancet in that gable (Pl.237), the S. side is more elaborate (Pl.234). The cyma moulding is lavishly used, there are three lancets crowned with a moulding below the gable in the wall of the nave, and the doors into the narthex and S. sanctuary have moulded lintels and jambs.

Over the narthex door there is a relieving arch above the lintel (Pl.235). It is characteristic of Mar Yakub that all the lintels are in the nature of straight arches; they are all composed of three parts, a key stone and two side blocks. This can be particularly well seen in Pl.235. Above the lintel of the S. sanctuary door there is a straight arch of stone voussoirs. Placed on the cyma moulding immediately above the door is a tiny bit of decoration consisting of a cross in a victor's wreath (Pl.236)[39]. On the W. facade it is to be observed that the upper part of the narthex wall above the arches is later work. The original wall was several courses lower and was crowned by a cornice which still remains in its old place. The original disposition is clearly visible at the left hand corner of Pl.234.The roof over the nave has also been raised. The old gable came down as far as the cornice which can be seen in the wall above the narthex roof. The piers supporting the W. arcade of the narthex have finely moulded capitals showing the usual cyma with a bead below it and two plain bands (Pl.232).

Mar Azaziel at Kefr Zeh[40] and Mar Kyriakos at Arnas.

The churches at Arnas and at Kefr Zeh are both of the same type. Mar Kyriakos has suffered more than Mar Azaziel at the hand of time and of the restorer and it will therefore be well to take the latter first as it illustrates the type better. Arnas and Kefr Zeh, like most of the villages of the Tur 'Abdin, stand upon the summit of a hill. Both villages are now miserable little collections of hovels inhabited partly by Moslems, partly by Christians; the great churches, memorials of a past civilization and prosperity, rising up over the rude dwellings of the present population give a most striking impression of splendour and decay. This is especially the case at Kefr Zeh, where the church stands clear of the modern village and is moreover exceptionally well preserved. Pl.153, a view taken from the N. W., shows its fine position on the mountain top. It is a landmark across many miles of rocky hills.

I do not think that Mar Azaziel (Fig. 8) was originally a monastic church, for I saw no signs of extensive monastic buildings[41]. In the courtyard S. of the church there is one small room N. of the gate which is at present occupied by an old nun who seems to have constituted herself guardian over the church. Though the walls are modern, the disposition of this court or atrium is no doubt ancient and I think it highly probable that it may always have contained a lodging for one or more clerks who had charge of the shrine. Monasteria clericorum were well known institutions in early Christian times; I have dealt with them more fully in my book on the Kara Dagh (Ramsay-Bell, *The Thousand and One churches,* p.416). The small exedra on the E. side of the court is a constant feature in the Tur 'Abdin (Pls. 156–157)[42]. The village priest at Khakh told me that these exedras were used for week-day prayer, only the Sunday prayers being recited in the church itself. Pognon states that they were used in summer and the churches in winter (op. cit., p. 93), and his authority for this observation is probably better than mine. The exedra at Mar Azaziel is dated in an inscription placed inside it. It was built in the year 1246

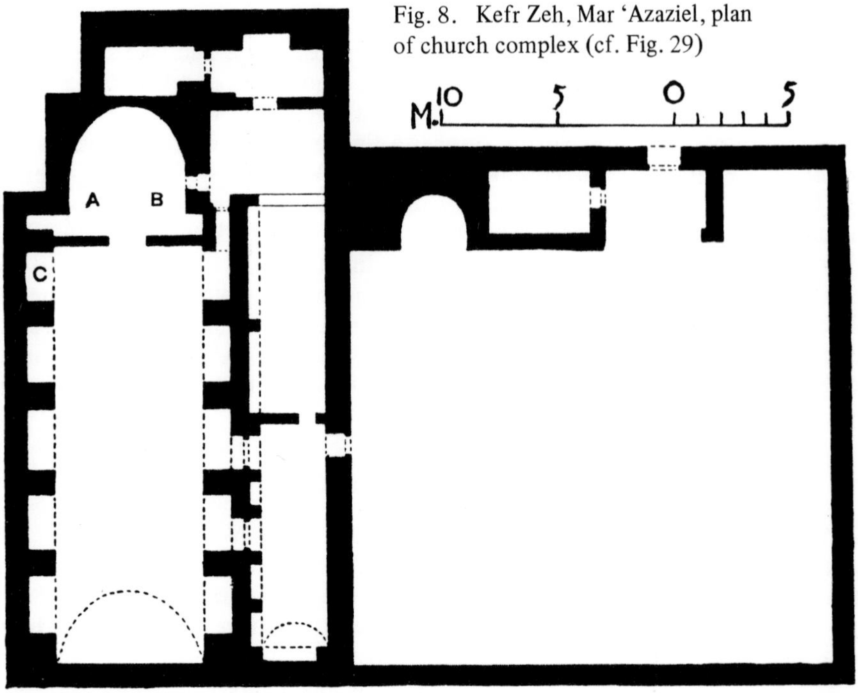

Fig. 8. Kefr Zeh, Mar ‘Azaziel, plan of church complex (cf. Fig. 29)

of the Greeks, i.e., about A. D. 934[43]. In every example I judged the exedra, on architectural grounds, to be later than the church to which it belonged; perhaps the fashion of placing exedras in the atrium did not arise till towards the 10th century. They are invariably decorated with a cross cut in relief upon the interior of the semi-dome, as are many of the church apses[44]. In Pl.156 can be seen the stone tables that held the liturgical books and scriptures, in this case three in number, one in the centre of the exedra and one on either side (see Pognon, p. 42).

A single door leads into the narthex which lies on the S. side of the church. The division across it is modern. The eastern half is very dark and heaped up with rubbish; I cannot be certain that the arcade which is to be seen along the N. wall of the western half of the narthex is not continued to the E. more regularly than I have indicated it on the plan[45]; probably it is. At Arnas the S. wall of the narthex is arcaded as well as the N. wall, but at Kefr Zeh it is plain. The narthex is covered with a brick vault, the bricks set in squares. Two doorways lead into a long vaulted nave, arcaded on either side. The sanctuary is raised a couple of steps above the nave and separated from it by a screen of four columns carrying an architrave (Pl.161). This screen is not, I think, as old as the church, though it is certainly not modern[46]. There are two columns with an acanthus capital (Pl. 163) and an uncut acanthus capital (Pl. 162). Both have the characteristic garland hung over the corners, and the acanthus capital looks as if it had been copied from the splendid engaged capital under the apse arch on the N. side, which can be seen in Pl.161. I give a detail of it in Pl.159; the capital under the S. end of the apse arch was much damaged. On the semi-dome of the apse is the cross in relief of which I have spoken. A fine moulding runs round the apse under the semi-dome (Pl.160). It is composed of a band of palmettes, a bead and reel, and a band of cross-shaped entrelac; the lowest member is a double band of dentils set alternately. The palmettes appear in every decorated moulding in the Tur 'Abdin. The apse arch is worked with two bands of palmettes with rinceaux between them[47]. It is horse-shoed and so are all the arches of the arcades in nave and narthex. The nave is covered with a brick vault (Pls. 164–165), the bricks set in squares on the system described in the church at Salah. A door in the S. side of the apse leads into a small chamber which communicates also with the nave by a narrow door, and communicated with the narthex by a door now walled up. Above it is an upper chamber, approached by a wooden stair and containing an altar. Another small dark chamber with an altar lies still further to the E. and leading out of it there is yet another, quite dark, lying behind the apse.

How much of all this building is the original work? It will be observed that the apse arch starts from within the screen; the capitals that support it are worked on the angles of masonry marked A. and B. on the plan. Further, it is evident that the pier C. has no architectural relationship with the apse. This can be seen in Pl.161, where the rudely moulded capital of pier C. obscures some of the fine mouldings of the apse arch. My impression is that the arcade on the N. side of the nave, and therefore the vault which it helps to support, are later work and this is borne out by the fact that some of the upper part of the N. wall seems to have been rebuilt (Pl.165)[48]. The S. wall of the narthex is certainly late (Pl.155); it is a patchwork of re-used blocks. But the nave wall above it, with its lancet windows and cyma cornice, is old. Pl.154 gives the windows of the W. wall in detail. They are three in number, one in the gable and two below. The moulded arches rest on short stumpy columns. Between the two lower windows there is a curious piece of decoration, two lions' heads with a cross between. Three rows of projecting blocks of stone can be seen in the N. and W. walls. They are so regularly placed that they must have been intended to have a decorative value. The E. end of the church has been much pulled about, but all the lower parts of the walls seem to be the original work, including even the wall of the curious chamber behind the apse, while bits of the cyma of the topmost gable are still in place (Pl.152). There is a window in the gable corresponding to the window in the W. façade.

There is fortunately epigraphic evidence with regard to the restoration of **Mar Kyriakos**[49] (Fig. 9). An inscription published by Pognon (op. cit., p. 99) states that the N. wall and vault were "restored and built" at the end of the 16th century[50]. I did not know of this inscription when I worked at the church, but I had independently come to the conclusion that the S. wall and arcades of the nave were old up to the top of the arcade arches, whereas in the N. wall only the foundations were old. It is satisfactory to find that the architectural evidence agrees so completely with the epigraphic. The plan of Mar Kyriakos is almost the same as that of Mar Azaziel. There had been an atrium

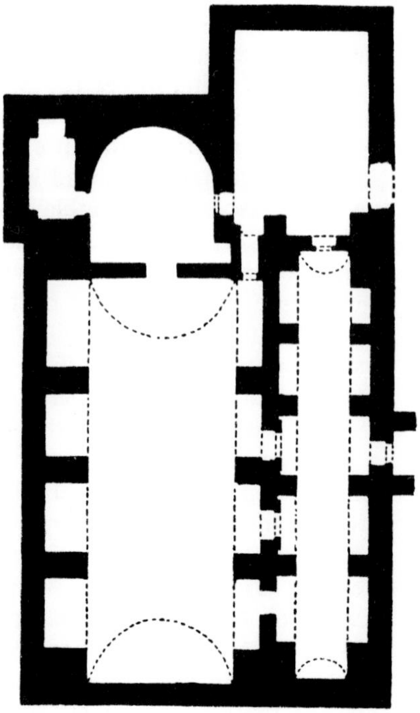

Fig. 9.

Arnas, Mar Cyriacus, plan of church
(cf. Fig. 34)

to the S., now partly built over by modern houses; the walls that remain are terribly ruined. Two exedras stand in the E. wall of this atrium (Pl. 98) ; that which lies to the N. appears to be the older of the two, but I do not think that it is as old as the church. The mouldings and decorations of the southern exedra betray a comparatively recent date. The S. wall of the narthex has been in part rebuilt; possibly, as Pognon suggests, there was here an open arcade similar to that of the narthex of Mar Gabriel and Mar Yakub. The present narthex is arcaded on either side, the arches here as elsewhere in the church being horse-shoed. Two fine moulded doors lead into the nave. The sanctuary is raised and divided from the nave by a screen as at Kefr Zeh (Pl. 158). Here, however, the screen is much later work; it is dated by an inscription in the 8th century (Pognon, p. 96) (Pls. 99–100) . Late work betrays itself infallibly when brought into comparison with the magnificent decorations of the early period; the two are so distinct that there can never be a moment's hesitation in deciding between them, whether there be a dated inscription or no[51].

The apse arch (Pls. 100–1) is carved with palmettes, rinceaux and entrelacs (Pl. 102) . It springs from garlanded Corinthinian capitals (Pl. 103) , the tops of which can be seen in Pl. 99. Again the N. E. pier of the nave arcade impinges upon the old capital, but here we know that the pier is part of the restoration.

A cross decorates the semi-dome, which rests on a moulding adorned with palmettes and vine scroll (Pl.104). An ornament is laid over the vine scroll in the centre of the apse. As at Kefr Zeh, a chamber containing an altar lies to the S. of the apse, communicating with apse, nave and narthex[52]. There is no chamber behind the apse[53], but a very small room lies to the N. of it, communicating with it by a door that corresponds to the door on the S. side. High-placed windows light the nave, and a bold cyma moulding forms a cornice and runs round the gable of the nave roof (Pl. 97).

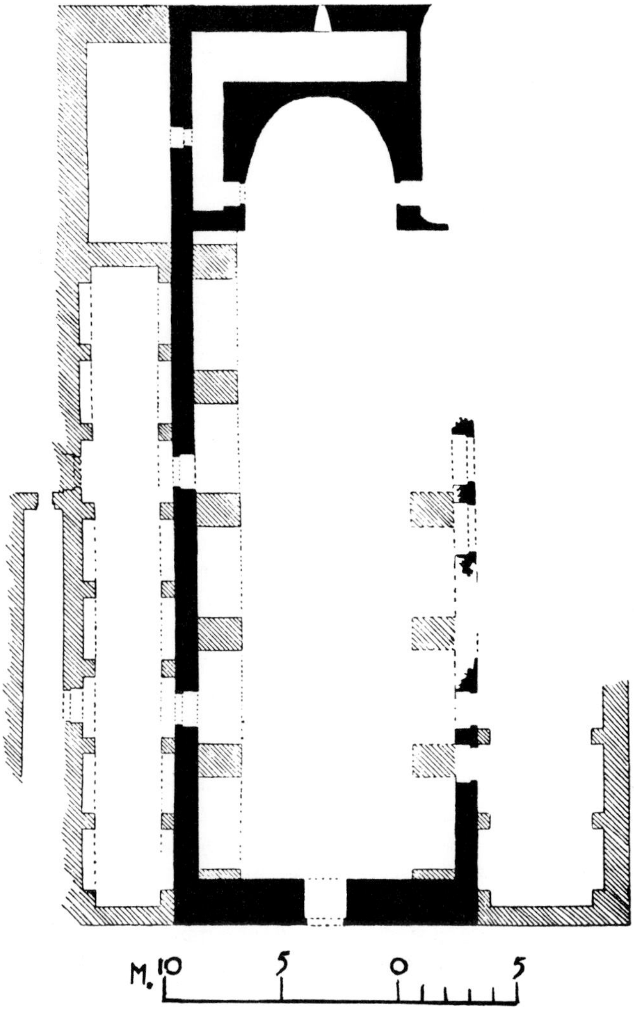

Fig. 10. Ḥaḥ (Khakh), Mar Sovo, plan of church

Mar Sovo at Khakh[54], and Mar Philoxenos at Midyat.

There are two other churches of the same type as those at Arnas and Kefr Zeh. They are both ruined, but since they must both be placed among the very early buildings of the Tur 'Abdin, they cannot be neglected. The most important of the two is the great church of Mar Sovo at Khakh (Fig. 10). It is by far the largest church of this type, the nave being 27.30 metres long by 11.10 metres wide. These measurements are from wall to wall, not from arcade pier to arcade pier. At Kefr Zeh the nave is 17.40 metres long by 8.97 metres wide from wall to wall, and at Arnas 13.65[54a] metres long by 8.90 metres wide.

Mar Sovo was standing at the end of the 15th century, for a bishop was buried in it in 1493 (Pognon, p. 121 et seq.). The ruins consist of a nave and apse and two aisles, but the N. aisle is certainly a later addition (Pl.119). Seen from the E. the point where the later wall joins the old wall of the chamber that runs behind the apse is clearly marked by a straight joint. The two doors in the N. wall of the nave are, however, part of the original plan; they are decorated on the outside, i.e. inside the aisle, with excellent mouldings (Pl.116). The pilasters and arches of the arcade of the aisle are set so close to the jambs that they do not allow them to stand out in relief from the wall as they were intended to do. In the interior of the nave the piers of the arcade are also a later addition. In the N. arcade a pier impinges upon the easternmost of the two doors (Pl.120); on the S. side the piers partly block the old doors which are here distributed in two groups of two (Pl. 125). These doors also are finely moulded on the outside and above each lintel there is a shallow relieving arch (Pl.124). The easternmost pier on either side of the nave is so placed with regard to the apse that it conceals the apse mouldings[55]. Behind the pier, on the E. wall on either side of the apse (the narrow space between pier and wall can be seen in Pl.122) I found a splendid moulding (Pl.116). It formed a cornice to the wall. There are remains of Corinthian capitals[56] under the horse-shoed apse arch, and a decorated moulding ran round the interior of the apse under the semi-dome[57], but it is unfortunately much weather-worn (Pl. 121). A trace of the moulding round the apse arch can be seen[58]; it appears to have been even more elaborately worked than the corresponding arches at Arnas and Kefr Zeh (Pls.101,161). There was a small door on either side of the apse. That which stands to the S. is entirely blocked with ruins; the N. door leads into a narrow vaulted chamber running round behind the apse. The vault is of brick and I believe it to be part of the original structure (Pl.123). A door to the N. opens into another chamber lying at the E. end of the N. aisle; it belongs to the later period. A tiny wedge-shaped window lighted the chamber behind the apse.

The arcade of the S. aisle is also later than the nave. One of the few pilasters that remain upon the N. side covers the mouldings of the westernmost pair of doors. Presumably what I have called the S. aisle was originally a narthex on th S. side of the church. This narthex must have occupied the same space that is now covered by the aisle, for there is some old masonry at the exterior S. W. angle (Pl.118). The W. door of the nave may be part of the original plan; it is perfectly plain. The nave had been lighted by windows high up in the wall; they can still be seen in the fragment of the old N. wall that rises above the N. aisle (Pl.117) There are also some stones of the cornice.

The question that chiefly occupied my attention while working on this church was the nature of the original roof. No doubt after the restoration the nave had been covered with a brick vault, like all the other churches in the Tur 'Abdin; but the arcades on either side, which were then put in, diminish the width of the nave by 3.80 metres, leaving only a space of 7.30 metres to be spanned. There is nothing to show that an arcade on either side of the nave existed in the early plan; on the contrary, if it had once existed, why was it not restored as it stood instead of putting in piers[59] that blocked the S. doors? But if there were no arcades, the nave was 11.10 metres wide. That implies a vault with a very large span, larger than any in the Tur 'Abdin where the widest vault known to me is that of Mar Gabriel, 10.70 metres. Moreover in Mar Gabriel the walls were much thicker than in Mar Sovo. I am inclined to believe that the original church at Khakh was not vaulted.

To the S. of Mar Sovo there is an atrium now filled with ruins. It contains an exedra in the E. wall. In the interior of the exedra here are memorial inscriptions of the 12th and 13th centuries[60], and the usual cross in relief is cut on the semi-dome (Pl.126). The mouldings are good, but not as good as those of the church; they look like careful copies rather than contemporary work (see sections Pls. 116 and 127–128).

To the E. of the apse there is a tower[60a]. High up on its W. face I saw a much worn inscription in a label and probably if it were legible it would give the date of the building, but the mouldings are decisive proof that it belongs to a later period than the church. I know of no early towers connected with churches in the Tur 'Abdin. There is a cusped arch over the niche in the W. wall of the tower which should be compared with the cusped arch over the S. door of Mar Philoxenos (Pls. 126 and 173).

The plan which I give of **Mar Philoxenos**[61] (Fig.11) shows the whole complex of buildings on the site, but the only part which is ancient is the much ruined church to the N. (Pls. 169–175). The apse and the S. wall of the nave are standing (Pl.174). I do not believe that the arcade against the S. wall (Pl. 175) belongs to the original plan for it blocks the windows in the upper part of the wall (Pl.173). There are good cyma capitals upon the piers (Pl.172). The N. wall has certainly been rebuilt and the arcade does not exactly correspond with the arcade of the S. wall. The N. aisle is completely ruined; without excavation it would be impossible to tell whether it is a late addition or no. The doors leading from the nave into the S. aisle have good mouldings on the S. side, but they are difficult to see because the aisle is exceedingly dark. Besides the mouldings, the central door has brackets set on either side of the lintel, a motive common in Syria but unknown to me elsewhere in the Tur 'Abdin. Except for the wall containing these doors, all the S. aisle is late; so are the chapel to the E. of it and the buildings S. of that chapel. Part of the old cornice still crowns the S. wall of the nave. The S. door into the aisle with the cusped arch over the porch is not part of the old work. Little can be made of this church until it is cleared out. I cannot even be sure that I have got the plan of the apse correctly; there was, however, certainly a chamber behind it (Pls. 169–171).

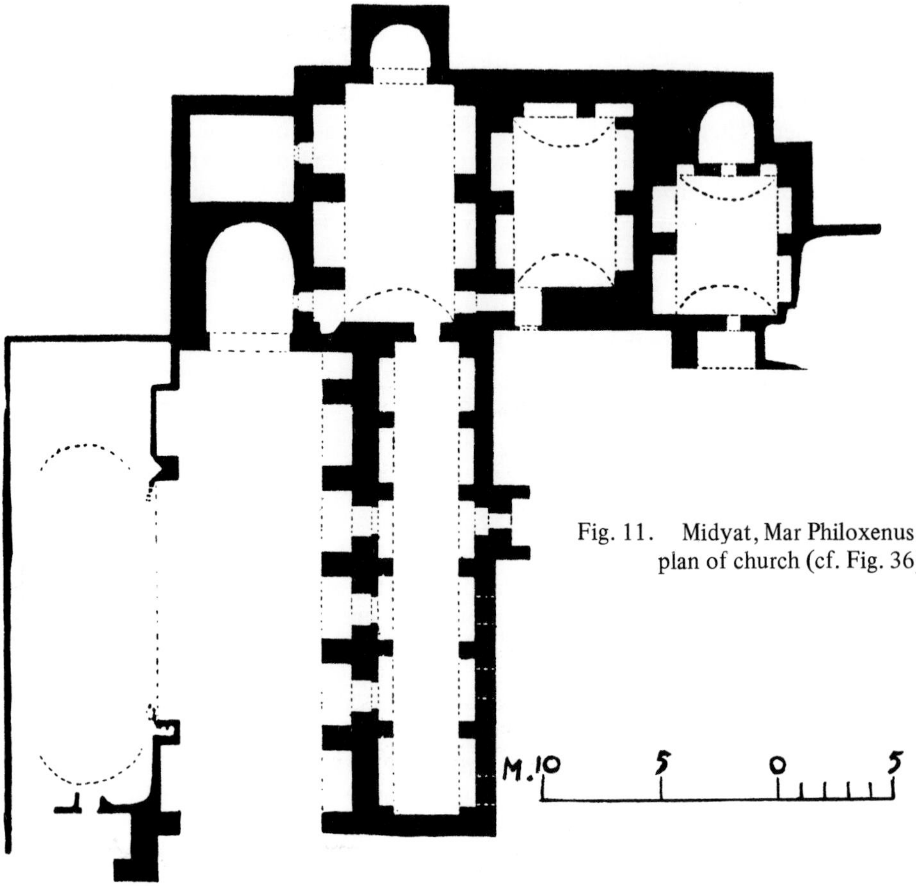

Fig. 11. Midyat, Mar Philoxenus, plan of church (cf. Fig. 36)

El Adra at Khakh[62].

The crowning glory of the Tur 'Abdin is the church dedicated to the Virgin at Khakh (Pl. 132: there is a sketch plan in Parry, op. cit., p. 328, where, too, the legends connected with the foundation may be found). Till two years ago it had stood absolutely untouched and unaltered except for the addition of the W. porch hatched in the plan. The interior is still as the first builders left it, but a thrice accursed priest conceived the idea of replacing the original roof with a dome. The old roof was perfectly good and never let in a drop of rain, so the village priest, who was bitterly against the alteration, told me; the present dome leaks, and unless some further repairs are carried out shortly the church will suffer. The new work (Pl.135) is easily to be distinguished from the old. There had been, said the priest, a tiled pointed roof covering the interior dome; this was removed and replaced by a round stone exterior dome [63]. It is quite clear that above the row of arched niches under the dome there was a small octagonal tower, the base of which still remains. From the tower rose the pointed roof of which the priest spoke; it was probably built with eight ridges converging towards a much flattened apex. From the foot of the niches a tiled roof had sloped down to a cornice which can still be seen, borne by pilasters with Corinthian capitals; but the wall has been raised above the cornice and the sloping roof is now of stone[64]. The niches are flanked by small columns with Corinthian capitals which again carry horse-shoed arches[65]. Very shallow pilasters with uncut Corinthian capitals are set along the N. and S. walls (Pl. 136), four on either side; the W. wall is concealed by the modern porch; there are no pilasters on the E. wall except at the corners (Pl. 133). Above the pilasters is a cornice. The W. porch (Pl. 134) is a clumsy addition to the old work and the W. door into the narthex is modern[66], though it must occupy exactly the same space as that which was occupied by the old door. The ends of the narthex, when I was at Khakh, were just filled with heaps of chalk for whitewash, which had, alas, been plentifully bedaubed over the interior, blurring the exquisite mouldings. I observed a blocked door at the N. end of the narthex, but none at the S. There is a semi-dome at either end of the barrel vault. The vault itself is divided by two stone ribbing arches into three compartments composed of bricks set in squares and bordered with the usual pattern of semi-circular tiles. Three doors lead into the nave; each is surrounded by fine bold mouldings, but the central door is the most elaborately treated (Pls. 139, 141). The mouldings of lintel and jamb are beautifully decorated with palmette, bead and reel and rinceaux. On either side of the door stand round columns carrying uncut Corinthian capitals with garlands hung over the corners. Above the columns and over the lintel of the door is laid an entablature decorated with rinceaux and dentils. A cornice decorated with two rows of dentils runs round the top of the wall under the vault; it can be seen in Pl. 139 together with the beginning of the vault.

The central part of the nave (Fig. 12) is covered with a dome, semi-domes lying to N. and S. of it and another over the apse to the E. The square inscribed by the four horse-shoed arches, to N., S., E.. and W. (the W. arch is over the narthex door) is turned into an octagon by means of squinches (Pl. 142). No attempt was made to change this octagon into a circle, for the dome itself is octagonal not circular (Pl. 140: it is an eight-sided *Klosterkuppel*). The angles are lost in the upper part and the top appears to the eye almost like an ordinary dome, though on close observation I came to the conclusion that the octagonal shape is in reality preserved almost to the summit[67]. Between the squinches are small oblong windows; a dentil moulding runs continuously round the horse-shoe of the squinches and the rectangle of the windows, and the same moulding is set at the base of the octagonal dome. The four arches are worked with rinceaux[68], that over the apse having a richer decoration than the others. The arches spring from garlanded Corinthian capitals (Pl. 143); below the acanthus leaves there is a band of woven entrelac. A moulding on the level of the top of these capitals passes over the

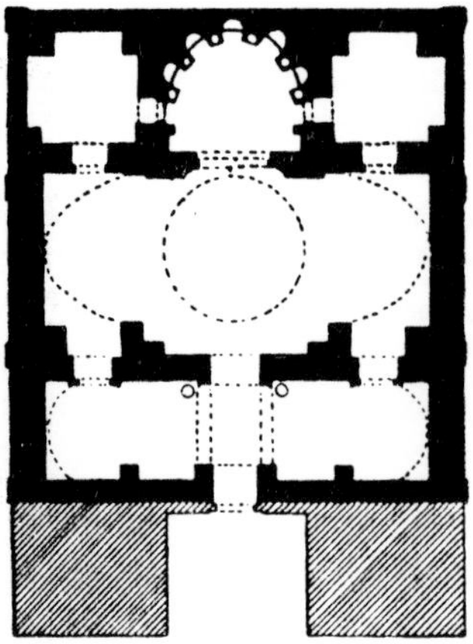

Fig. 12.

Ḥaḥ (Khakh), el 'Adhra, plan of church (cf. Fig. 37)

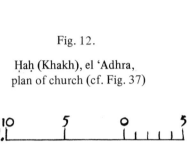

W. door and under the semi-domes. It is worked with palmettes, bead and reel and a band of interslung circles with a diamond shaped motive along the centre where the circles intersect (Pl.144). In the original plan the arch over the entrance of the apse had been left open, but it is now blocked by a stone screen filling the whole arch and pierced by a door – a vestige of it can be seen in the bottom left hand corner of Pl. 142. The apse is thus concealed, which is much to be regretted as it is extremely beautiful[69]. It is set round with six columns carrying four small horse-shoe arches (Pl.145 & Fig.38). Between the columns are five niches each furnished with a stone seat and covered by a tiny shell-shaped semi-dome. (I must apologise for the bad photographs of the apse. The difficulty of photographing in a space extremely exiguous and blocked by the altar was almost insurmountable.) The capitals are some of the most singular with which I am aquainted. They give the effect of an acanthus capital, but when you observe them more closely, you find that they are composed entirely of cords and tassels[70]. The arches are decorated with dentils and an interwoven band; above them is the moulding that runs round the base of the semi-dome. The two columns standing immediately to the E. of the doors leading into the side sanctuaries bear acanthus capitals. Each of the two small sanctuaries to N. and S. of the apse contains an altar.

It would be difficult to over-estimate the importance of this church in the history of architecture. It is probably the earliest example that still exists of the type called by Strzygowski the Kuppelquerschiff, which is, as he points out, the prototype of Sta.Sophia, Constantinople *(Byzantinische Denkmäler* III, p. XVI). Its almost perfect preservation gives it an inestimable value and the setting of the dome is of the highest interest. I may say without hesitation that the Persian system of squinches would be predicted here by every one who is acquainted with Oriental architecture. Whether the dome be ancient or mediaeval, scarcely any other method of setting it on the square is known in the Mosul and Diarbekr districts, although I have seen in the churches E. of Mosul a few mediaeval examples of small domes set on a straight corbel across the angle of the square substructure. But the arched Tromp, the squinch, is by far the most frequent device employed. Whenever and wherever it appears strong Oriental influence may be assumed. (I have given other examples of domes set on corbels and squinches in a book on the *Thousand and One Churches* of the Kara Dagh, written in collaboration with Sir W. Ramsay[71].)

The church of El Adra contains a copy of the Gospels (modern) in an interesting old silver binding which represents the descent into Hades (Pl. 146).

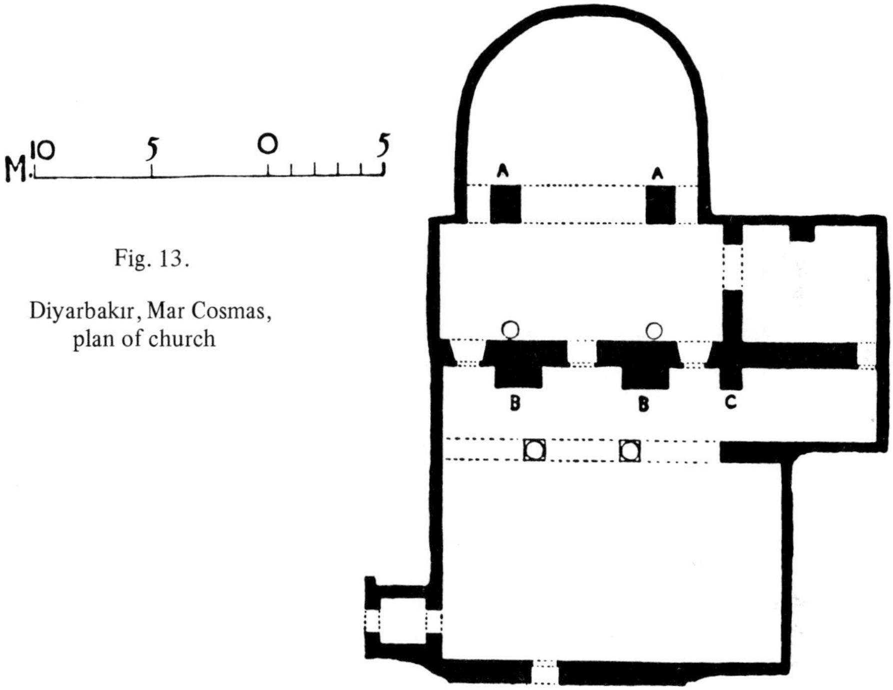

Fig. 13.

Diyarbakır, Mar Cosmas, plan of church

Mar Cosmas, Diarbekr[72].

Of the church of Mar Cosmo (Greek Orthodox) little remains, but that little is enough to show that it belongs to the early group of ecclesiastical buildings which are so plentifully distributed through the Djebel Tur 'Abdin. The parts of the older structure still to be seen in Mar Cosmo (Fig. 13) include the apse and the rectangular chamber which lies before it, possibly also the small chambers to the south. The west side of the present narthex is later work, though the piers on the east side and parts of the wall belong to the original building. I take it therefore that the west side of the narthex of the original church has disappeared and been replaced by the present make-shift piers and wall. The present west wall of the church, which has evidently been much patched and pulled about, bears out this view (Pl. 12). The church is built of stone and mortar, but the semi-dome of the apse is of fine brickwork [73]. The chamber west of the apse is laid so that its greatest length runs from north to south ; this is not unusual in the churches of the district, but I cannot feel certain whether, in the case of Mar Cosmo, we have the original disposition or no. The piers AA and BB look as if they had been intended to support a dome, which would give an entirely different character to the whole building. I think it quite possible that the original form of Mar Cosmo may have resembled closely the church of El Adra which still stands at Khakh [see above, pp. 20ff. and Fig. 37 below]. At the northern end of this lengthways nave there is an altar resting on a mediaeval tomb (Pl. 11). The most significant fragments in the building are to be found on and near the southernmost engaged pier of the east wall of the narthex, marked C in the plan. On the north side of this pier there is a bit of moulding which indicates the existence of an arch that ran from east to west. It must have separated the southern end of the narthex from the central portion, forming a small chamber to the south of the narthex, such as that which still exists (Pl. 9). Above it, built into the east main wall, is a fine Corinthian engaged capital, with garlands hanging over the corners among the acanthus leaves [74]. At a lower level, on the west face of the pier, is another fine capital of uncut acanthus leaves (Pl. 10) [75]. These capitals and mouldings belong to the same period as the work in other churches of the Djebel Tur 'Abdin and the old parts in the Court of the big Mosque in Diarbekr; the profile of the arch moulding resembles many that are to be found on the lintels and string-courses of those buildings.

The court to the west of the church and the bishop's house still further to the west are modern. I was unable to approach from the east owing to the houses which are built up against the apse and therefore do not know the appearance of the church from that side.

El-Hadra, Diarbekr [76].

By far the most important church which I saw in Diarbekr was that of El-Hadra (Jacobite). I had the good fortune to find the bishop at home – his house lies on the south side of the inner south court – and he gave me a short history of the building. The church, said he, was once part of a very large monastic foundation, the precincts of which stretched as far as the Aleppo Gate. (See Parry, *Six Months in a Syrian Monastery,* p. 49. He mentions, but with incredulity, the fact that the present church is but the sanctuary of a far larger building, p. 44. His opinion in matters architectural is not, however, to be trusted.) The part that stands at present had originally been no more than the choir of a large circular church in the centre of which was the tomb of the patriarch Yuhanna ibn Shurban who died, so the bishop said, about 1000 years ago. The site of the tomb is marked by a wire grille, but on measuring the ruins, I found that the bishop had used the word "centre" very loosely, for the tomb lies 15 metres from the east side of the circular church and 41 metres from the west side. The bishop then pointed out to me the remains of the original building. The foundations of the circular church can be traced at intervals, parts of them being hidden by the school and other modern structures which have been erected over them. The school occupies almost the whole of the north side. On the south east side the curve of the foundations took an outer spring which I have indicated in the plan (Fig. 14). With a little excavation the outer line of the walls could be recovered with complete accuracy [cf. Fig. 51, ed. 1981].

Turning to the existing church, the bishop observed that the curious curved

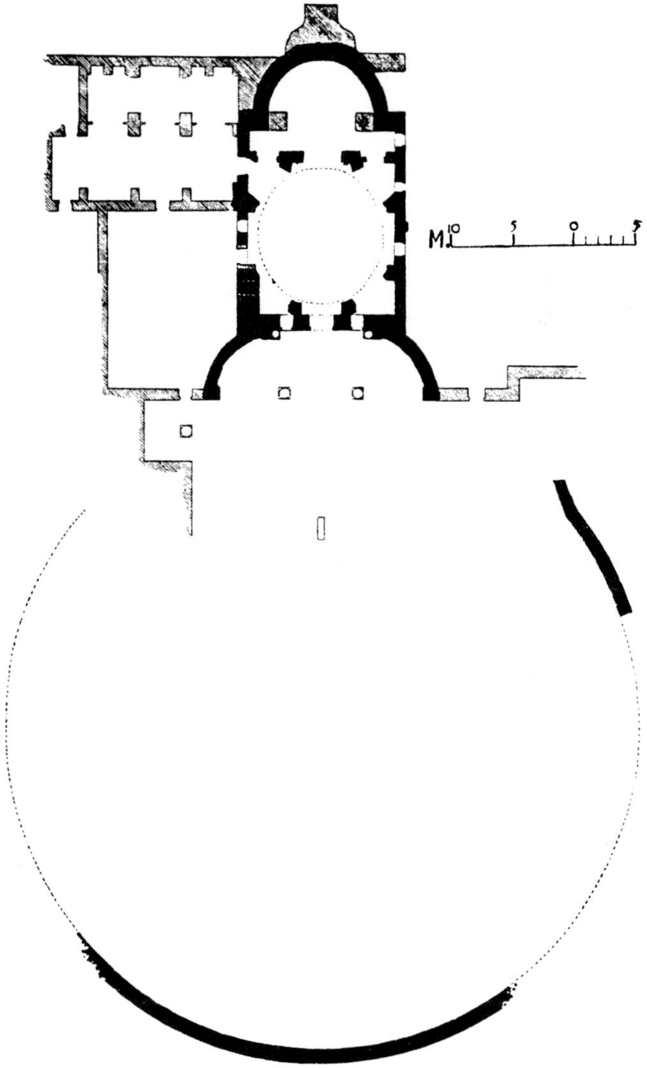

Fig. 14.
Diyarbakır, el 'Adhra,
plan of church and chapel of Mar Ya'qub on N (cf. Fig. 51)

narthex (Pl. 13) had formed the east end of the round church. The four columns (Pl. 22) on the west side of the narthex[77], together with the roof they support, are clearly modern additions. I think it possible that the west door of the existing church, with its two flanking windows, are not part of the first plan. The opening into the ancient choir was probably as wide as the full extent of the arch resting on short columns, that covers door and windows. There are no mouldings round the door, such as one would certainly expect to find if it were early work. Above the narthex roof there was a gaunt fragment of old wall, pierced with pointed windows of different periods, some of which have been filled up. The bishop was positive that this wall had formed the east wall of the circular church. How the original choir was roofed I am unable to say. The present dome is modern and the engaged piers supporting it seemed to me to be all later additions[78]. They are irregular in shape and are placed without any regard for the older structure. They block the western opening of the choir, whether it were originally single or triple; they impinge on the width of the original apse and are set quite irregularly in respect of the two old doors, the one in the north and the other in the south wall. Of these doors, the northern alone remains. Its age is proved by the fine bold mouldings of lintel and jambs (Pl. 14 and section). The south door has been filled up, but a trace of it remains in the brick relieving arch visible on the outer wall (Pl. 17) . It corresponds to the relieving arch over the north door. All the existing windows are modern. The apse has been buttressed and built round on the outside, but its line can easily be made out (Pl. 16). Inside, the opening of the apse has been narrowed by two bits of wall, hatched in the plan. The interior of the church being thickly plastered with whitewash, it might have been difficult to discover that the present arch of the apse is narrower than it once was, but fortunately there remain, high up on the wall on either side, the original engaged capitals that supported the apse arch, together with fragments of the moulding that ran round the arch and was extended on either side to the outer walls of the church (Pl. 18). I was obliged to photograph these capitals from below, but the picture gives a sufficient indication of their character (Pls. 20–21). They are the same garlanded acanthus capitals that appear in Mar Cosmo, Diarbekr, in the churches of the Tur ‘Abdin and in the courtyard of the big Mosque of Diarbekr. On the moulding above the capitals I could make out the egg and dart motive and a band of palmettes[79].

To the north of the church lies a chapel dedicated to Mar Yakub, all of which is modern[80]. Modern, too, are the north and west walls of the small court that lies to the west of this chapel. In the south west corner the court is blocked by the curve of the north east wall of the present narthex (Pl. 15) which, if I am correct, is a part of the old building. In it can be seen the traces of a window, now blocked up, covered by a brick arch or relieving arch. The original structure of the choir, so far as I can judge on a brief study, consisted therefore of a small rectangular building, the greatest length being from east to west, terminating to the east in a wide apse and to the west in a wide opening into the circular church beyond. I should conjecture that it was barrel vaulted.

THE ṬÛR 'ABDÎN AND NEIGHBOURING DISTRICTS

In the spring of 1909 I journeyed through the mountains of the Ṭûr 'Abdîn and found there a group of churches which, though they are of great moment in the history of early Christian art, had received little attention from previous travellers. At the request of Professor Strzygowski I published the results of my observations in the work on Amida which he and M. van Berchem were then preparing for the press [81]. Last year I returned to the Ṭûr 'Abdîn and I avail myself of the kindness of the editor of the Zeitschrift für Geschichte der Architektur to correct some errors in my former plans, to add further photographs and drawings of the Ṭûr 'Abdîn and to compare the churches of that district with others which I visited this year. We may hope to have in the future, from archaeologists whose authority is greater than mine, a record of most of the churches with which I shall deal. Dr. Preusser was in the Ṭûr 'Abdîn in 1909, a month earlier than my first visit, and studied the buildings at Qarṭemîn and at Ṣalaḥ. His book is on the eve of publication (*Nordmesopotamische Baudenkmäler*, 17. Wissenschaftliche Veröffentlichung der Deutschen Orient-Gesellschaft). I have not seen his plans, but he was so kind as to show me his photographs when I was at Qal'at Shergât last year. M. Violett was at Midyâd in 1910 and I believe he visited Ṣalaḥ. Dr. Guyer spent some time in the Ṭûr 'Abdîn last year, prior to my arrival. He tells me that he has collected a considerable body of material, both there and in the region north of Urfah, but I have not yet had the advantage of seeing his drawings.[82]

Fafî

I entered the Ṭûr 'Abdîn this year from Mârdîn, but I was careful not to follow the usual road to Midyâd. Dr. Andrus, a member of the American Mission at Mârdîn, well known for his intimate acquaintance with the surrounding country, had given me the names of certain villages which were not marked in Kiepert's map, telling me that he had heard that ruins were to be found in them (Fig. 15). Following his advice, I travelled by paths unspeakably steep and rocky through a mountain district which has been little explored. In these hills, remote from civilization and inhabited mainly by Mohammadan

Kurds who speak no language but Kurdish, I seemed to have come upon an older stratum of monuments than any which has remained in the comparatively open plains and wide cultivated valleys round Midyâd. The first of these buildings was a much ruined tower tomb in the village of Fafî[83] (Pl. 110). (Mentioned by Pognon, *Inscriptions de la Syrie et de la Mésopotamie,* p. 16, note 1. He compares it with the Towers at Serrîn, published by him in the same work and by me in *Amurath to Amurath,* p. 36 [one of these is dated A.D. 73],with the Qâmu'a Hurmul near Baalbek [*Desert and the Sown,* p. 190], and with a tower tomb near Edessa [*Amida,* p. 268][84].) The S.E. corner stands to a height of two storeys. At the angles of the lower storey are placed shallow engaged pilasters crowned with Corinthian capitals of unworked acanthus (Pl. 111). Between the capitals and on a level with them, supporting the entablature, human torsos are set upon a bunch of acanthus leaves, two figures to each facade (Pl. 112). They are headless and, as far as can be made out in their battered condition, their arms are bent back behind them.

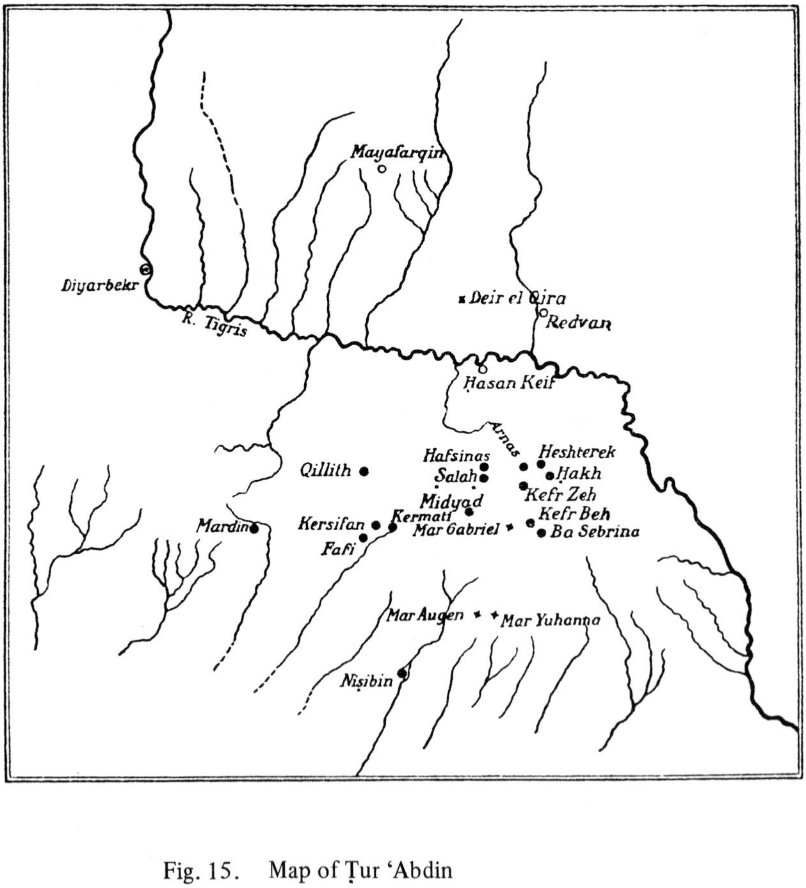

Fig. 15. Map of Ṭur 'Abdin

Above them runs an architrave consisting of a couple of fasciae and a projecting cornice, well and sharply moulded (Pl. 109). Above the architrave are fragments of a frieze decorated with rinceaux in which the garlands of acanthus encircle heads of men and animals and small squatting figures. For this type of decoration, well known in Syria and in Egypt (*Desert and the Sown*, p. 246; Strzygowski, *Koptische Kunst*, p. 54), there is a later North Mesopotamian example upon the exterior of Deir Za'ferân, the famous Jacobite monastery near Mârdîn (Pl. 189). The date of the Fafî tomb was probably recorded upon a tablet on the S. wall, part of which still exists; but the Greek inscription is almost illegible (Pl. 108). Sir William Ramsay, to whom I sent the photograph, replies: "So much is lost that the whole is not capable of restoration, except after an amount of conjecture which would deprive the restoration of almost all value as evidence. It is in a script very regular and peculiarly difficult to date, but it may well be of the second or third century after Christ, not earlier. The inscription is metrical, and metrical inscriptions cannot be restored except by valueless conjecture. A prose inscription in regular formulae can often be restored with comparative certainty, the other is a mere exercise in Greek verse and I have found that when even 1/8 part of each line has to be restored, the restoration is very remote from the original when discovered"[85]. The evidence of the inscription, so far as it goes, bears out the conclusions which I had formed from the architecture, namely that the building is a monument of the pagan era and dates, in all probability, from the 3rd century. The tomb, so I was informed by the inhabitants of the village, was destroyed some 70 years ago by the cannon balls of Ḥâfiẓ Pasha who came up to quell the unruly Kurds of Fafî. Their lawless independence must go back far into the past, for their village still shows the evidences of ancient fortification. Fafî stands, like most of the villages of the western Ṭûr 'Abdîn, upon a headland of rock jutting out between two converging valleys. The whole of the bluff had been surrounded by a massive wall built of undressed stones laid dry (Pls. 113-114). On the S.W. side of the hill the wall, reinforced by huge solid bastions, ran down towards the western valley. The gateway had lain to the N. where the walls, partly rock cut, partly built of immense stones, had enclosed a spring. The tower tomb stands in the southern line of the wall. S. of it, outside the fortifications, a sacred grove of oaks marks the burial ground, and below the grove there are rock cut tombs. I cannot attempt to date the fortifications of Fafî[86]. Dr. Andrus has described to me a somewhat similar site N. of Qullith which he believes to be Assyrian. That the civilization of these mountains is very ancient, is clear from the fact that Midyâd is mentioned in cuneiform inscriptions (Lehmann-Haupt, *Armenien Einst und Jetzt*, vol. 1, p. 370); the peasants of the western villages brought me small seals, some of which may go back to late Hittite times, and Dr. Thom, a colleague of Dr. Andrus at Mârdîn, has in his possession a bronze figure[87], found in the Ṭûr 'Abdîn, which has strong affinities with Hittite art.

Kersifân and Kermâtî

Before I reached Midyâd I came upon two shrines which I believe to be pre-Christian. The first and larger of the two was at the village of Kersifân (Fig. 16)[88]. It is composed of three open courts, set back into the hill-side, so that the eastern end was partly rock-cut (Pls. 167-168). The E. wall (the orientation is not quite exact) is formed entirely out of the living rock, the irregular apses in the N. and central courts are hollowed out of

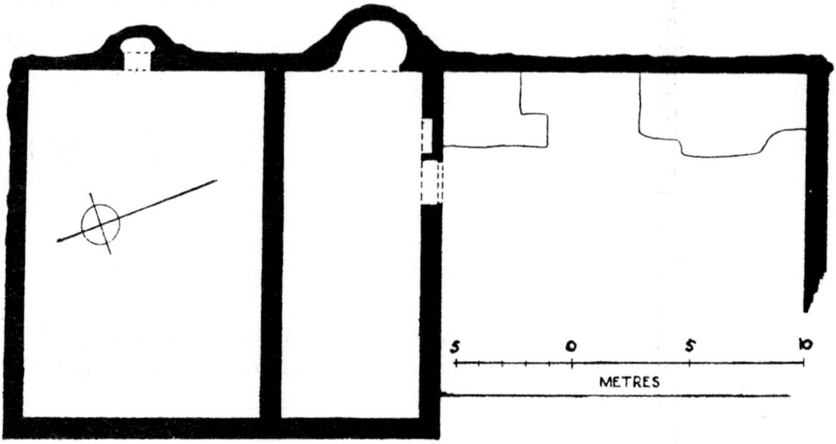

Fig. 16. Kersifan, plan of shrine

(Below) Figs. 17 & 18. Kermati, plan of shrine, and drawing of two figures in low relief

the hill, and the platforms on the E. side of the S. court are outcrops of rock. Above the rock cutting, the dividing walls are built of huge blocks of stone; most of the W. wall has fallen away down the hill, but the stones that remain on this side are not quite so large as in the dividing walls. Owing

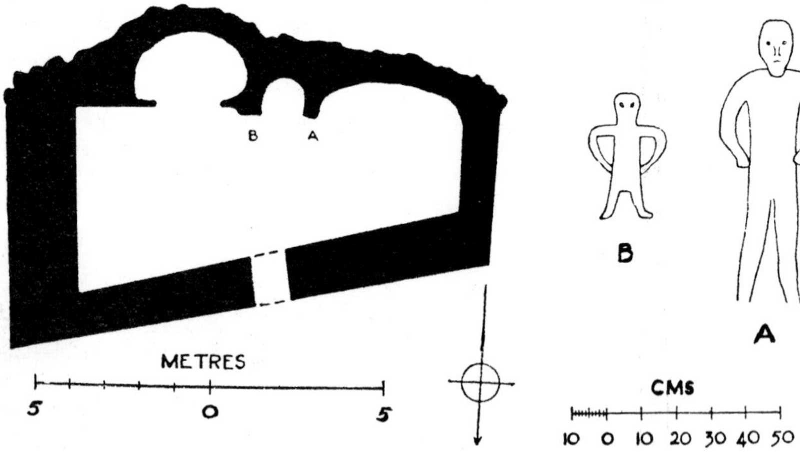

to the approximate orientation, I was in doubt as to whether this strange sanctuary might not have been of Christian origin, but close to the neighbouring village of Kermâti [89] I found a smaller shrine of the same character in which the apses lay nearly due S. (Fig. 17). Here too the structure runs back into the hill and the apses and S. wall are rock cut. Between the apses, at the points marked A. and B. in the plan, two rude figures are carved in flat low relief, one being that of a man, the other, about half the size, of a woman (Fig. 18). The court N. of the apses had been covered by a roof of great slabs, resting at the N. end upon a masonry wall. On the slopes of the hill below the village I saw two chambers which seemed to belong to very ancient dwellings. The roof was constructed in the same manner with huge slabs corbelled forward between a rock cut wall and a wall built of large stones. The innumerable deep stony valleys and steep ridges with which the Ṭûr Abdîn is intersected make the district peculiarly difficult to explore exhaustively, but I believe that a careful archaeological survey would yield many valuable results.

Mâr Gabriel, Qarṭemîn?[90]

I revisited the great monastery of Mâr Gabriel and give here a corrected plan (Fig. 19). The chambers on the N. side of the church were inaccurately drawn [91]. That which lies E. of the octagon is a very late structure, and I do not think that any part of the monastry is as old as the principal church. The church dedicated to the Virgin, which lies at the S.W. angle of the monastery has a different, and a more accurate, orientation. It is of a considerably later period. Belonging perhaps to the same date as the church of the Virgin is the church of the Forty Martyrs, which stands at a higher level on the opposite side of the small W. court, i.e. in the N.W. angle of the monastery (Fig. 20). Below it, and partly below the level of the ground, are some chambers cut down into the rock which are shown in the N.W. angle of the ground plan (Fig. 19). Two of these, approached through a small vestibule leading into a short passage, contain tomb niches; a third, N. of the vestibule, has been used as a chapel and contains an altar. None of these rooms are lighted by windows. In the present plan I have placed the octagonal tomb of the Egyptian monks in its correct position N. of the monastery (Pl. 208) [92]. The principal church, dedicated to Mâr Gabriel, I believe to be the church built by Anastasius about the year 500 (Pognon, Inscriptions, p. 39). The vault of the oblong nave is covered, like the rest of the church, with plaster, but the plaster has peeled away in many places, revealing the materials used in the building (Pls. 217-218). The vault is divided into three sections by a couple of stone transverse arches springing from projecting corbels. The corbels are not placed as low down as the spring of the vault, but at the point where the curve becomes abrupt. I make no doubt that the stone masonry of the walls is carried up to the corbels; between the stone transverse arches, however, the vault is of

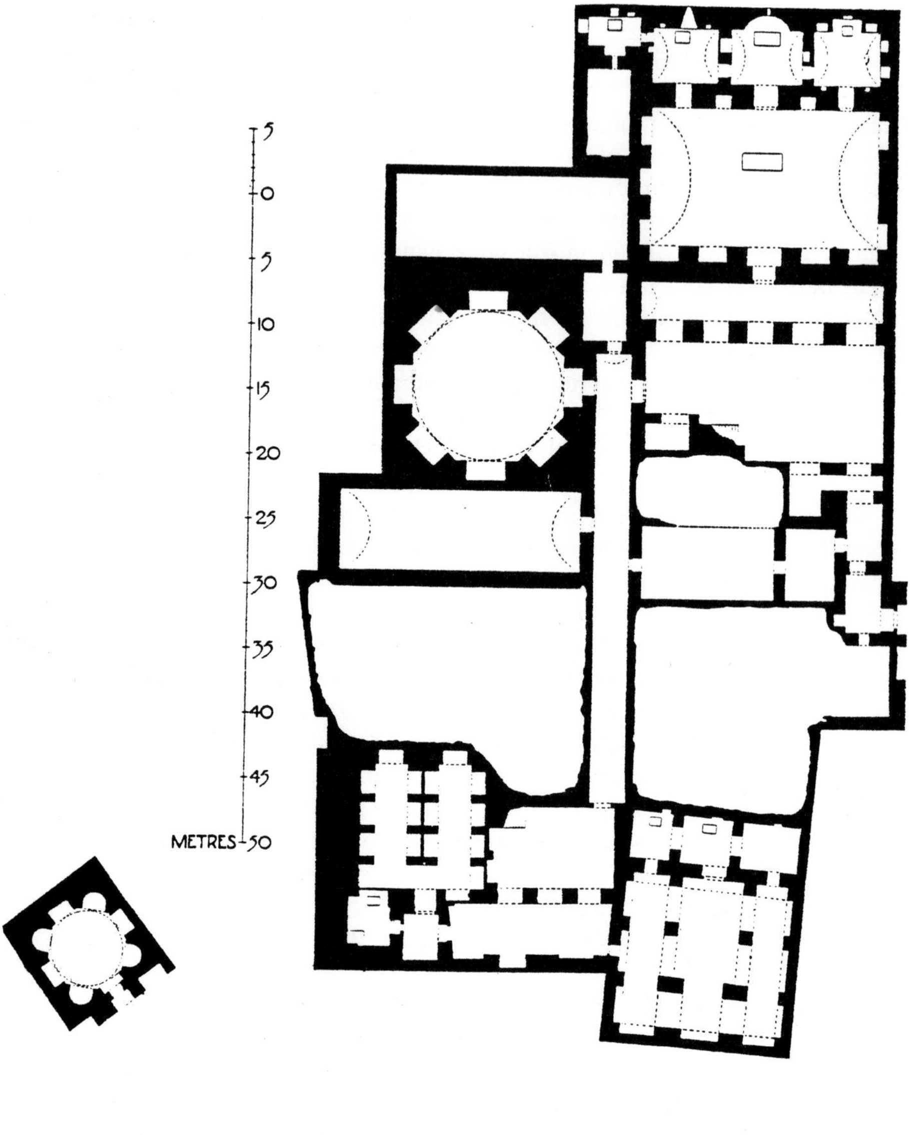

Fig. 19. Mar Gabriel, plan of monastery (cf. Fig. 5)

brick, and according to the system universally followed in the Ṭûr 'Abdîn, the bricks are laid in squares stretching from arch to arch. But the brickwork has not the finish of the exquisite vaults of Ṣalaḥ (Pl. 244), which are the finest in the district, nor even of the vault of Kefr Zeh (Pl. 164); it is without the bands of herring-boning and of semi-circular tiles which give so beautiful an effect in those two churches and in the narthex of Ḥâkh, and it is evident that at Mâr Gabriel the brick was not intended to be seen. Local tradition insists that the vault of the nave was once covered with mosaic like the vault of the presbyterium; possibly a careful examination of the brickwork might yield some evidence as to the truth of this tale. Of the presbyterium mosaic a precious fragment remains [93]. The barrel vault is covered with a spreading vine, the spirals of which encircle leaves and bunches of grapes (Fig. 21). The drawing is made from a photograph and from a sketch of mine done on the spot. Every spiral of the vine contains a leaf or a bunch of grapes, but only those are drawn which could be made out distinctly. The vault is much blackened by smoke; if it were cleaned every detail would be visible. At each of the four corners, the vine springs from a double handled vase. The body of the vase is divided into two zones by a narrow band; in the lower zone a geometric design springs up from the pointed base. In the centre of the vine, at the top of the vault, there is a rayed crux gemmata enclosed in a circle (Fig. 22) [94]. The vault is bordered by three bands of ornament. The first is a forked pattern worked in three colours [95]; the second a row of hollow 8-pointed stars with a white dot in every point and an ivy leaf in the hollow centre; the third a series of rhomboids, separated from each other by a cross band of three jewels, the whole closely resembling the jewelled bands which occur in Byzantine mosaics of the 6th century. On the S. wall of the chamber, under the vault, there are fragments of mosaic in which it is possible to make out a small domed tabernacle, the dome carried on two pairs of columns [96]. On the N. wall also there are traces of mosaic [97], and upon the floor there is a pavement of different coloured marbles [98]. The mosaic on the vault is carried out

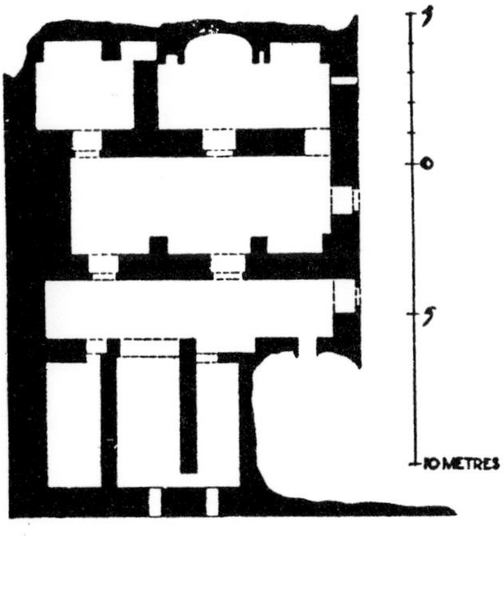

Fig. 20. Mar Gabriel, plan of church of Forty Martyrs

in red, a pale greenish blue, and white, upon a gold ground; there may be shades which in the darkness and dirt escape detection, but I do not think that the range of colours is large[99]. I see no good reason for doubting that the mosaic is contemporary with the church. The execution of the vine is fine and

Fig. 21. Mar Gabriel, drawing of mosaic on vault of main church

delicate in detail, and the realistic treatment is unlike mosaics of the Moslem period. The decoration of Mâr Gabriel belongs to the same family as the creations of Byzantine mosaicists. Involuntarily the spectator compares it with the trailing vines that encompass the golden figures of the Evangelists in the vaults of Galla Placidia's tomb at Ravenna (Phot. Ricci, No. 69), or with

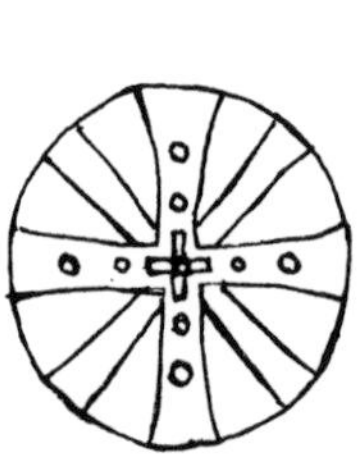

Fig. 22. Mar Gabriel, drawing of mosaic on vault of main church

the rolling branches springing from many-coloured baskets on the walls of San Vitale (Phot. Ricci, No. 25)[100]. It is singularly instructive to place the Ṭûr 'Abdîn fragment side by side with the drawings of the mosaics in the Qubbet eṣ Ṣaḥrah in Jerusalem (De Vogüé: *Le Temple de Jérusalem*, plates 21, 22, 23)[101]. The 8-pointed hollow stars, an exceedingly common motive, reappear in the border of the earlier of the Jerusalem mosaics (finished in AD 691) but the fantastic vegetation of 'Abdul Malik's work bears no relation to the vine scrolls of the Christian church. New influences have come into play, Persian artistic themes proclaim the conquest of the Hellenistic world by artificers steeped in the traditions of the Sasanian kings. ("The home of this strange vegetation is to be sought not in Constantinople, Greece or Egypt, but in Mesopotamia and Persia where it had been employed for several centuries." Dalton, *Church of the Nativity at Bethlehem*, p. 35.) Nor was that conquest to prove transitory; the Qubbet eṣ Ṣaḥrah bears evidence of its enduring nature. The second series of mosaics (completed in AD 1027) exhibits the same characteristics as the first, and a hundred and fifty years later El Malik eẓ Ẓâhir decorated his madrasah at Damascus (finished in 1279) with mosaics of which the elements still show a strong Persian feeling[102]. All these have nothing to do with the vine scrolls of Mâr Gabriel, which belong to an earlier age and were born of a different tradition.

Mâr Ibrahîm and Mâr Ubil[103].

A church of the same type as Mâr Gabriel is that of Mâr Ibrahîm. The monastery of Mâr Ibrahîm and Mâr Ubil stands upon the outskirts of Midyâd (Fig. 23). The larger church, according to the information given to me by the monks, is dedicated to Mâr Ibrahîm, while a smaller church to the N. is dedicated to Mâr Ubil. It would be more accurate to describe the northern church as a tomb chamber with a single sanctuary to the E. These burial chambers are usually outside the church, and not uncommonly they are connected with a chapel, as at Mâr Gabriel. Like Mâr Gabriel, the Midyâd monastery also contains a church dedicated to the Virgin. It is in this case a small domed building lying immediately to the S. of the main church. I planned the monastery when I was at Midyâd in 1909, but I did not publish it in *Amida* for the reason that it has been almost entirely rebuilt at a recent date. It was, so the monks informed me, reduced to a state of complete ruin, and little of the present structure is old. The restoration was however carried out on the original foundations, and any part of the walls that were standing are included in the present monastery. The churches of Mâr Ibrahîm and Mâr Ubil, together with the monastic buildings, form three sides of a court, the fourth (western) side of which is bounded by a wall wherein is the principal entrance. The monastic buildings are all modern, and are not included in the plan. The church of the Virgin opens onto a small inner court which has been entirely rebuilt. To the

E. and S. of the existing house there are traces of ruined walls among the vineyards, showing that the monastery must once have occupied a larger area. The plan of the main church is exactly the same as Mâr Gabriel except that the narthex is closed on the W. side by a solid wall instead of by an arcade. I doubt whether this is the original arrangement. Traces of an arcade exist in the W. wall of the narthex of Mâr Ubil; the piers, with their moulded capitals and horse-shoed arches, are clearly visible in the body of the wall, though the openings of the arcade have been filled in with modern masonry (Pls. 176-177). This arcade is continued along the N. wall of the narthex of Mâr Ibrahîm, which projects beyond the face of the narthex of Mâr Ubil. A single arch springs from the corner pier, now concealed (A. on the plan) to the pier (B)

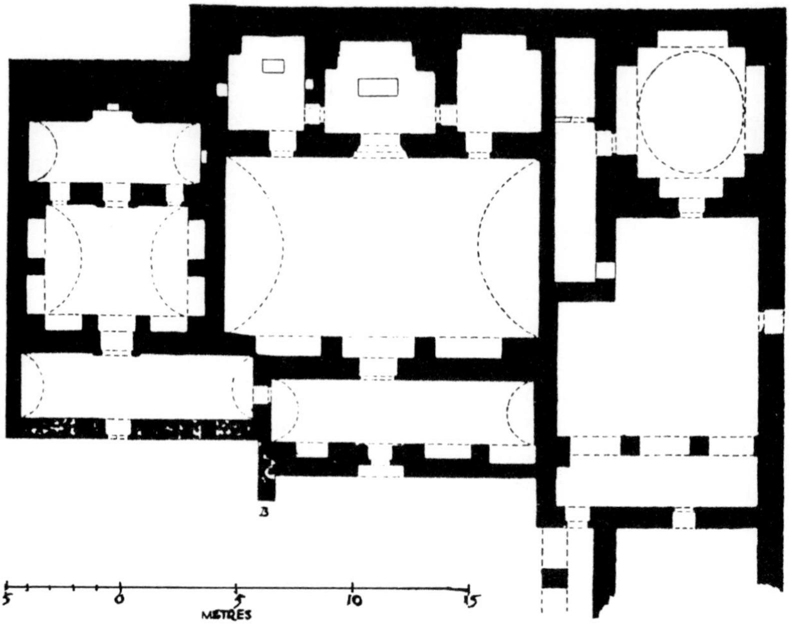

Fig. 23. Midyat, Mar Ibrahim and Mar Ubil, plan of churches

which juts out into the court (Pls. 177-178). It looks as if the narthex of Mâr Ibrahîm had at one time been wider than it is at present and had been closed by an arcade of which B. is the angle pier. A great part of the E. wall of Mâr Ibrahîm is ancient (Pl. 180). It is moreover crowned by the original heavy cyma cornice which must have been picked up among the ruins and relaid – a piece of it, built into the wall, can be seen in Plate 177. In Mâr Ubil the moulded doorways from narthex to nave (Pl. 181), and from nave to sanctuary are part of the old work, and so too are the horse-shoed arches over the tomb niches – probably a considerable amount of the tomb chamber was standing at the time of the restoration, but the walls here and in the adjoining church are covered with whitewash, and it is impossible to detect the differences of structure which must exist. The door mouldings of Mâr Ubil are shallow and poor. The domed church of the Virgin is rebuilt from the foundations, and the structure of the dome is not therefore of any importance. The main gate of the monastery, in the W. wall, has lintels and jambs decorated with bands of geometric ornament in shallow relief (Pls. 182-183). There is also an almost obliterated Syriac inscription running round the door opening[104]. The stones here have all been relaid and the gateway is a mere patchwork of fragments which cannot themselves, judging from the decoration upon them, belong to a very early period.

There is an interesting problem connected with the religious house of Mâr Ibrahîm and Mâr Ubil. As is well known, the history of monasticism begins in the Ṭûr 'Abdîn with the foundation of St. Eugenius, who was an Egyptian from the island of Clysma and a disciple of St. Anthony. He died about the year 362 (*Livre de la Chasteté* ed. Chabot, p. 4; *Histoire de Seert*, Patrologia Orientalis, vol. 4, p. 235 where his correspondence with Constantine is mentioned; Budge, *Book of Governors*, vol. 1, pp. XLV and CXXV). The monastery which he founded near Nisibis on Mount Îzlâ I identify with the establishment which is still called by his name, Mâr Augên, situated on the heights of the Ṭûr 'Abdîn overlooking the Mesopotamian plain (*Amida*, p. 225). It is recorded in the life of Mâr Augên (published by Bedjan in the *Acta Martyrum et Sanctorum*, part 3)[105] that he and his disciples were empowered by Sapor to build monasteries wherever they pleased. In the list of disciples who profited by this permission occur the names of Mâr Ibrahîm and Mâr Ubil, but they are not specially connected with one another[106]. There was however a second, and a more famous, Mâr Ibrahîm, a native of Kashkâr (Wâsiṭ) who founded a monastery in Mt. Îzlâ near Nisibis towards the middle of the 6th century (Hoffmann, *Auszüge aus "Syrische Akten persischer Märtyrer"*, p. 172, *Book of Governors*, vol. 2, p. 37, *Livre de la Chasteté*, p. 8). This monastery, which was extremely renowned and is frequently mentioned by the Syriac chroniclers, I have not been able to identify, unless it be one and the same with the monastery of Mâr Ibrahîm and Mâr Ubil near Midyâd. There is a certain amount of negative evidence in favour of this theory in the absence of any fragments of architecture which could be referred to a date earlier than the end of the 6th century, but the association of Mâr Ubil with Mâr Ibrahîm of Kashkâr would be difficult to explain, and a more exhaustive exploration of the Ṭûr 'Abdîn may reveal another site which can be accepted with certainty as that of the Great Monastery of Mt. Îzlâ. (Hoffmann, *Auszüge* p. 170, identifies the monastery of Mâr Ibrahîm of Kashkâr with a ruined monastery of Mâr Bauai, mentioned by Taylor [*Journal of the Royal Geographical Society* 1865, vol. 35, p. 52] which he believes to be identical with

Cernik's Marbâb [*Petermann's Mitteilungen*, Ergänzungsheft No. 45] a village at the foot of the hills a little to the S.E. of Qal 'at edj Djedîd. I rode through the foot hills in 1909 on the way from Qal 'at Ḥâtim Ṭayy to Qal 'at edj Djedîd and neither saw the monastery of Bauai nor heard of it, but in the broken ground I may have passed close by without catching sight of it, and I was that day without a guide and therefore got no information concerning villages not directly on my path. The description of the site of the "Great Monastery" which Hoffmann quotes [p. 167] from an Arab author of the 13th century, and applies to the monastery of Mâr Ibrahîm of Kashkâr is not conclusive, for it would apply equally well to the monastery of Mâr Augên, as I know from having visited the latter. Michael the Syrian gives "Îzlâ" in a list of monasteries existing about the year 518 [ed. Chabot, vol. 2, p. 171]. He must mean the monastery of Mâr Augên, since that of Mâr Ibrahîm of Kashkâr cannot have been built at that time. Ibrahîm was an old man in 596 and must therefore have been too young to found monasteries in 518. I suspect that there is in the chroniclers a considerable amount of confusion between Augên's foundation, the earliest in Mt. Îzlâ, and the Great Monastery of Ibrahîm of Kashkâr, which superseded the other in importance[107].)

Mâr Malkâ[108].

Between Mâr Augên and Midyâd stands the monastery of Mâr Malkâ. Like Mâr Gabriel it stands alone, the nearest village being a mile or two away, and like Mâr Gabriel its appearance is that of a little fortress (Pl. 222). I visited

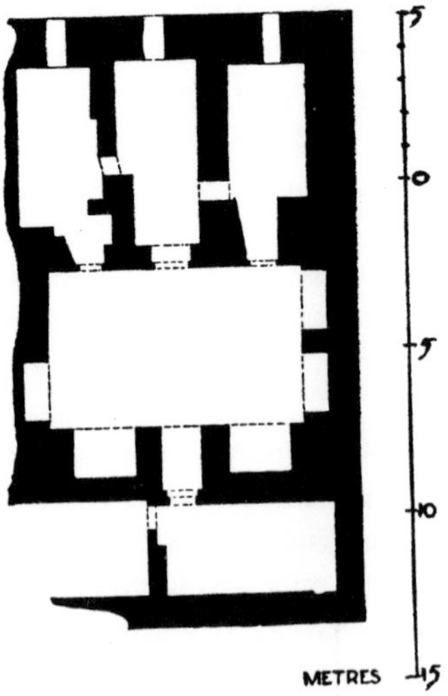

Fig. 24. Mar Malka, plan of church

Mâr Malkâ in 1909 and at that time planned the little church which it contains (Fig. 24), but I did not publish the plan in *Amida* because it is impossible to hazard any conjecture as to the date of the building. The church is not detached, but forms an integral part of the monastic complex. It is somewhat raised above the level of the ground, and below it are windowless and half subterranean burial chambers. The masonry is rough and indistinctive, there are no mouldings or decorations, much of the monastery had recently been repaired or rebuilt, and if there were any walls of an earlier date they were hidden beneath plaster and whitewash. The church is of the usual monastic type, with an oblong nave lying across the three sanctuaries. The narthex, I was specifically told, is used by the women during the services. The tomb of the patron saint is in a niche in the N. wall of the nave. Above it is a rude picture of Mâr Malkâ overcoming the Devil, and I was informed that the tomb possesses miraculous powers of healing and it is visited by persons of all creeds who are afflicted with fits or madness (Niebuhr heard of the wonder-working fame of Mâr Malkâ, *Reisebeschreibung*, vol 2, p. 388). In spite of its lack of architectural interest the monastery is an ancient foundation. It existed at least as early as the 7th century, for it is mentioned as the convent in which Athanasius of Balad pursued his studies in Greek philosophy (Athanasius became patriarch in the year 684. Wright, *Syriac Literature*, p. 155; Assemani, *Bib. Or*, vol. 1, p. 498)[108a]. The name of Mâr Malkâ occurs in the list of the disciples of Mâr Augên who founded monasteries, and local tradition describes him as the nephew of the Egyptian Ascetic[109].

Mâr Yaʻqûb el Ḥabîs, Ṣalaḥ[110].

There was an important correction to be made in the plan of this church: the exterior of the apse is polygonal, not circular as I first drew it (Fig. 25). I was mistaken in saying that the church is no longer used nor the monastery inhabited. I found this year two monks, who told me that services are regularly conducted. The buildings to the W. of the church which the monks occupy are modern. On revisiting Ṣalaḥ I was impressed even more than before by the beauty and solidity of the architecture. The masonry is better finished here than anywhere in the Ṭûr ʻAbdîn, except in the church of the Virgin at Ḥâkh, and the brickwork of the vaulted roofs is the finest in the district[111]. Plate 244, a view of the northern end of the nave vault, gives some idea of the surface of the stone and the decorative effect of the brick. As at Mâr Gabriel, the vault is divided into three compartments by stone transverse arches, but at Ṣalaḥ, where the roof was intended to be seen, these arches are painted to imitate brick. The laying of the bricks in squares gives to each compartment the effect of a hollow pyramid, but this is an optical illusion, the curve of the vault being in fact uninterrupted. In the wide band of herring-boning which borders the squares, there is, at the centre of each compartment, a diamond-shaped ornament. The diamond contains a circle, which in turn encompasses a small Greek cross. The Greek cross reappears at either end of the church upon the moulding which runs round the nave under the vault. On the N. side this moulding is carried straight through from wall to wall, as can be seen in

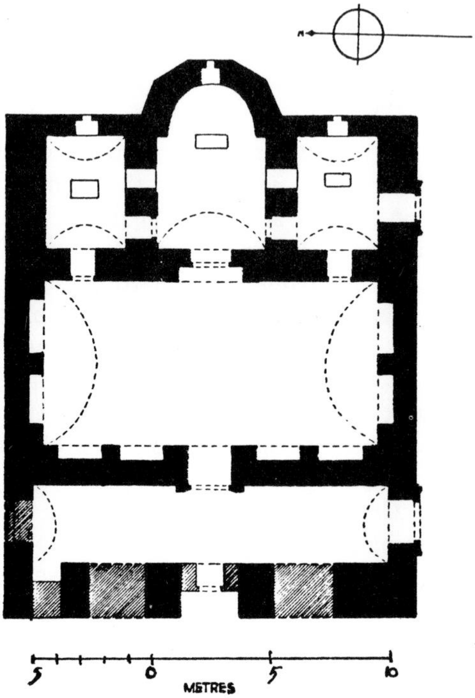

Fig. 25. Ṣalaḥ, Mar Ya'qub Ḥabisha, plan of church (cf. Fig. 6)

Pl. 244, but on the S. side it forms a ramp which is carried over the three windows. It was impossible to photograph the S. end of the church, owing to the fact that the only light comes through one of the three southern windows (the other windows are all blocked up) but Fig. 26 gives the elevation[112]: the two niches below, the three windows placed high up in the wall, with long sills splayed inwards to the interior face of the masonry, and the moulding decorated with a cross above the central window. The same moulding, with its band of dentils between a cyma and a half-round, is carried round the interior of the sanctuary, under the barrel vault and under the semi-dome of the apse, interrupted only by engaged capitals of uncut acanthus from which springs the arch of the semi-dome. On the narthex wall the cornice is simpler, the dentils being omitted (Fig. 27a). Round the foot of the narthex wall runs a moulded base (Fig. 27b) corresponding to the base of the piers which carry the arcade on the W. side. Upon the door leading from the nave into the central sanctuary were expended the chief efforts of the builders[113] The lintel and jambs of the doorway are richly moulded (Pl. 246). On either side of the doorway stands a pilaster adorned with carved bands. The pilasters carry capitals composed of flat leaves arranged alternately in two regular rows. A broad strongly marked rib appears in the upper part of each leaf, and the tip of the leaf falls

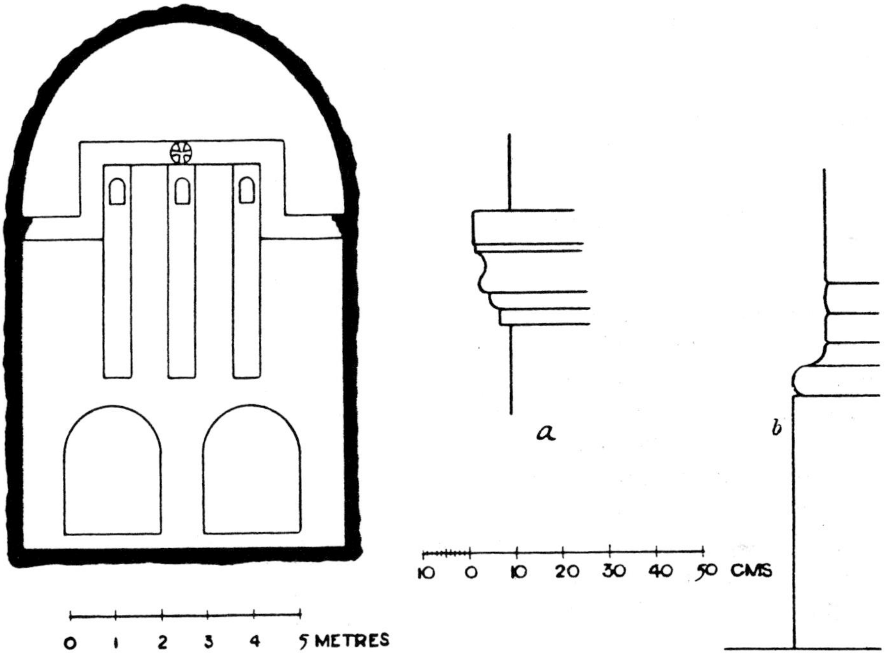

Figs. 26 & 27. Ṣalaḥ, Mar Ya'qub Ḥabisha, church, drawings of S wall of nave and of mouldings in narthex

over slightly onto the rib. From the central rosette of the abacus a thin garland hangs down round the upper series of leaves and is caught back onto the abacus at either side of the capital. Upon the capitals rests a moulded architrave which springs up over the door into a horse-shoed archivolt. In the tympanum there are traces of fresco. To return to the decoration of the pilasters: a plain fillet, 8 mm wide, runs round the face of each pilaster. Within the fillet there is a band of vine rinceaux, within the rinceaux a band of shallow mouldings, while the space that remains in the centre of the pilaster is filled with a strip of carving in relief (Fig. 28, Pl. 247). The vine rinceaux are much broken and still further defaced by whitewash. Within each curve of the vine branch springs an upright leaf. The surface of these leaves is delicately worked, the swell of the lobes from the central rib is given with great fidelity, and the texture of the leaf is reproduced in the stone. The stalk on which the leaf grows ends in a small trefoil at the root of the lobes. Below each leaf hangs a bunch of grapes. The lower band of the rinceaux is much broken. The branches seem to grow out of a vase, standing on a high foot, with a couple of birds drinking from it. In the central strip of carving the vine does not reappear. The upper part is filled with six birds, each standing upon a small branch. They are short in the leg and long in the bill, and resemble water birds. Below them are two alternating motives. The one is a fantastic acanthus blossom: two leaves with curving tips, facing one another, spring upwards from a smaller pair of leaves hanging downwards. A drill hole marks the centre of the smaller leaves, and a third drill hole emphasizes the point where the upper leaves curve apart. The second motive is a fir cone outlined by tendrils, the points of which roll away from the tip of the cone. The pilasters at Ṣalaḥ furnish a clue to another much contested monument, a marble niche which is now built into the outer wall of the Khâṣakî Djâmi' at Baghdâd and serves as a miḥrâb. Viollet, who first published a photograph of the niche (Descrip. du palais de al-Moutasim, *Mémoires présentés à l'Acad. des Inscrip. et Belles Lettres,* tome 12, deuxième partie, p. 11), pronounced it to be of Christian origin; Herzfeld (*Der Islam*, vol. 1, p. 35, Die Genesis der islamischen Kunst) is persuaded that it dates from the time of the foundation of Baghdâd in AD 762, and conjectures that it may have come from N. Syria or the Diyârbekr district [114]. The work of the miḥrâb is less delicate than that of the pilasters.

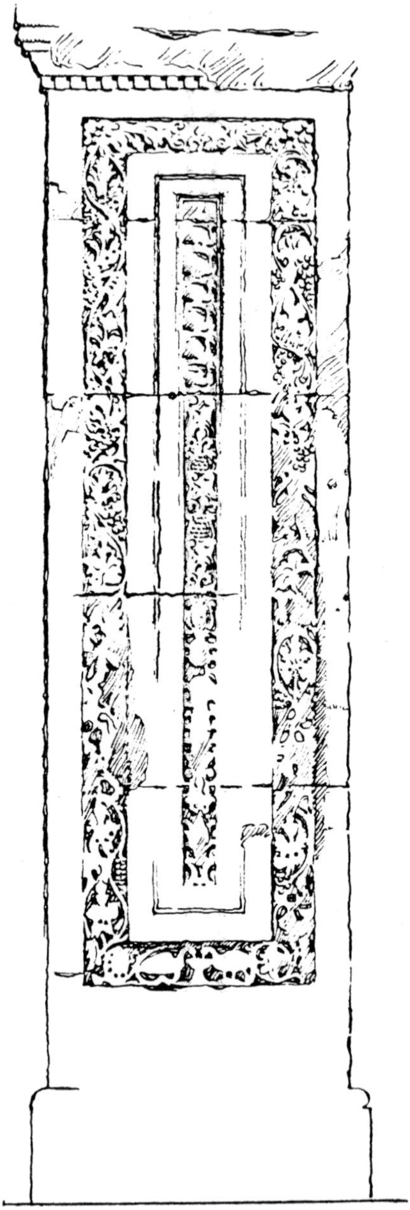

Fig. 28. Ṣalaḥ, Mar Ya'qub Ḥabisha, church, drawing of pilaster (cf. Fig. 7)

The vine leaves are much flatter than those on the outer bands at Ṣalaḥ, but they show the same feature of a trefoil at the end of the stalk, though it is more rudely expressed. (Herzfeld has drawn it as three berries, and it has almost that appearance. In Coptic work the vine stalk frequently ends in a triple berry; for examples see the illustrations given by Strzygowski in *Mschatta*, p. 304. At Mschatta the motive varies from a fully developed vine leaf placed inside the larger leaf at the base of the lobes, not unlike the Ṣalaḥ example, to a swelling at the end of the stalk. Sometimes it is omitted entirely.) The pine cone reappears at Baghdâd, though the tendrils on either side are treated there more like acanthus leaves. Above all, the singular decorative scheme of an upright strip of ornament which distinguishes the miḥrâb, is found also at Ṣalaḥ. The capitals at Baghdâd are unlike any known to me in N. Mesopotamia. They seem to be more nearly related to Syrian work.

Concerning St. James the Hermit, to whom the church is dedicated, Procopius relates the following story in his account of the besieging of Amida by Kobad in the winter of 502–3 (*De Bello Persico*, 1.7, Bonn Edition 1833, pp. 34–35. Assemani alludes to the tale: *Bib. Or.* vol. 1, p. 256 and 275)[115]. Many years earlier, James had retired to a place in the territory of the Endieli, a day's journey from Amida, where an enclosure had been built for him by the people. Here he lived like an ascetic. At the time of the war, some Epthalites discovered him and drew their bows on him, but before they could shoot, their arms were stiffened so that they could not hold their weapons. They remained thus until Kobad heard of it. He came to see the miracle and begged James to undo the mischief. This he did with a single word, whereat Kobad offered him any reward he chose to ask, expecting that he would demand a sum of money. But James asked for immunity during the war for all fugitives who should take refuge with him. His request was granted and many persons were thus saved. According to Taylor (Travels in Kurdestan, *Journal of the R. Geographical Soc.* [1865], vol. 35, p. 31) there is an old convent dedicated to the same saint at Sâ'irt. Little is known concerning the history of the monastery at Ṣalaḥ, and there would seem to be no mention of it at an early date. It occurs once in the list of bishops which is given at the end of the Chronicle of Michael the Syrian (Ed. Chabot, vol. 3, p. 459): "John, bishop of Sarûdy, of the monastery of Ḥabîsa, which is in the Ṭûr 'Abdîn". The tomb of this bishop is still to be seen in the narthex of Mâr Ya'qûb and the inscription, dated in the year of the Greeks 1219 (AD 907) has been published by Pognon (*Inscriptions*, p. 64). None of the other inscriptions from Ṣalaḥ published by him bear so early a date [116]. There exists in the church an unpublished Syriac inscription, but it is placed in a position which makes it exceedingly difficult to decipher. It is painted upon two stones of the vault, immediately below the brickwork on the E. side of the nave, above the main sanctuary door. It appears in one of my photographs of the vault and I sent it to Dr. Cooke, who consulted Professor Margoliouth as to its interpretation. It is a list of subscribers with a notification of the amounts subscribed, and both authorities agree that the writing is decidedly late, not more than three or four centuries old. It would probably relate, therefore, to some restoration of the church or monastery and can give no clue as to the date of the foundation[117]. Beyond the likelihood that a church dedicated to Mâr Ya'qûb el Ḥabîs cannot be earlier than the 6th century, there is no definite conclusion to be drawn from the epigraphic and historical evidence which we possess.

I saw another monastic church built on exactly the same plan as those which I have described. It was at Deir el Qirâ in the Djebel el Qirâ north of Hasan Ḳeif[118]. The church is smaller than Mâr Gabriel (the measurements of the nave are 12.80 m x 6.10 m as against the 18.25 m x 10.70 m of Mâr Gabriel) but in other respects the two were almost exactly alike, even the open narthex of Mâr Gabriel being reproduced at Deir el Qirâ. I planned the latter (Fig. 54), but I do not here reproduce the plan because, except as an example of the repetition of a type, the building is devoid of interest. It has been frequently repaired, it contains no mouldings or inscription, the brick-work vault, so typical of the Ṭûr 'Abdîn is absent, and even the monks did not claim for it an earlier date than the middle ages. The fact, however, that this peculiar scheme of church should have been imitated at a much later period, is worth noting.

Mâr Azîzael, Kefr Zeh[119]

There were some slight corrections to be made in the plan of Mâr Azîzael (Fig. 29). The E. end of the narthex is blocked with modern masonry which

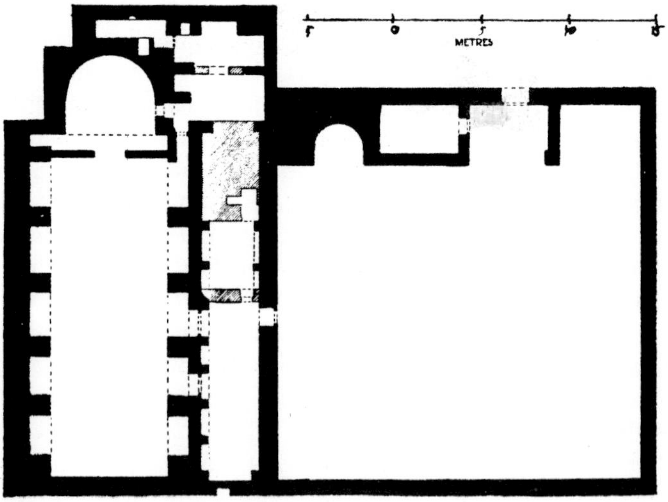

Fig. 29. Kefr Zeh, Mar 'Azaziel, plan of church complex (cf. Fig. 8)

extends as far as the E. door. A very small chamber is included in the W. end of the modern work: whether the masonry behind it is solid or not, I do not know. The narthex is not in its original form[120]. The S. wall has been rebuilt, as I mentioned in my first account of the church. The outer roof of the vault, which must have been pitched as high as the base of the clerestory windows, is now flat (Pl. 155). But I was mistaken in supposing that there had been equally extensive reparations in the nave [121]. The fine brick vault is original work (Pls. 158, 165). The whole of the vault is here of brick, instead of being carried up for a certain distance in stone, as at Ṣalaḥ and Mâr Gabriel; the transverse arches spring from above the decorative border and are themselves of brick, not of stone (Pl. 165). The pilasters rest upon a moulded base (Fig. 30). In the centre of the nave there is a round stone pulpit approached by steps from the E. (it can be seen in Pl. 158)[122]. According to Pognon (*Inscriptions*, p. 92) the western part of the nave, behind the pulpit, is reserved for women, but the low wall across the nave, of which he speaks, has almost disappeared. The profile of the capitals of the pilasters is a simple bevel. The enriched mouldings of the chancel arch consist of an outer band of split palmettes, a pearl string, two beads and a reel, a fillet, rinceaux with two small

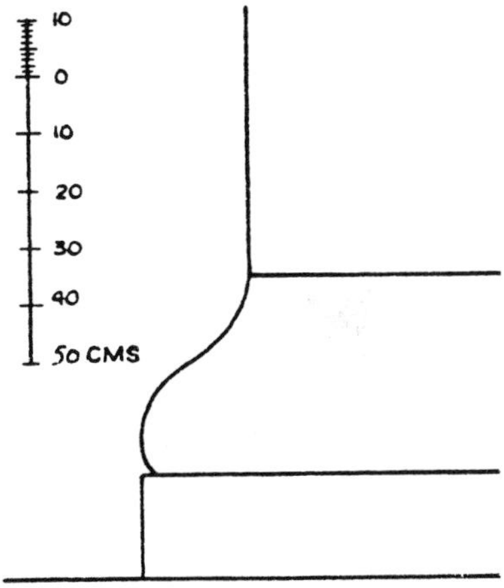

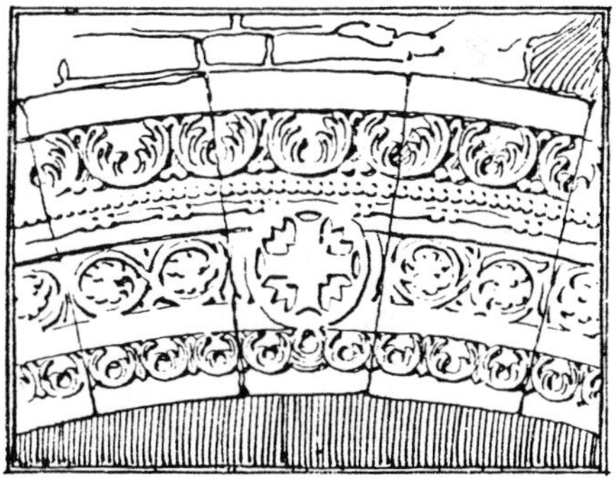

Figs. 30 & 31. Kefr Zeh, Mar 'Azaziel, profile of base of pilasters, and drawing of moulding of apse arch

leaves in each curve of the stem, another fillet, and a second band of split palmettes. Upon the keystone there is a cross in an indented circle (Fig. 31). Garlanded capitals carry the ends of the apse arch (Fig. 32, Pl. 159). They are crude in execution. The stiff upright acanthus leaves are scored with even ribs, and the heavy tip of the leaf falls forward in a singularly clumsy fashion. The garlands hang down over the upper row of leaves and are woven together on the abacus by a triple plait, which takes the place of a rosette. The same triple plait covers the astragal. Very curious is the treatment of the cornice, which runs round the apse under the semi-dome (Pl. 160). It is composed of a cyma filled with split palmettes, a reel with two beads, and a band of cross-shaped ornaments, separated by shallow mouldings from a double row of dentils

Fig. 32. Kefr Zeh, Mar 'Azaziel, church, drawing of apse capital.

placed alternately. This cornice is carried onto the pier of the apse arch and the lower part of it forms a ramp and runs under the capital both at the side and on the face of the pier. The screen which stands on top of the steps leading into the sanctuary (Pl.161), 88 cm. above the level of the floor of the nave, is probably contemporary with the church[123]. The moulded architrave is carried by two columns with acanthus capitals. The northern capital is composed of unworked leaves and wreathed with a garland (Pl. 162), the southern of worked acanthus, also garlanded (Pl. 163). Although the capitals are dissimilar, they are of the same style and they fit the columns. The architrave accords with the mouldings round the apse. There is therefore every reason to suppose that the various parts of the screen were worked for the position they now occupy, and that the difference between the capitals is intentional. The entrance to the apse is in the centre, between the two columns. A low wall, pierced with windows, fills the space between the columns and the apse piers, and as Pognon observed, the screen is closely allied to the iconostasis of a later date. There is a moulding under the semi-dome round the interior of the small exedra which stands on the E. side of the atrium (Pl. 156) but the profile is carelessly worked and the medallions, containing Greek crosses, which are placed under the centre of the semi-dome are far more shallow in cutting than any ornament in the church (Pl. 157). The exedra, according to an inscription, was built in the year AD 914 [124]. Mâr Azîzael, to whom the church is dedicated, was the son of a governor of Samosata who suffered martyrdom in Rome during the persecution of Diocletian in 304 (Michael the Syrian, ed. Chabot, vol. 1, p. 188. Chabot quotes the date from a Syrian MS of the Acts of St. Azîzael which exists in the Jacobite church at Jerusalem).

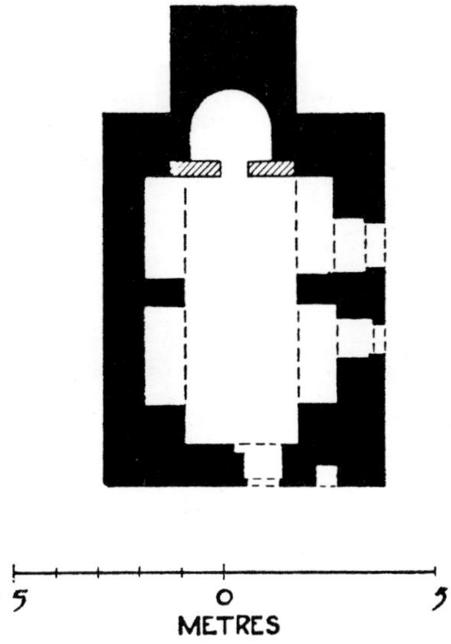

Fig. 33. Kefr Zeh, chapel of el 'Adhra, plan

Besides the church of Mâr Azîzael, there are three small chapels in the village of Kefr Zeh. One is completely ruined; the other two are very similar to one another. I do not believe that any of them belong to an early period, but I give the plan of one of the three, which is dedicated to the Virgin[125]. It stands not far to the N.E. of the church of Mâr Azîzael (Fig. 33). The vaulted nave is divided by pilasters into two bays. There are two doors in the S. wall, and one in the W. wall. To the S. of the W. door there is a small niche in the wall of the church. The second chapel[126], much the same as this in plan, has a tiny detached exedra to the S.(Pl. 166). It stands on the eastern side of the village.

Mâr Cyriacus, Arnâs[127].

St. Cyriacus was martyred, together with his mother Julitta, at Tarsus in Cilicia in the same year as St. Azîzael. According to the History of the Patriarch Mâr

Jabalaha III (Ed. Chabot, p. 134) the church of St. John the Baptist at Marâgha in Adherbâidjân contained a relic of him, and in the Chronicle of Michael the Syrian (Ed. Chabot, vol. 2, p. 191) there is an account of the visit of the wife of the Persian king Kobad to a monk called Moses who inhabited a monastery near Dârâ. The Persian queen was possessed of a demon, and having cured her, the monk gave her a part of the relics of Mâr Cyriacus. Kobad reigned from AD 488 till 498 and again from 501–530. The connection at that date of the relics of the saint with a "monastery near Dârâ" is interesting. The church at Arnâs is not monastic. It belongs to the same type as Mâr Azîzael, which it closely resembles (Fig. 34). The plan which I made in 1909 needed consider-

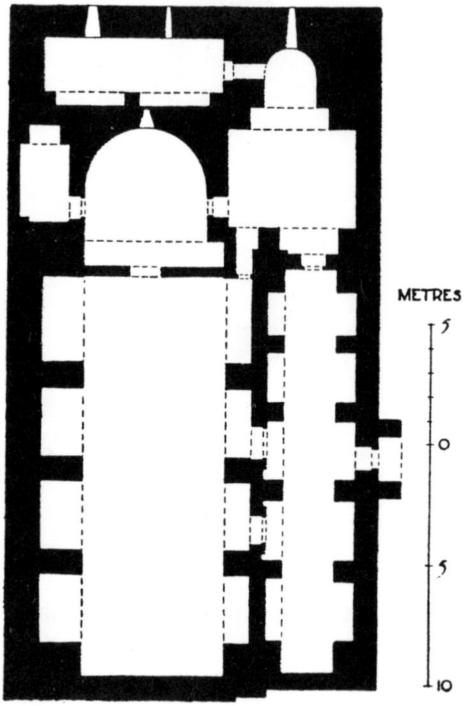

Fig. 34. Arnas, Mar Cyriacus, plan of church (cf. Fig. 9)

able correction. I found on my second visit that the chamber to the S. of the apse was part of the original work. It is covered by a vaulted brick roof which is certainly old. A moulding runs round the interior of the apse here, under the semi-dome; the profile is flat (a cyma and fillets) but the summary character of the workmanship is probably due to the fact that the moulding was intended for a subsidiary apse. Acanthus capitals, much injured, but apparently not quite alike, carry the apse arch. The chamber to the E. of the main apse is also a part of the original design, though I neglected it in my first plan, thinking it to be a later addition. (There were some grounds for this view. On the outer side of the N. wall there is a straight joint 4.52 m from the E. end, which led me to think that the E. chamber had been added to the original building. But in early Christian architecture straight joints are often present in masonry which is all of the same period.) Mâr Cyriacus had therefore from the first the chamber behind the apse which exists in all other churches of the same type in the Ṭûr 'Abdîn. It is even more fully developed here than at Kefr Zeh, and it seems to have communicated with the sanctuary by a small wedge-shaped window, placed in the centre of the apse. The chamber built in the thickness of the wall to the N. of the main apse is peculiar to Arnâs[128]. The N. side of the nave is all rebuilt, but the pilasters on the S. side belong to the older work. These S. pilasters carry bevelled capitals like those at Kefr Zeh, but the N. pilasters are without capitals (Pl. 99). A fragment of the original brick vault can be seen at the E. end of the S. side[129], incorporated in the later stone vault. When the vault was rebuilt, its span was narrowed by placing the pilasters on the N. side of the nave further forward; consequently the crown of the present vault does not fall over the centre of the apse arch, but slightly to the S. of it, and the easternmost of the pilasters on the N. side impinges upon the pier which bears the chancel arch, and conceals the capital. All this can be seen clearly in Pl. 99, where the fragment of the first vault appears on the S. side, the curve being different from the curve of the later stone vault. The two doorways on the S. side of the nave are also old, as is shown by the mouldings on lintel and jambs (Fig. 35). The central of the three southern pilasters of the nave narrows by 15 cm. the opening of one of the doors. The S. wall of the narthex has been rebuilt, the vault is of stone like the vault of the nave, and the outer door with its porch are modern. Pl. 97 gives a view of the S.E. end of the church. Parts of the original cyma cornice can still be seen on the S. wall of the nave and on the wall of the main apse, together with bits of ancient masonry patched with more recent stone work. The re-examination of the church led me to the following conclusions: The apse and the chambers round it are all old; the foundations of the W. wall of the nave and of the N. wall between the pilasters are also old, so are at any rate the two eastern piers on the S. side (the easternmost is engaged in the E. wall) and the fragment of brick vault above them. I think it most probable

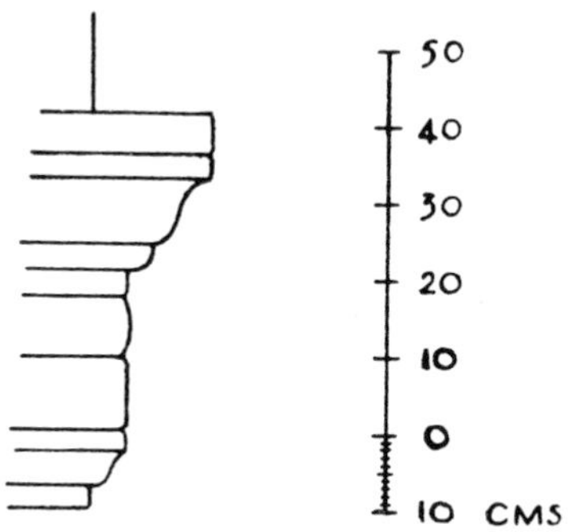

Fig. 35.
Arnas, Mar Cyriacus, profile of door moulding

that the three other piers on the S. side are also in their original position, in spite of the fact that one of them slightly blocks an old doorway. In sum, the ruined parts of the church were reconstructed on the original foundations, the general disposition and proportions being maintained, except that the northern arcade was brought further forward. Fortunately, there is in the church a dated inscription which gives some security to these conjectures (Pognon, *Inscriptions*, p. 99). It states that the N. wall was restored and built together with the barrel vault of the church (i.e. the nave) in the year 1591–2[130]. At what date the original church was built is nowhere recorded, but a slight clue is afforded by an inscription on the easternmost of the S. pilasters which states that the screen was built in AD 760–1. The inscription is full of errors and Pognon has shown reason for believing that the date of the screen should be AD 754–5; but he believes the inscription to have been written not later than the end of the 8th century or the beginning of the 9th. We may conclude that the screen was erected in the middle of the 8th century. The date is of significance. The architrave carried by the four columns of the screen is moulded and carved, but the decoration bears no relation to the enrichments of the chancel arch, and belongs without doubt to a later period, and to a different artistic tradition[131]. The capitals of the screen columns are also of considerably later date than the capitals under the chancel arch[132]. So great is the disparity, that if the inscription refers to the existing screen, which seems probable, the older parts of the church must be relegated to a period before the Moslem invasion[133]. (A detail of the chancel screen is given in Pl. 100.) The apse mouldings and capitals at Arnâs are more closely related to those of the church of the Virgin at Ḥâkh than to Kefr Zeh. The chancel arch (Pl. 101) shows almost the same outer and inner band of palmettes as at Kefr Zeh (Pl. 161, Fig. 31) (the lower side of the palmettes is not connected by the two small fronds of Kefr Zeh and Ḥâkh) but the rinceaux motive is more delicately cut than at Kefr Zeh and is (as far as can be judged under the veil of whitewash) exactly like the rinceaux round the arches at Ḥâkh (Pl. 140)[134]. A geometric pattern under the rinceaux again recalls the decoration at Hâkh (Pls. 143–144). The keystone of the arch (Pl. 101) is worked with a dove which should be compared with the doves upon the exterior of the tambour at Ḥâkh (Pl. 137)[135]. In the wreathed capitals which carry the apse arch (Pl. 103) the plaited astragal of Kefr Zeh and Ḥâkh is absent, but the acanthus leaves are exactly like those on the Ḥâkh capitals (Pl. 143). In both cases we have a fan-shaped leaf, with a thick bulbous central rib. The rounded tip hangs over very slightly, while the side lobes of the leaf spring up higher than the rib and meet above the overhanging tip. The enriched cornice round the apse under the semi-dome (Pl. 104) is not continued under the capital as at Kefr Zeh.

Mâr Philoxenus, Midyâd[136].

In the complex of buildings dedicated to Mâr Philoxenus, only the north church belongs to an early period, and even the N. church has undergone restoration. It is now in a state of complete ruin. I have redrawn the plan, making some slight corrections in the nave and the sanctuary of the N. church

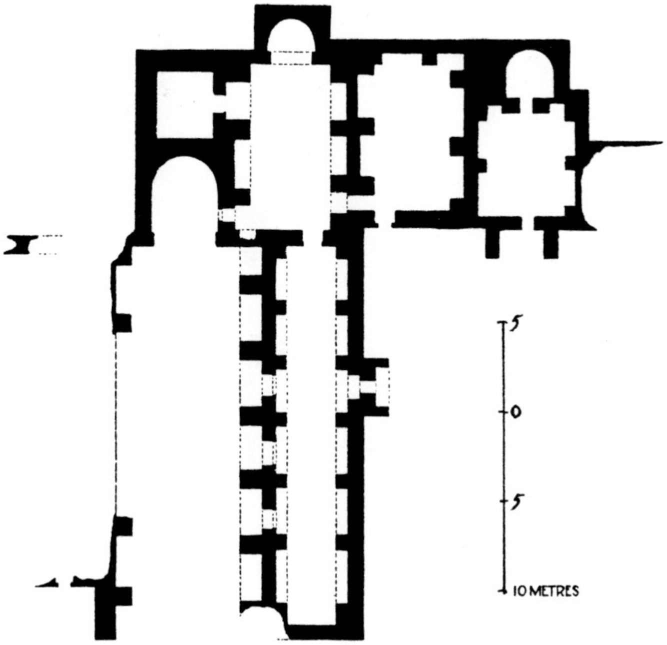

Fig. 36. Midyat, Mar Philoxenus, plan of church (cf. Fig. 11)

(Fig. 36). The N. aisle I believe to be a later addition. At the E. end it terminates in the ruins of an arch; in all probability there was a chamber to the N. of the sanctuary communicating (as at Mâr Sovo)[137] (Fig. 10) with the aisle by a doorway. The semi-dome of the apse is standing, but it does not seem to have been decorated like the chancel arches at Arnâs and Kefr Zeh; there are no capitals under the chancel arch, and the cornice round the interior of the apse is very poor. The heavy cyma which forms the capitals of the pilasters (Pl. 172) reappears upon the outer cornice (Pl. 173) where it is worked with great irregularity. These mouldings have the same character as the mouldings upon the cornice and pier capitals at Mâr Ibrahîm and Mâr Ubil (Pls. 177, 180) and I should be inclined to assign the two buildings to much the same date. The saint to whom the church is dedicated, Philoxenus, bishop of Manbidj, was born in a village of Beth Garmai, a bishopric on the Lesser Zab (Hoffmann, *Auszüge*, p. 253). He was murdered in AD 523 (Wright, *Syriac Literature*, p. 72)[138].

To the same architectural group, which I have called the parochial as distinguished from the monastic type, belong several other churches in the Ṭûr 'Abdîn. The most important of these is Mâr Sovo at Ḥâkh (Fig. 10)[139]. It has frequently been repaired and is now in ruins, but there are indications which

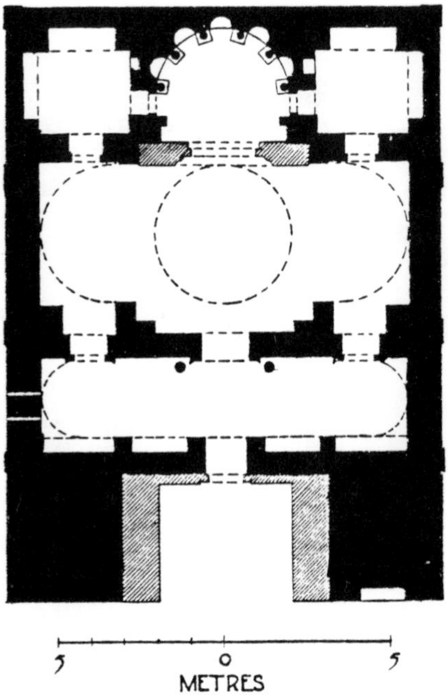

Fig. 37. Ḥaḥ, el 'Adhra, plan of church (cf. Fig. 12)

point to its being one of the oldest of the ecclesiastical buildings in the district. The mouldings on either side of the main apse are as fine as any in the mountain (Pl. 122) and there are traces of exquisite decoration round the chancel arch. The piers that supported the vault are a later addition, and the dimensions of the nave, together with the comparative thinness of the walls, show that it must originally have been covered by a wooden roof. None of the remaining churches of this type are as ancient. At Bâ Sebrînâ the church dedicated to Mâr Dodo (Pl. 105)[140] is dated by an inscription in the closing years of the 12th century. (*Amurath to Amurath*, p. 204. I have described Mâr Dodo as belonging to a monastery, but I doubt whether this statement is correct. The buildings round the walled enclosure of the court are so exiguous that they were probably only intended for the lodging of the priests who served the church.)[141] In the village of Kefr Beh, not far from Mâr Gabriel, there is a large church dedicated to Mâr Stephanus and Mâr Yuhannah[142], dated by an inscription AD 1465 [142a]. It is in perfect preservation and is still in use. There are scarcely any mouldings here, and the chancel arch is not decorated. Between Ḥâkh and Ṣalaḥ I passed through the village of Heshterek and found there a ruined church (Pl. 151)[143] which I should conjecture to belong to about the same period as the one at Kefr Beh. Finally at Hafsinâs, N. of Ṣalaḥ, there is a church[144] of the same type, and here the chancel arch is adorned with split palmettres and rests upon acanthus capitals, but the work is so rudely executed that it is obviously only a later attempt to carry out the old traditional decoration. There is also a small monastery[145] at Hafsinâs containing a church of no architectural interest which had either been completely rebuilt or was in origin a mediaeval foundation. One notable feature this monastery does however possess. In the courtyard stand the remains of a round tower set upon

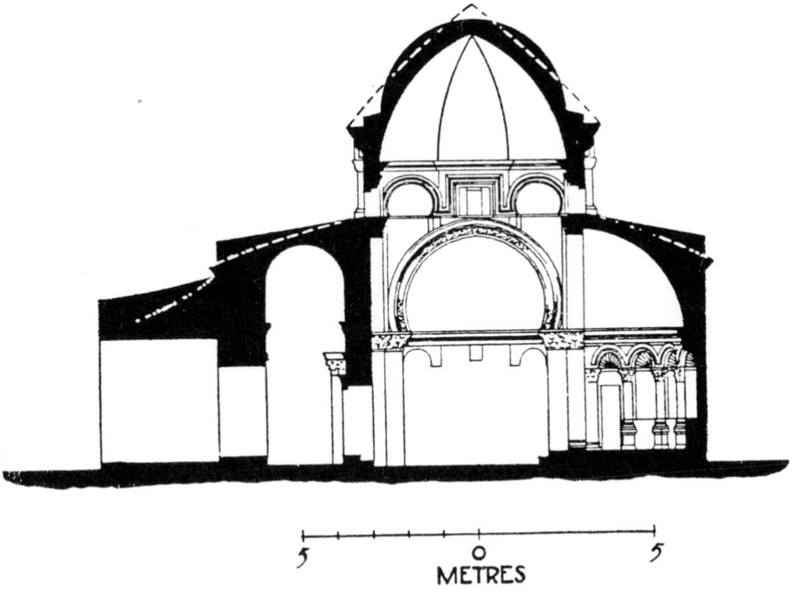

Fig. 38. Ḥaḥ, el 'Adhra, section from W to E

square base which is divided into four steps (Pl. 115). The masonry of the tower is of better workmanship than that of any other part of the church and I should judge it to be older. The priest informed me that it was a bell tower. There is no other bell tower in the Ṭûr 'Abdîn save at Ḥâkh where a square tower stands to the E. of Mâr Sovo (Pl. 126) but this tower is late work of the Mohammadan period. In any case the Hafsinâs tower is the only round tower attached to a Christian church which is known to me in Mesopotamia or in Syria.

El 'Adhra, Ḥâkh [146].

There was very little to correct in my original plan of the domed church of the Virgin at Ḥâkh (Fig. 37). I found on re-examining the building that I had been wrong in stating that the whole of the masonry of the porch was a recent addition. The door itself is new (it is due to the restoration which took place in 1907 [147] when the tiled roof of the dome was replaced by stone) but on either side of it there is a block of ancient masonry with a moulding running across its western face rather more than half way up between the ground and the cornice (Pl. 134). The niche, covered by a moulded arch, to the S. of the W. door, is also part of the old work. The original opening in the porch must therefore have been much wider than it is at present; the modern addition is represented in the plan by hatching. In addition to the plan, I give a section taken through the centre of the church from W. to E. (Fig. 38) and, through the kindness of Mr. O.H. Parry, I am also able to provide a photograph of the church taken in 1892 before the alterations, which were effected in 1907 (Pl. 131). I have indicated in the section the lines of the original roof. When I was at Ḥâkh in 1909 I was told by the priest that the church had been restored two years earlier [148]. He said that no change had been made in the interior, but that on the exterior the tiled, pointed roof, which originally covered the inner dome, had been replaced by a stone outer dome. From Mr. Parry's photograph, as well as from the indications furnished by the building, it is possible to determine that the roof over the narthex and apses have also been altered in the manner shown in the section; it is now covered, not with tiles, but with stone slabs. The roof of the porch seems to have undergone several alterations at different periods; a small cornice which still exists below the masonry of 1907, appears to me to give the line of the roof when Mr. Parry took his photograph, and I have so represented it in the section. The most important problem is the original form of the roof over the central part of the church. There are one or two examples in early Christian architecture where a stone tambour, provided with interior arched niches as though to receive a dome, can never, owing to the want of solidity of the walls of the tambour, have been covered by anything heavier than a tiled wooden roof. (For example, the side chambers of the basilica of St. Sergius at Ruṣâfah [Sarre, "Ruṣâfah", in the *Monatsheft für Kunstwissenschaft*, 1910, p. 102] and the basilica at Aladja Khân [Khodja Kalessi, Supplementary Papers, No. 2 published by the Hellenic Society] according to Dr. Headlam, whose views are supported by Dr. Herzfeld, after a careful examination of the ruins.)[149] It is therefore open to question whether the whole of the dome at Ḥâkh, the interior as well as the exterior, is not due to the restoration of 1907, and whether the original roof was not wholly of wood. I do not think this to have been the case for the following reasons: 1. The low tambour at Ḥâkh was always sufficiently stable to carry the dome, as it does at present; there was therefore no reason for the omission of the dome. 2. Mr. Parry's photograph shows a slight convexity in the pitched roof which points to the settlement of the timbers that rested upon the haunch of the dome, i.e. the original roof was an interior dome protected by wooden rafters which were covered with tiles. 3. This explanation accords with the account of the restoration given to me by the priest who had been present when it took place. It is important therefore to observe that we have here an early example of a dome carried on a true tambour, lighted by windows in the tambour.

Not only is the dome set upon arched niches, but the semi-domes to N. and S. of it are borne by similar arches bracketed out from the wall. This construction can be seen in the section. The five sedilia round the apse are divided by columns placed upon very high bases (Fig. 39) [150]. The pair of columns at the back of the apse carry wreathed acanthus capitals, the next two pairs of columns further west are crowned by the curious barocco capitals of which an illustration is given (Pl. 145). I described them in *Amida* as being composed of ropes and tassels, but it would be more correct to term the rope a woven garland; and the member of which I spoke as a tassel is in reality a slender flask slung between the garlands, which pass through its handles [151]. W. of the sedilia a square-headed door opens on either side into the chambers to N. and S. of the apse. The shell niches which cover the sedilia are continued over the doors and carried on the western side by columns set on low bases and crowned by unwreathed acanthus capitals. There is one other feature of great interest in the decoration of the church which I omitted to mention in my former account. The niches on the exterior of the tambour are divided from one another by pairs of dwarf columns supporting small moulded arches (Pl. 138). The moulding runs through over the capitals of the columns from arch to arch, and at the angles of the tambour it is returned upwards and carried across the top of the arches. (Compare for this treatment of the moulding the façade of the basilical hall of Mshatta [*Mschatta*, pl. 4] and a very early Syrian example, possibly Naba-

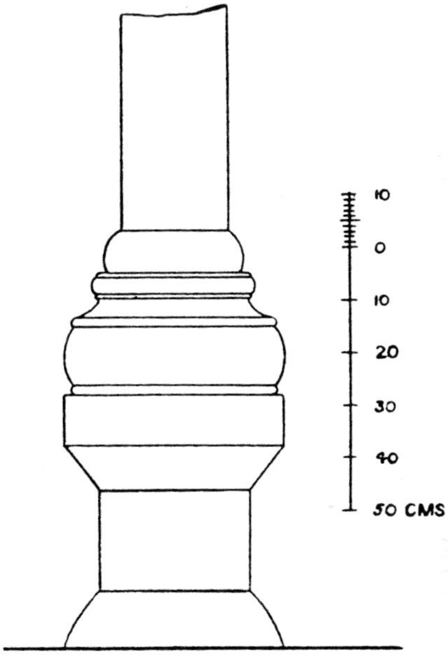

Fig. 39. Ḥaḥ, el 'Adhra, profile of column base in apse

taean, at Umtâ'îyeh [Butler, *Ancient Architecture*, Section A, part 2, p. 89].) In each arch there is a decorative motive. On the W. side of the tambour the central arch contains a Greek cross, each of the arms of which is finished by volutes. The three arches on either side are filled with a dove with outspread wings (Pl. 137). Finally in the tympanum, at the angles of the tambour, there is an upright leaf with a broad rounded tip. On the other three sides of the tambour the leaf reappears in the central arch, while the other arches contain a plain projecting boss or ball. The tambour is crowned by a cornice consisting of a cyma of good profile and a torus covered with a triple plait. The low octagonal wall round the base of the dome above the cornice is modern.

I have already alluded (p. 8 above) to the problem presented by the two types of ground plan which prevail in the Ṭûr 'Abdîn, the monastic church, so placed that the longer axis of the nave lies N. and S. and the parochial church with its longer axis lying E. and W.[152]. I suggested that the monastic churches preserve a Babylonian architectural tradition, the latitudinal chamber of palace and temple with doors in the centre of the long sides, whereas the parochial churches recall the later Assyrian scheme of longitudinal chambers, a scheme which Dr. Andrae conjectures to have been borrowed from Western Asia[152a]. It is curious to observe that even the second type seems to have been considered by the Christian builders of this region in the terms of the first. The longitudinal nave of the parochial churches is always approached from the broad side, the doors are invariably in the S. wall, never at the W. end, where a complete adherence to the longitudinal type would place them; the narthex and atrium lie to the S.; the whole conception is that of the latitudinal chamber, although the nave is actually disposed in the contrary fashion with relation to the apse. Thus an old architectural tradition may be said to be still perceptible, to a greater or lesser degree, in all these buildings, though they are stamped so profoundly with the impress of Western artistic influences.

It is singularly instructive to compare this type with that which had been developed in adjacent regions many centuries earlier by the Hittites. We have as yet no certain evidence with regard to monumental Hittite architecture in the northern Mesopotamian plains and the mountains which bound them, save that which has been afforded by the excavations at Sendjirli, though the work undertaken by Professor Garstang at Sakche Geuzi, by the British Museum at Karchemish, and by Baron Oppenheim at Râs ul 'Ain cannot fail to provide us in the near future with valuable data. Fortunately the excavations at Sendjirli have been peculiarly fruitful in the domain of architecture, and since the publication of the second part of the report in 1898, we have been possessed of sure knowledge of the Hittite plan of palace and temple, which was known to the Assyrians as the Hilâni. Professor Koldewey has pointed out (*Ausgrabungen in Sendschirli*, p. 183) that it is the local fortress gate adapted to royal, domestic and religious requirements, and he has insisted that the essential characteristic of the structure is the latitudinal arrangement of the chambers[153]. It is startling to place the plan of Hilâni 2 at Sendjirli (I select this example because it was in all probability a cult building) beside the plan of the parochial churches of the Ṭûr ‘Abdîn. Here is the same entrance chamber or porch (the Christian narthex) with its door in the long side, the same latitudinal main chamber (the Christian nave) with the small room that contained the cult image at one end (the Christian apse) giving, as in the churches, a slight longitudinal emphasis which was never fully expressed in the architectural scheme. The original flanking towers of the city gate had already in Hittite times undergone considerable modification. In Hilâni 2. only one of them remains; in the small Hilânis of the upper palace (*op. cit.*, plate 22) the latest monumental buildings on the site, the solid towers have given place to a side room or rooms. In the Ṭûr ‘Abdîn, though the latitudinal disposition characteristic of the Hilâni is retained, the towers have disappeared, and the memory of them is perpetuated only in the plan, by the subsidiary room at the southern end of the narthex. In N. Syria and central Asia Minor the development took an exactly contrary direction. There (for example at Turmanîn and at Binbirklisse)[154] it was the towered facade which was perpetuated, while the longitudinal main chamber of the Hilâni gave way, as in Solomon's Temple in Jerusalem, to a longitudinal nave with true architectural emphasis imparted by the sanctuary.

I should like to suggest that this ancient ground plan may have played a part also in the development of ecclesiastical architecture in Southern Syria. An exceedingly interesting group of churches has recently been published by Mr. Butler in the section of Ancient Architecture in Syria, which deals with Umm edj Djemâl in the Southern Ḥaurân (Section A, part 3, p. 171). It begins with the church of Julianos which is dated by an inscription in AD 345, and is the earliest dated church in Syria. This church belongs to the type which Mr. Butler has christened the hall type. It consists, like the parochial churches of the Ṭûr ‘Abdîn, of a nave without aisles, but the brick vault of the Ṭûr ‘Abdîn is replaced by what may be termed the Ḥaurân vault, a series of transverse arches carrying stone slabs. In the S. wall there are three doors, and the narthex and atrium lie to the S.; the corresponding doors in the N. wall open only into subsidiary chambers, probably living rooms; the single door at the southern end of the W. wall leads into a similar chamber, it is not a main entrance and bears no relation to the main W. door of a longitudinal nave. The nave of the Julianos church is structurally a latitudinal chamber like the naves of Arnâs and Kefr Zeh. There are at Umm edj Djemâl five more hall churches (one of them being part of a double church); with one exception (the double church) they all have doors in the S. wall, but in no case are the S. doors the principal entrances. The main doors are placed in the W. wall and are usually emphasized by a narthex borne on columns at the W. end of the church. That is to say, that in all these examples the nave has become a true longitudinal chamber.

Whether the two types of the Ṭûr ʻAbdîn are equally common in the Urfah district I do not know[155]. I have found no example of them save in the immediate vicinity, at Deir el Qira (Fig. 54)[156], but the ruins at Djindeirmene, planned by Dr. Guyer[157], look uncommonly like a modification of the monastic church. The existing remains of ancient churches at Diyârbekr all show some form of centralized plan. (Dr. Guyer tells me that I was mistaken in representing the church of the Virgin as round; it is in reality closely allied to the martyrium at Ruṣâfah, a typically Mesopotamian form of the centralized plan [see Fig. 51 below].)[158] At Mayâfârqîn, which I visited this year, there are two churches of exceptional interest; in one of them the scheme is that of a basilica, while the other is a centralized building.

Basilica, Mayâfârqîn[159].

The basilica is probably the older of the two. Its dimensions are exceptionally large, 25,75 m wide x 38,65 m long, excluding the apse (Fig. 40). The columns

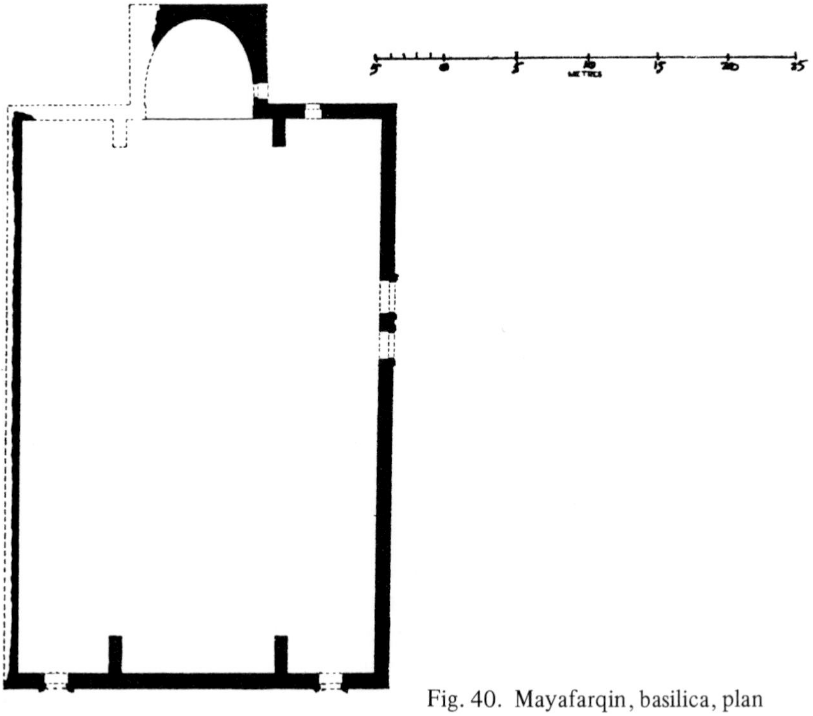

Fig. 40. Mayafarqin, basilica, plan

which separated the nave from the aisles, are gone, but they have not travelled far, for I conjecture that they are the very columns now to be seen in the oldest part of the mosque of Ṣalaḥ ed Dîn el Ayyûbî[160] which lies immediately to the S. of the church (Pls. 38, 47). They carry their original capitals of uncut acanthus, and in some cases they stand upon their original bases (Pl. 48). If I am right in this supposition, the church must have been in ruins before the end of the 12th century. Nothing now remains but the outer shell, nor is that perfect. The N. wall has almost disappeared; the apse has fallen and its northern side is completely obliterated by modern buildings. The area which was occupied by the nave and aisles has been turned into a mulberry garden. But the existing ruins and the highly finished masonry are enough to show how magnificent the building must once have been. The main entrance is from the S. where the two doorways are placed together, not in the middle of the S. wall, but nearer its eastern end (Pl. 39). The lintel and jambs of the doors are decorated with mouldings (Fig. 41). Above the lintels there are high stilted relieving arches, similarly moulded. At the W. end two smaller doors, with the same mouldings and relieving arches, give access to the aisles, but there is no W. door to the nave. An unmoulded opening, either door or window, is to be seen at the E. end of the S. aisle, and there is a small unmoulded door on the S. side of the apse. The apse, a stilted circle within, is rectangular without. There are no chambers to N. and S. of it. (It is interesting to compare this apse with that of the newly discovered Constantinian church of the Ascension on the Mt. of Olives [*Revue Biblique*, 1911, p. 219]. The apse there is much shorter, but it projects in the same way, without side chambers, from the body of the church. The exterior form is not yet determined; P. Vincent in his conjectural reconstruction makes it polygonal, rejecting the rectangular shape on account of the useless mass of masonry which it implies. His reasoning is not quite conclusive, as the Mayâfârqîn example shows, and a rectangular exterior would seem to accord better with the facts revealed up to now by the excavations of the Pères Blancs.)[161] The church was abundantly lighted by windows placed high up in the walls. Two square-headed windows at the E. end (Pl. 40) and one arched window at the W. end of the S. aisle (Pl. 41) are still preserved. Lehmann Haupt (*Armenien, Einst und Jetzt*, p. 422) mentions 15 large windows in the S. wall, but of these only the upright divisions of 6 openings remain towards the western end. At the W. end of the nave there are at present similar remains of four window openings, but when Lehmann Haupt saw the church there was yet another row

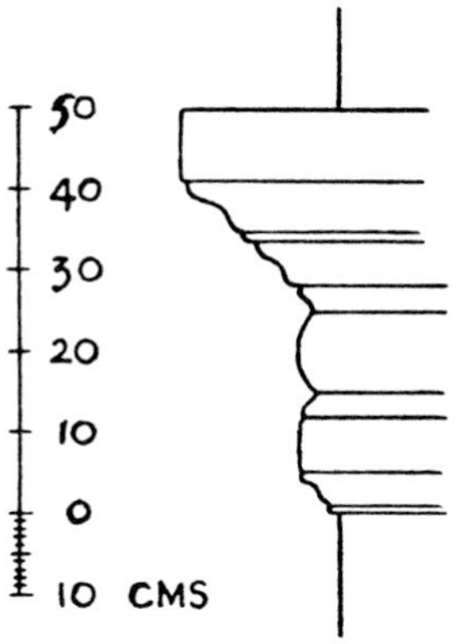

Fig. 41. Mayafarqin, basilica, profile of moulding of S doors

of four windows above these, and his illustration (*Ibid.*, 399) shows that they were all arched. At the E. end of the nave, part of an arched window can be made out; it must have been one of a group of windows, perhaps four in number, in the upper wall above the apse. All the walls of the church were crowned by a bold cyma cornice, remains of which can still be seen, both on the aisle wall and above it on the angle of the nave wall. The nave was covered by a gable roof (the angle stone of the gable is still in place) and the aisles with similar sloping roofs. Though the arcades on either side of the nave have been entirely removed, there remain, most fortunately, three of the returning piers with their engaged capitals and fragments of the arches which they carried [162], together with the capital under the S. end of the chancel arch and a few stones of the arch itself. The arches between the nave and aisles are moulded (the torus of the door mouldings plays a conspicuous part in their profile) and markedly horse-shoed. On the chancel arch the mouldings were richly carved (Pl. 42). The capitals of the S. aisle differ slightly from the sole remaining capital of the N. aisle. They consist of two rows of acanthus leaves with curving tips, and an upper row of acanthus calyxes, from which sprang flat fronds which have now almost entirely disappeared. On the western capital (Pls. 43–44) the deep abacus is decorated with palmettes, not the split palmettes of the Ṭûr 'Abdîn, but the true palmette of classical architecture. They spring from a curving stem and are placed alternately pointing up and down. The rosette is decorated with a woven basket pattern. On the E. capital, which is more broken, the palmettes on the abacus appear to be all placed point upward (Pl. 42) and they are carried round the rosette. The eastern capital has also a band of decoration below the bell, probably an egg and leaf, and below that a dentil, like the capital of the chancel arch. Moreover, like the chancel arch capital, it was wreathed with a garland, of which a small vestige remains [162a]. On the capital of the N. aisle there is the same double row of acanthus leaves, but the volutes spring directly from between the upper row of leaves, not from a calyx (Pls. 45–46). The abacus is carved with stiff vine rinceaux. Finally the capital under the chancel arch (Pl. 42) is similar to that which stands at the E. end of the S. aisle, save that the abacus is covered with acanthus rinceaux. A single moulded and enriched block is all that remains of the cornice that ran round the apse under the semi-dome[163]. No capitals in the Ṭûr 'Abdîn can show acanthus leaves so finely modelled as those of the capitals at Mayâfârqîn, but in the Ulu Djâmi' at Diyârbekr there are many examples (derived from buildings older than the mosque) in which the workmanship is exactly similar (see for instance *Amida*, Fig. 260) [164] . To the S.E. of the church there is an archway which now serves as one of the entrances to the precincts of the mosque (Pl.49). The cross upon the keystone shows its Christian origin, though what part it played in relation to the temenos of the church it would be difficult to determine. The work is rather coarser than that of the church but the vine rinceaux is a close repetition of the rinceaux on one of the capitals [165].

El 'Adhra, Mayâfârqîn[166].

The second church, dedicated to the Virgin, belongs to a wholly different type. It is a domed basilica and so far as my knowledge goes its plan cannot be exactly paralleled, except at Salonika in the church of Sta. Sofia[167] (Fig. 42).

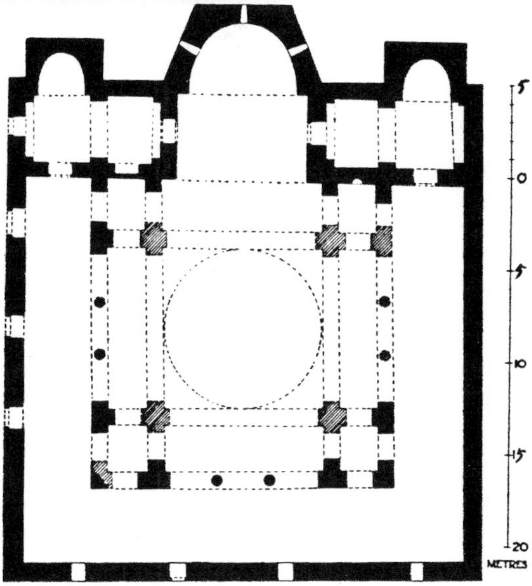

Fig. 42. Mayafarqin, el 'Adhra, plan of church

Its close resemblance to Sta. Sofia, Salonika, depends upon the reconstruction, which I have indicated on the plan, of four inner corner piers supporting the dome. All of these have been carried away by the fall of the dome, and the place where they stood is covered with heaped up masses of ruin; but the fact that they once existed is assured by the returns in the E. wall on either side of the apse, and by the returns in the five remaining outer piers (Pls. 57–58), which were connected with the inner piers by arches of narrow span. The remains of these arches are still to be seen upon the western piers (Pl. 57). Since I do not know the shape of the inner piers, I have restored them in the manner which seemed best to accord with the existing piers, cruciform, not square as at Salonika. The columns between the two western piers are standing(Pl. 60), together with the arches they carry, the cyma cornice above the arches and the bases of the second order of columns. On the N. and S. sides similar columns can be restored with complete certainty; intermediate supports between the piers are called for by the span of the arches that spring from the piers, and it would be inconceivable that those supports should not correspond to the columns on the W. side. We have therefore a plan which, as Strzygowski has said of Sta. Sofia, Salonika, implies that the builder distinguished imperfectly between the domed basilica and the domed cruciform (*Kleinasien*, p. 119). He has placed his dome upon an inner cruciform, but instead of carrying through the thrust to the outer walls, he has encompassed it with another series of piers and columns and turned his church into a domed basilica. No doubt here, as at Salonika, he was instigated by the fact that he had not yet learnt to transfer the thrust of the dome to the outer wall; he was therefore obliged to double his corner piers so that they might be sufficiently strong to take the thrust of the dome upon themselves. The form of the triple sanctuary differs slightly from that of Sta. Sofia. The prothesis and diaconicum are placed in line with the N. and S. walls, which leaves a space, filled by a small vaulted chamber, between them and the central sanctuary. At Salonika the side apses are rounded on the exterior. At Mayafarqin they are rectangular, but in both cases the central apse has a polygonal mantle and is lighted by three windows. The N. sanctuary is old work. The semi-dome of the apse and the vaults over the two chambers are intact. It is the only part of the church which is at present in use. The S. sanctuary has recently fallen into ruin and been rebuilt; it was full of planks and building material when I saw it. The semi-dome over the main apse is gone; the wall of the apse has been relaid, so that the windows are probably not in their original form, and the existing chancel arch is modern (Pls. 54, 57). But the small arched niche in the wall between the southern piers is old work (Pl. 58). The N. wall is all old (Pls. 55, 57). There is a door into the N. sanctuary with a window above it. Three doors lead into the N. aisle; they are square headed with a very shallow relieving arch over the lintels. Above the eastern and the central door there are two arched windows, and another pair of arched windows breaks the wall between, making two rows of three windows. The N. end of the W. wall is old (Pl. 56). It contains three square-headed windows, and there must have been a row of small arched windows above them, only one of which remains. The southern half of the W. wall seems to have been rebuilt, but not recently; and the greater part of the S. wall is due to an ancient restoration. The inner side of the later walls do not show the vaulting corbels which appear on the interior of the old walls. I think it probable that at some period, after the dome had fallen, the church was patched up and covered with wooden roofs. To the W. of the church the ground slopes away rapidly, which would account for the absence of a W. door. The original superstructure must have differed from Sta. Sofia chiefly in one point: the roof of the galleries that ran round three sides must have been pitched considerably higher. Instead of the low arched openings of the Salonika galleries, it is clear (Pl. 57) that the stilted arches of the upper storey ran up as high as the arches on the ground floor beneath them. In Pl. 56 it can be seen that the corbels that took the roof were placed very little higher than the intrados of the narrow arches between the angle piers. As at Salonika, the low wall above the corbels was broken by small windows lighting the space under the arches that carried the dome. The wall is crowned by a cyma cornice. The upper row of arched windows in the outer wall (Pls. 54–55) lighted the galleries. The corbels that carried the floor of the galleries can be seen in the N. wall just above the lower row of arched windows (Pl. 57). The piers and columns carry a very remarkable series of capitals. Those upon the piers are impost-capitals (Kämpferkapitell) divided into three horizontal fields of ornament, corresponding roughly to astragal, bell and abacus. The lower field is a narrow band decorated with a running pattern; the central field is completely covered with geometric designs; the upper field is an abacus of slight projection, which in all the lower capitals is very much broken, but in the better preserved capitals of the upper storey is decorated with a triple plait (Pl. 63). The pattern upon the central field of this capital is repeated in the lower storey on the engaged pier immediately to the S. of the door leading into the N. sanctuary (Pl. 65). It is composed of interlacing bands forming ovals, which are filled alternately with a whorl and with a many-petalled blossom. A vine leaf occupies the space between the ovals, above and below. On the S. side of the capital the geometric design gives place to a pair of vine branches, hanging downwards and bearing leaves and bunches of grapes. In the centre, between the vines, there is a ring containing a heavily veined leaf. The lower half of the ring is decorated with a concentric band, the upper half with small bosses. Above the ring are two small upright bands with voluted ends, connected by a triple stripe. The lower part of the capital bears a double plait. On the pier to the W. of this engaged pier, the lower part of the capital is worked with a flowing vine, the central field with interwoven bands encompassing alternate whorls and blossoms: the design is in fact the same as that upon the face of the engaged capital, but the bands are woven more closely so as to allow for three rows of the whorls and blossoms (Pl. 64). This decoration is repeated upon the sole remaining eastern capital of the upper storey. The W. piers all carry, in the lower storey, capitals of which the central field is covered with a lozenge-shaped entrelac, each lozenge being filled with leaves forming a 12-pointed star (Pls. 61–62). In the lower field there is an egg and leaf. All the upper storey capitals at the W. end are the same as Pl. 63. The columns between the piers carry basket capitals (Pl. 66) with moulded imposts. The bell of the capital curves very sharply inwards so that its lower circumference is considerably smaller than the circumference of the column upon which it rests. The basket work, bulging upwards, is terminated by a torus, ridged, rope-like, with a spiral line. Upon this torus is placed a square abacus, the corners of which project abruptly from the circular bell. No attempt is made to adjust the square of the abacus to the circle of the bell. Below the abacus, the echinus is decorated on one of the capitals with vine rinceaux and on the other with a laurel wreath. On the corners of the abacus there is a small half leaf, or half palmette, doubled backwards on a curving stem.

(It is scarcely to be seen in Pl. 66, but is well preserved on the other capital.) I know of two other Mesopotamian examples of the basket capital. At Niṣîbîn, outside the church of St. James[168], I found one of them in a fragmentary condition (Pl. 83). As at Mayâfârqîn, the basket work covers the whole of the bell; the abacus is decorated with a zigzag; the echinus is a bead and reel, and in this case the rectangular corners of the abacus are accommodated to the bell by a triangular projection. The other example is in a courtyard at Dârâ[169], close to the ruins of the church (Pl. 67a). Here there is a rope torus above and below the basket work; the remainder of the capital is much defaced; the abacus is however rather higher than at Niṣîbîn or Mayâfârqîn; the angle bosses are almost completely broken away; between them there are faint traces of a geometric pattern. The nearest parallel to this group of capitals is to be found in two capitals in and near the church of the Holy Sepulchre at Jerusalem (they are reproduced by Strzygowski, Felsendom und Aksamoschee, *Der Islam*, vol. 2, pl. 5)[170], but even these are not quite so unmitigatedly geometric, for the volutes of a Corinthian capital emerge from above the basket work. The other well known examples of the basket capital, whether they be found in Egypt or at Parenzo, Constantinople or Salona, are all composite[171] (with the exception of one example from Egypt given by Strzygowski in *Kleinasien*, Fig. 86). Another form of composite basket capital has been found at Edjmiadzin (Strzygowski, *Byzantinische Denkmäler*, vol. 1, p. 10); it is probably to be dated in the middle of the 7th century[172]. The basket capital continued to be used in Armenia until a late period. (Strzygowski, *Mschatta*, p. 361. The funnel capitals on which the net work gives place on each of the four sides to an ornament in a trapezoid field, as for instance in the lower order at San Vitale, are closely akin to the basket capitals, but I have seen no example of them in Mesopotamia.) In the same courtyard at Dârâ stood another capital so interesting that I reproduce it here (Pl. 67b). Above a rope torus the bell of the capital is covered with a vine motive. Upon another rope torus, or echinus, is placed the abacus, which seems to have been decorated with a band of rhomboids. From the corners of the abacus depend heavy, tassel-like ornaments. (Compare with this the capitals of the engaged piers at *Mschatta*, 36. I should like to point out the remarkable resemblance of these bell-shaped capitals, finished above and below by a rope torus, with certain bell-shaped Hittite bases, which also show the rope torus on the upper and lower edge of the bell. *Ausgrabungen in Sendschirli*, p. 142, Abbildung 47.) For the pilaster capitals at Mayâfârqîn the closest parallel is again near at hand; it is the capital which now stands in front of the serail at Urfah and serves as a fountain (I do not reproduce my photograph because the capital has already been published several times by Strzygowski from a photograph of Baron Oppenheim, *Mschatta*, p. 256. [It is added here as Pl. 86, ed. 1981][173]. Here the scheme of Pl. 62 is repeated almost exactly, even to the egg and leaf of the astragal. The same rhomboid ornament appears upon some of the smaller capitals of Sta. Sofia, Constantinople (Salzenberg, pl. 17, fig. 4, or more closely pl. 20, fig. 8, a capital of unknown origin which was found in the church. Capitals of the same kind are to be seen in the Sultan's dais), and there is a remarkable instance in N. Syria [174] of a capital dated as early as AD 414 which is decorated by intersecting bands forming lozenges (Butler, *Ancient Architecture*, section B, part 4, p. 159). The interlacing circles of Plate 64 are also found at Constantinople in a somewhat similar form (Salzenberg, pl. 17, fig. 3), but my own impression is that the prototypes both of the pier capitals and of the basket capitals at Mayâfârqîn are to be sought in Armenia[175], and it is certain that Armenian influences must have been strong in this region. Whether the same can be said of the plan of the church is open to question. The domed basilica is a creation of the Hellenistic coast lands where, up to the present, it has exclusively been found, the most easterly example being Qaṣr ibn Wardân[176]. The close resemblance which the Mayâfârqîn church bears to Sta. Sofia, Salonika, as well as the character of the capitals, would point to a date in the 6th century. Now we know from Procopius that Justinian refortified the city of Martyropolis (Mayâfârqîn) [177], but no mention is made of the building of a church. There is however another record which might apply to the edifice. Abul Faradj (*Hist. Dynast.* ed. Pocock, p. 98)[178] says that Khosrau II, after his restoration to the throne in AD 591, gave back Dârâ and Mayâfârqîn to the Emperor Maurice and built two churches in Mayâfârqîn, one dedicated to the Virgin and one to St. Sergius. (Michael the Syrian, ed Chabot, vol. 2, p. 372, gives a variant of this story. He says that the towns restored by Khosrau were Dârâ and Resayna [Râs ul 'Ain] and that he built three churches, dedicating one to the Virgin, one to the Apostles, and one to St. Sergius, but where these churches were erected he does not mention.) It is very tempting to see in the existing ruins of the church of the Virgin the foundation of the Persian king, and the evidence with regard to date which is to be derived from the decorations would not conflict with this theory. (Taylor, *R. Geographical Soc. Journal*, vol. 35, p. 24, says that the interior of the church was ornamented "by a broad belt representing clusters of grapes and foliage".)

As regards the date of the basilica, I should not like to place it, on architectural grounds, much later than the beginning of the 5th century, and it may well be as Lehmann Haupt supposes (*Armenien*, 421) a foundation of the famous bishop Marutha who was a diligent collector of the relics of martyrs. (Assemani, *Bib. Or.* vol. 1, p. 178. Marutha was bishop of Mayafarqin as early as 381, when he attended the Council of Constantinople, Assemani, vol. 3, p. 363.) Lehmann Haupt, who identifies Mayâfârqîn with Tigranokerta, quotes from the Armenian historian Faustus a statement to the effect that St. Eugenius erected a martyrium chapel at Tigranokerta in the days of the Armenian king Pap (AD 369–374)[179]. He believes this martyrium to have been the precursor of a martyrium built by Mârûthâ in the reign of Theodosius (AD 408–450) with which he identifies unhesitatingly the ruins of the basilica[180].

Citadel, Diyârbekr[181].

In the citadel of Diyârbekr there is another building which falls into the class of domed basilica though it has certain peculiarities which are not found elsewhere (Fig. 43). It is difficult of access since it is now used as a depôt for military stores, and it has been known to us hitherto only through a sketch plan made by de Beylié and published in *Amida*, p. 173. It consists of two parts,

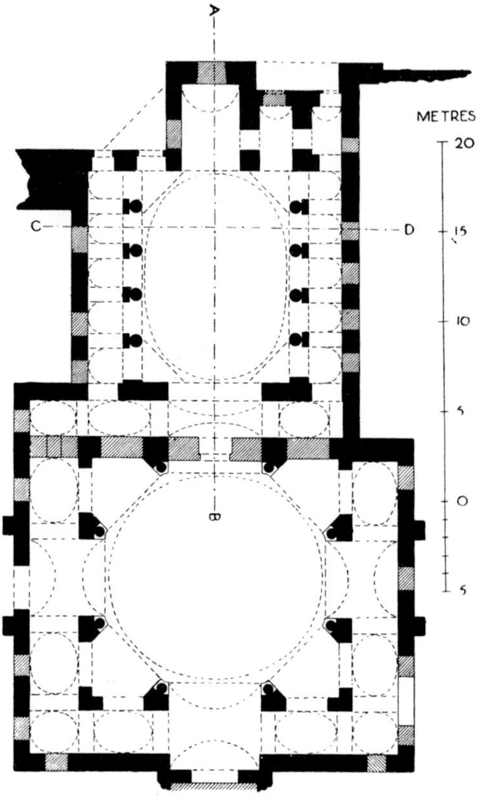

Fig. 43. Diyarbakır, citadel buildings, plan

of which the eastern building is probably the older, and to the eastern building alone is it possible to assign a Christian origin. It stands upon the city wall, overhanging the steep bank that runs down to the Tigris. The unusual shape of the E. end (Pl. 27) may have been dictated by the line of the wall on which it was built. The main sanctuary is an oblong chamber with windows in the E. wall and a large opening, now blocked up, to the N. A doorway at the S. side leads into a smaller chapel which communicates both with the nave and with a second chapel lying at the E. end of the S. aisle. The nave is divided from the aisles by arcades of five arches, carried by columns which are backed by small piers. The piers are needed to support the transverse arches across the narrow aisles. The aisles are not roofed with a continuous barrel vault, but each bay between the transverse arches is covered by a small barrel vault running N. and S. and ending against the outer wall in a semi-dome. Pl. 29 is a flash light photograph of one of these semi-domes; the top of the transverse arches can be seen on either side; the floor which intersects the archways is that of a wooden gallery, extending through both aisles and on either side of the nave, and used for storage purposes. The gallery is shored up by planks which completely cover the walls of the aisles and enclose the columns and piers; it was therefore impossible to get a general view of the lower part of the church, indeed the Commandant begged me as a personal favour not to take any photograph in which the military stores should appear. These conditions are not favourable to an accurate examination of the building, and it was only by peering through the cracks in the boards that I could determine the shape of the columns and piers. The two sections, Figures 44 and 45,

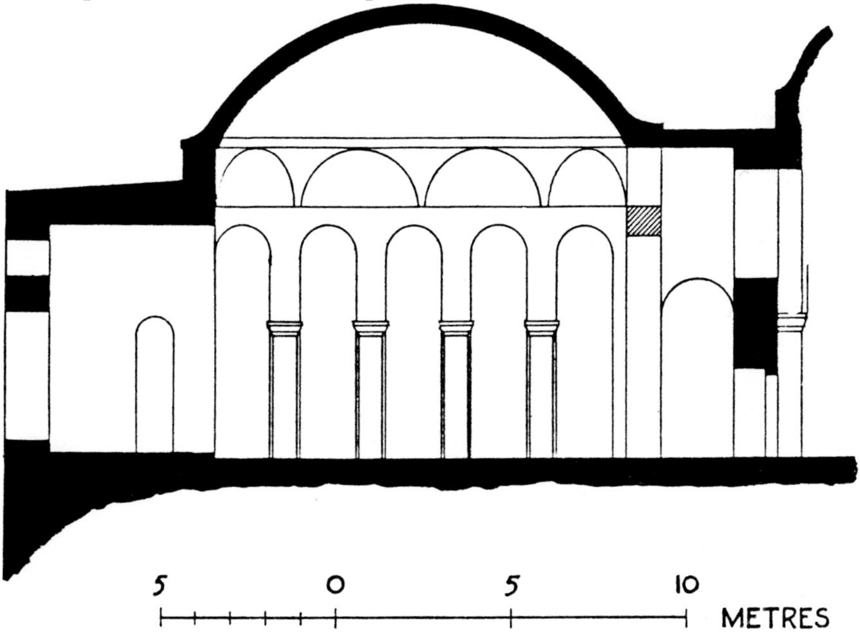

Fig. 44. Diyarbakır, citadel buildings, E half, section A–B

will help to an understanding of the interior. The columns carry simply moulded capitals which are without any other form of decoration. Plate 28 shows the construction of the upper part of the nave. The stilted lower arches belong to the arcade of the S. aisle. Above them shallow arches carry the oval dome, the angle arches springing across the corners of the nave. The central arch at the W. end is left open for the lighting of the nave. The wooden stair, which runs across it in the picture, connects the galleries on either side of the nave. The pendentives between the arches are decorated with stalactites worked in plaster. In the whole building there is no trace of any other decoration, and the rough masonry, a mixture of stone and brick, precludes the idea of delicate profiles or elaborate friezes. The dome is all of brick; so are the

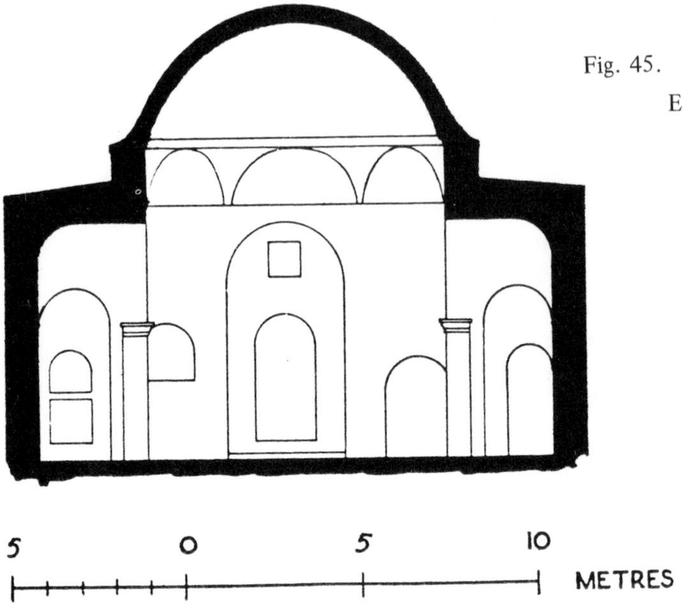

Fig. 45. Diyarbakır, citadel buildin
E half, section C–D

semi-domes and transverse arches of the aisles, but the nave arcades, so far as they were visible, are of good dressed stone. The aisles were once lighted by a number of windows; they are invisible on the inside, by reason of the boarding which covers the walls, but on the exterior their brick arches appear above the level of the ruin heaps (Pl. 26). The nave and aisles open at the western end into the second building, which consists of a central octagonal area, covered by a slightly oval dome (the greater width being in this case from N. to S.) and girdled by a series of domed or vaulted cells, the whole forming a rectangular edifice. The dome rests upon eight supports, each being composed of a column and an irregularly shaped pier. Piers very similar in form occur in the church of the Virgin at Diyârbekr, but neither they nor the dome they carry belong to the original structure (Fig. 14). The top of the dome has fallen in, but enough remains to give an accurate idea of the construction (Pl.30). It is undoubtedly Moslem of a late period. The columns are re-used material. In each one the lower part is a small shaft complete up to the necking; it was not high enough for the requirements of the builders and another piece of shaft was added. The main door was to the W. It is blocked up on the outside by heaps of grassgrown ruin, but on the inside the wooden lintel is visible, as well as the relieving arch over it. The present entrance is from the N; on either side of it there are two other doorways which are now blocked up.

There are two more blocked doors on the W. side (visible from the interior) and four to the S. The roofing system of the outer girdle of cells is symmetrical. The three angle cells at each corner are covered with oval domes, the elongated cell in the centre of each side with a barrel vault. An outer door communicated with every cell. The eastern cells have been blocked on the W. side with walls which convert them into a kind of narthex to the domed basilica; I think it possible that this narthex was an integral part of the basilica and received its present form only when the western building was added, and this conjecture is supported by the fact that on the S. side the symmetry of the western building is broken by the absence of the S.E. corner cell – at this point the old narthex was not lengthened, though at the N. end it received the necessary addition. The doorway leading from the centre of the narthex into the octagon, together with the wall in which it stands, seem to belong to the same building period as the rest of the western building. How much of the domed basilica is old work? I may say at once that the superstructure, so far as it is visible, all appeared to me to belong to the Moslem period, and the dome to be of the same date as the dome of the octagon. The walls, both inside and outside, are a patch-work of re-used material; the masonry of the nave arcades betrays its Moslem origin by its character (the small size of the stones and the manner of the arch building is quite unlike early Christian work) and the absence of all decoration, even at important points like the chancel arch, is very significant. The columns and piers are hidden by boarding, and the lower part of the walls are boarded up on the interior and half buried in ruin heaps on the exterior; on the E. side, only, the whole wall visible, and here again there are evidences of reconstruction and alteration (Pl. 25). Since so little of the building can have been preserved in its primary form, it is open to question whether it should be considered as a Christian church or no. The orientation and the basilical plan are in favour of the local tradition, but it is not a subject on which I should like to dogmatise. As to the date of the possible original building, the evidence is purely negative: there are no evidences, structural or decorative, which point to an early period. The citadel wall, immediately to the S. bears an inscription of the Merwânid Abu'l Qâsim Naṣr, dated 1071–2, but the wall on which stands the building just described is of a different character and bears no relation to the inscribed wall (Pl. 27).

Deir ez Za'ferân, near Mârdîn[182].

I visited two other domed churches in N. Mesopotamia, one at Deir ez Za'ferân near Mârdîn, the other at Niṣîbîn, but the first I did not plan [see Fig. 53 here], because I knew that it was shortly to be published by Dr. Preusser. The four-sided dome, which has been rebuilt, rests directly upon the walls, not upon columns; the decoration is overloaded and poor in execution. The church seems to be a late example of the ornate architecture of N. Mesopotamia and it is interesting as showing the last developments of the Hellenistic tradition. The plan is a modification, or perhaps it would be better to say a simplification, of the 'Adhra at Ḥâkh, but it is more definitely cruciform. The trifoliate bays of Ḥâkh are represented by three deep apses, the largest being that to the E. which contains the altar. A heavy, richly decorated moulding runs round the church and springs up into an archivolt over the apses and over a western bay leading to the W. door. The arch of the eastern apse is set higher up than those of the other three bays, and the moulding forms a ramp at the eastern end of the N. and S. walls in order to reach the necessary level, and projects forward over the massive acanthus capitals on either side of the chancel arch (Pls. 194–197). Not content with covering every member of the moulding with carving, the architect has placed upon it strange basket-shaped ornaments [183] which I have not seen in any other building. One of these ornaments, on the W. wall, is more like a vase (Pl. 194) than a basket. It recalls the vases on the capital at Ḥâkh (Pl. 145), though it is bigger and rounder than they. On either side of the archway leading to the W. door there are niches (Pl. 198) with acanthus capitals carrying enriched arches, and similar niches are found on the exterior (Pls. 190–191) of the building on either side of the W. door, as well as in the small court to the S. of the church (Pls. 192–193) [184]. (I have photographed all these but I do not give illustrations because they will probably be published by Dr. Preusser [they have been included here, ed. 1981].) I have already spoken of the cornice which runs round the outside of the church (Pl. 189). It is no doubt of the same date as the rest of the building, but it has been relaid (in a somewhat fragmentary condition), most of the upper part of the wall having been rebuilt (Pl. 188).

Mâr Ya'qûb, Niṣîbîn[185].

The church of St. James of Nisibis has also, I believe, been planned by Dr. Preusser, but since I was delayed at Niṣîbîn by torrents of rain, I spent the time in examining the building (Fig. 46; cf. Fig. 55). I do not suppose that we have in the present structure the whole of the original church; there must have been something more upon the S. side, for at the S.E. corner there is a fragmentary wall, continuing the line of the E. wall, and the series of arched openings upon the S. side (Pls. 70–71) corresponding to the doors in the opposite wall, must have led either into a narthex or into another church like the existing N. church. A good deal of the present building is due to restoration[186]. The W. wall of what is now the S. church is all modern, and in the N. church one of the doors has been completely blocked and the other narrowed. The piers which carry the vault of the N. church are all later work, but they belong to different periods of construction. The S. piers carry moulded capitals, and they and the arcade above them are of better workmanship than the N. piers, which are without capitals. I conjecture that the original vault of the N. church sprang from wall to wall, for there is no sign of arcades belonging to the earliest building period. The dome of the S. church is rebuilt, but a dome there must always have been in this position (Pl. 78)[187]. The whole of the wall up to the cornice is old, including the piers on the W. side and the garlanded acanthus capitals which they carry (Pls. 79–80). The western side of these capitals is not worked, and on the E. side the cutting of the acanthus leaves is very perfunctory[188] and the garland is broken off before it reaches the abacus. All round the interior of the domed chamber runs a moulding springing up, as at Deir ez Za'ferân, into an archivolt over the apse arch and the W. arch, as well as over the relieving arches of the doorways (Pl. 79). (The top of one of the door arches can be seen in Plate 78.) Every member of the moulding is enriched, the sequence of the ornament being a bead and reel, vine rinceaux, dentils, egg and leaf, flutes, rhomboids and acanthus palmettes[189]. Almost the same moulding, but without the acanthus palmettes in the crowning cyma, is carried continuously over the relieving arches of the doorways on the outer sides; in one case it is visible upon the exterior of the S. wall of the S. church

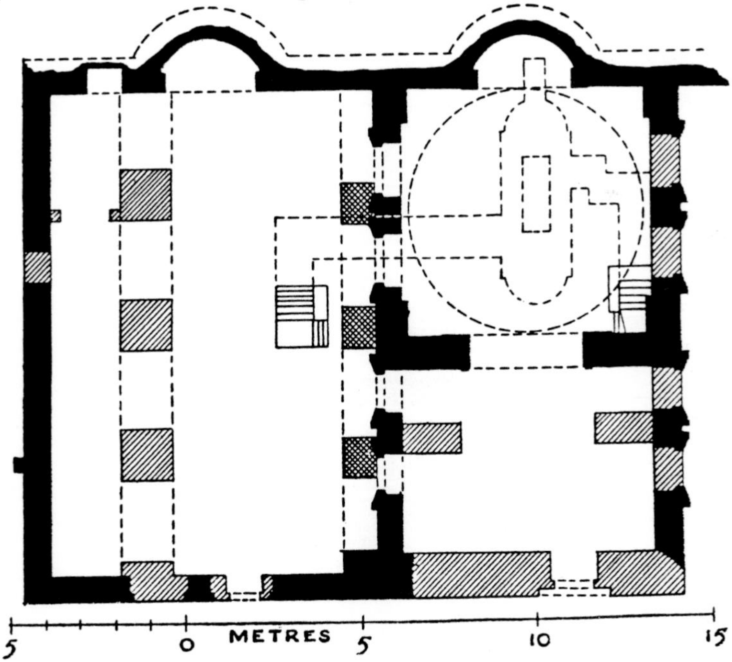

Fig. 46. Nisibin, Mar Ya'qub, plan of church (cf. Fig. 55)

(Pls. 74–76), in the other on the S. wall of the N. church (Fig. 47, Pl. 77). The relieving arches are slightly horse-shoed. The lintels and jambs of the doorways are only visible in the interior of the church. They are elaborately moulded and decorated with a band of split palmettes, each alternate pair being placed in a reversed position (Pl. 81)[190] . Between the lintel and the relieving arch there is a heavy frieze and cornice composed of a torus covered with alternate palmettes, dentils, egg and leaf, a row of small consoles, flutes, a bead and reel and a cyma. In Fig. 47 the moulded capitals on either side of the relieving arch belong to the S. piers, which are a later addition and cover the moulding which runs continuously from arch to arch. The vault at the W. end of the S. church has been completely rebuilt. Both churches are now pitch dark, but there would seem to have been square-headed windows in the E. wall above the apses. These can be seen in Plate 78 above the apse of the S. church where they are three in number. Both apses are shallow; the exterior wall is here hidden by earth. The dome of the S. church covers a crypt which can be entered by a flight of steps in the S.W. angle of the domed chamber, or by a second flight of steps leading out of the N. church[191]. The chamber containing a tomb[192], which is connected with the staircases by short vaulted passages, lies a little to the S.E. of the centre of the dome. At the E. end there is a deep niche which runs back under the main apse.

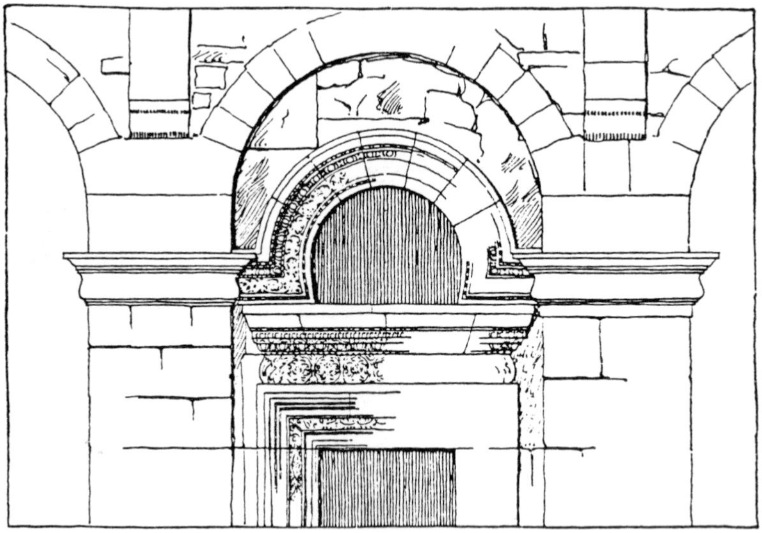

Fig. 47. Nisibin, Mar Ya'qub, drawing of door in S wall of N church

The saint whose body once lay in the sarcophagus in the crypt was James, bishop of Nisibis, who successfully defended the town against Sapor II in AD 338, and died in the same year after the close of the first siege. It is stated in the *Livre de la Chasteté* (Ed. Chabot, p. 4) that it was he who built the cathedral church of Nisibis, but architectural evidence does not point to any part of the existing church being as old as the 4th century[193]. An important clue is given in Baethgen's *Fragmente syrischer und arabischer Historiker*, where under the year AH 141 (AD 757) it is recorded that the building of the sanctuary and the concha (apse?) of the great altar of the church of Niṣîbîn was completed by Cyprian the metropolitan, who consecrated it on Whitsunday of that year[194]. When Southgate saw the church in 1837 (I quote from Ritter, *Erdkunde*, Vol XI, p. 437) one part (the N. church) was used as a military magazine, the other (the S. church) was roofless and in ruins, though the walls were beautifully decorated with sculpture. He saw no trace of the crypt, which had, however, been visited by many travellers before him, for example, by Tavernier in the middle of the 17th century (*Travels*, [London 1688], p. 71), and by Niebuhr in 1766 (*Reisebeschreibung*, Vol. 2, p. 380). In Niebuhr's time the church was standing, as it is today, deep in masses of earth and ruin. Most of the travellers who have left an account of the building have supposed either that it was erected out of the ruins of a temple, or that the decoration was taken from classical monuments[195]. I do not hold that there is any ground for these conjectures. The ornament was undoubtedly intended for the place it now occupies, it is of the same character as other Christian work in N. Mesopotamia and more closely related to the late decoration of Deir ez Za'ferân than to capitals and mouldings of earlier date[196]. In the S.W. corner of the church there is an interesting octagonal font (Pl. 82). It stands upon a moulded base above which there is a narrow band of zigzags and two rows of dentils, set alternately. The shaft is covered with a zigzag pattern enclosing in the centre of each side a rhomboid in which there is a cross. Above and below, the zigzags are filled in with a palmette. The bowl of the font is set upon a double row of zigzags and ornamented with basket work. The whole recalls the motives upon the capitals of the church of the Virgin at Mayâfârqîn (Pls. 61–65). Upon the modern roof of the two churches there is now a dwelling house, approached by an exterior stair at the N.E. corner.

All the churches of N. Mesopotamia bear witness to artistic influences which are not solely to be derived from classical traditions. The latitudinal chamber is to be traced back to an architectural scheme which was born in the Ancient East, the trifoliate plan of Ḥâkh is one which was common to Western Asia, the continuous moulding, springing unbroken over the arches, or lifting itself by ramps upon the face of the wall, is a motive dear to Syrian architects in the 5th and 6th centuries. (The architrave combined with archivolt, which is the underlying principle of the decorative scheme at Niṣîbîn and Deir ez Za'ferân, appears in Syria as early as Nabataean times [Butler: The Temple of Si', in the *Florilegium Melchior de Vogüé*] and in Europe first in the palace of Diocletian at Spalato, which was probably built under Syrian influence [Strzygowski: *Spalato, ein Markstein der romanischen Kunst*]. At Spalato too the plaited motive occurs frequently.) The woven patterns on moulding and capital exhibit Oriental principles of design. From the earliest to the latest of the buildings the same forms reappear with a persistence which can be attributed only to a strong local tradition, and the brilliant inference which led Strzygowski to group together Edessa, Amida and Nisibis in a common artistic school (*Mschatta,* p. 335) is amply justified by the evidence of the monuments. It was a school which was bound by the closest links to the arts and the architecture of Syria. The very details of the decoration are the same in both regions, the plait (Butler, *Ancient Architecture, passim*; there are several good examples in section B, part 4), the wreathed capital (Golden Gate at Jerusalem, De Vogüé, *Le Temple*, pl. 12, and several examples in Butler, for instance at Ksedjbeh, sec. B, part 4, p. 159), the split palmette (*Mschatta*, p. 282), and Syria, like N. Mesopotamia, was dominated, notwithstanding all divergencies, by the Hellenistic spirit. I cannot exemplify this better than by comparing the churches which I have just described with a building that lay beyond the pale of western authority.

Mâr Tahmazgerd, Kerkûk[197].

Fig. 48. Kerkuk, Mar Tahmazgerd, plan of complex

E. of the great mound on which stands the citadel of Kerkûk, upon a little hill near the mosque and tekîyyeh of Pîr Daniel, is the Nestorian church dedicated to Mâr Tahmazgerd. The history of this saint forms a famous episode in Nestorian chronicles. Tahmazgerd was a Magian in the service of the Sasanian king Yazdegerd II. He was converted by witnessing the fortitude exhibited by the Christians during the great persecution which he was conducting at Kerkûk, by the king's command in AD 446 (Hoffmann, *Auszüge*, p. 57), and was himself crucified by order of Yazdegerd. When the persecution was over, Mârôn, bishop of Kerkûk, built and consecrated a monastery[198] in memory of the martyrs on the mound outside the city where the massacre of the Christians had taken place, and ordered a yearly festival to be held in their honour. This festival is still observed by the Nestorians of Kerkûk on the 25th of September, which was the day of Tahmazgerd's death. (Wigram, *History of the Assyrian church*, p. 140. He gives the date of the martyrdom of Tahmazgerd as 448, but according to Labourt [*Le Christianisime dans l'Empire Perse*, p. 126] the persecution began in the 8th year of Yazdegerd, who came to the throne in 438.) Of the monastery nothing remains (Figs. 48 and 49). The church, with its complex of small domed and vaulted rooms and its long grave

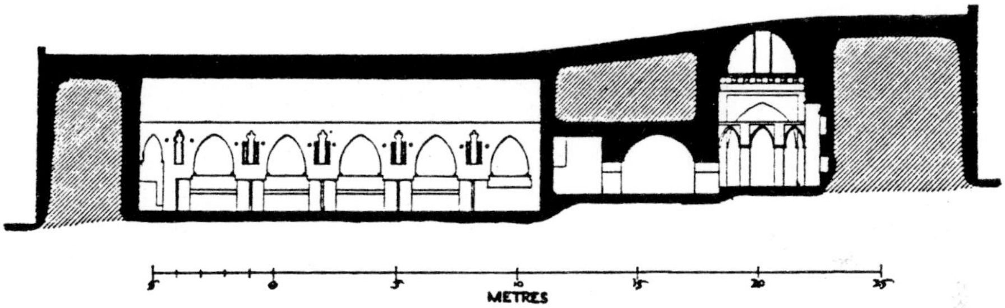

Fig. 49. Kerkuk, Mar Tahmazgerd, section A–B

chamber containing the tombs of the martyrs, stands alone upon the summit of the little rocky hill. Opposite to it the city of Kerkûk climbs up the great citadel mound and extends over part of the low ground, a patch of cornfields and gardens occupying the intervening space between the town and the church. A high wall, recently rebuilt, encloses the area to the W. of the church, which is now used as a cemetery. The only entrance into the graveyard is a door on the N. side, which is indeed the only opening in the outer wall, for the church has no doors or windows upon the exterior. The building is covered with roughcast without, and within by a coat of stucco. The masonry, including the vaults, is of unsquared stones set in a thick bed of mortar. The solidity of the vaults is due to the excellence of the mortar. The church itself is at the S. end of the complex. It is composed of three domed divisions lying approximately E. and W. The westernmost of these chambers is lighted by a window in the W. wall opening, into the court, and approached by a door in the N. wall. The small oblong room, into which the door gives, is modern, and so is the niched room outside the church to the W. The W. division of the church is covered by an ovoid dome set on arched niches (Pl. 32) and is connected with the next division by a broad doorway. This central division, which is of exactly the same construction as the first, is in turn connected by an arched opening with a passage room to the N., as well as with the sanctuary to the E. The church is almost entirely dark, the only light being that which filters through the doors and through the W. window, but I managed to obtain some photographs by flashlight. The sanctuary is raised by two steps above the level of the divisions to the W. of it (Pl. 33). It is prolonged to the E. by a rectangular recess (not quite rectangular on account of the irregularities of the building) and in the recess is placed an altar which is set back into the wall. The screen, carried by two columns which stands before the recess, is a later addition. Four pointed arches support the dome (Pl. 34). The walls are outlined by a shallow panel, above which there is a plain band of masonry. Then follows a band of large dog-tooths with a plain band above them. The four-sided dome is divided across the centre by transverse arches lying E. and W., and N. and S. In the walls of all three divisions of the church (and also in the hall of tombs) are small irregularly placed niches, the taqcheh found in every Persian building, ancient or modern. One of these can be seen under the arch in Plate 34. A door in the N. wall of the sanctuary opens into an oblong vaulted chamber at a lower level, which was, according to the priest who accompanied me, originally the baptistery. Besides the door, it communicated with the sanctuary by a crooked window, now almost entirely blocked by the altar screen. The baptistery is connected with the domed chamber which lies to the N. of the central division of the church. Here, and in the chamber still further to the N., the domes have recently been rebuilt. There is a window in the W. wall of one of the chambers, which gives into the modern room above mentioned, and a door in the W. wall of the other, the northern chamber. In the E. wall of the latter there is a small door which opens into a tiny windowless room (connected also with the baptistery) and further N. a short passage ending in a door which leads into the hall of tombs (Pl. 35). This hall lies N. and S. and is provided on either side with recesses containing tombs, five on the E. side and four on the W., where one recess is taken up by the door. The tomb of Mâr Tahmazgerd occupies the recess facing the door. The recesses are divided from one another by pairs of stumpy columns without capitals (the northern end of the hall has a column and a pier instead of two columns), and covered by semi-domes set over the angles on small squinches. The semi-dome is set forward from the walls of the recess (Pl. 36). Between the slightly pointed arches of the tomb recesses, the walls are decorated with lancet-shaped niches flanked by engaged columns, also without capitals. The lancet terminates in a pointed trefoil (Pl. 37). On either side, round holes, obviously so placed merely for their decorative effect, make a black disk upon the wall. At the northern end of the E. wall the final lancet niche is without engaged columns (Pl. 36). Beyond it to the N. a shallow and narrow pointed arch fills in the wall space, but there is no tomb below it, and it is absent on the W. side of the hall. The curve of the vault begins in fact from immediately above the pairs of columns, for from that point the whole wall slopes inwards, but the actual barrel vault springs from above the recesses, oversailing the wall. It is slightly pointed. Three very small windows, placed in the vault, light the northern end of the hall; towards the southern end there is a fourth window, rather larger than the others, which opens into a modern room. The floor of the hall is considerably lower than the present level of the ground to the W. of it, and the windows, though they are set high up in the vault, appear on the outside immediately above ground level. They can be seen to the left in Pl. 31. Moreover, this upper part of the building, owing to the slope of the wall and the curve of the vault below ground, falls within the outer line of the foundations, as I have endeavoured to indicate on the plan. I conjecture that the tomb recesses of the hall were always below the level of the court. On the E. side, the hill falls away abruptly and the outer wall is visible to its full height, i.e. to the level of the floor of the hall. According to my measurements (and the fact is apparent in the photograph, Pl. 31), there must be a mass of masonry at the northern end of the hall, but as I cannot be certain whether it is solid, it is partially hatched in the plan. A similar space exists between the S. side of the church and the southern outer wall. The E. side of the roof slopes gradually upwards from the hall to the sanctuary dome; there must therefore be a space between the surface of the roof and the low barrel vault of the baptistery.

The construction of the recesses in the hall of tombs at once recalls two chambers in the Sasanian palace of Sârvistân (Dieulafoy, *L'Art ancien de la Perse*, vol. 4, pls. 3 and 7, the plan is better given by Flandan & Coste, *Voyage en Perse*). Here we have the same pairs of stumpy columns without capitals, and the same semi-domes set on squinch arches, the sole essential difference being that at Sarvistan the columns stand free from the wall and are connected with it by an arch, whereas at Kerkûk they are engaged in the wall. The architectural scheme is, however, in principle, identical. Herzfeld believes Sârvistân to have been built by Bahram V. Gors, who reigned from 420 to 438 (*Iranische Felschiefs*, p. 131); the martyrium of Tahmazgerd was founded by Mârôn shortly after 446[199] , but though the existing building seems to retain the true Sasanian tradition, how much of the original work remains is doubtful. The systematic use of the pointed arch before the Moslem conquest appears to me to be improbable (Herzfeld, Die Genesis der islamischen Kunst, *Der Islam*, Vol. 1, p. 111). It is found at Qaṣr ibn Wardân in the 6th century (Butler, *Ancient Architecture*, section B, part 1), but at the castle of Ukheiḍir, which cannot be earlier than the age of the Umayyads, both pointed and ovoid arches are used [200], and my impression is that at that period the pointed arch was not completely established. Some of the vaults in the substructures of Qaṣr-i-Shîrîn are pointed, but in very rough construction, such as that of these vaults, the ovoid is apt to slip almost insensibly into the point [201]. Moreover, the wall decoration of Mâr Tahmazgerd can be paralleled in Mohammadan work. Something not very different from these lancet niches exists at Ukheiḍir, where also the round disks are to be found in a rather more elaborate form, and there are yet closer resemblances to the stucco work of the Arba'în at Tekrit (*Amurath to Amurath*, fig. 130)[202]. In the chambers between the hall and the church two of the domes have certainly been restored, but their original construction was probably exactly as it is now, and the same construction would be used at Kerkûk today. More distinctive is the dome over the sanctuary, with its intersecting arches. Here too the evidence of Sasanian tradition is strong. The dog-tooth ornament is to be found both at Sârvistân and at Firûzâbâd (Dieulafoy, op. cit., pls. 5 and 15). But the peculiar form of the dome is not known to me earlier than Ukheiḍir, where the intersecting arches appear in the semi-domes of the mosque, though these have not the four-sided plan (*Amurath to Amurath*, fig. 101)[203]. On the whole the evidence points to a date not earlier than the 8th or 9th century for the main part of the structure of Mâr Tahmazgerd, though it is possible that the hall of tombs, with its 5th century plan, may rest upon the original foundations of Mârôn.

There is another old church in Kerkûk upon the citadel hill. It is now used as a mosque, but it keeps its Christian dedication and is still called the mosque of the Lady Mary [204]. It is a basilica with a nave divided from the aisles by arcades of three arches, resting upon heavy stunted piers without capitals. The piers are so broad that the division between nave and aisles is more like a wall broken by three arches than an arcade. The oversailing vaults are high and pointed. At the E. end of the nave two piers stand forward so as partially to conceal the sanctuary, which is covered by a dome set on arched niches. At the E. end of each of the aisles there is a vaulted chapel. Doors are placed at the W. end of the nave and aisles, but the main entrance is at present to the N. On the N. side of the nave, against one of the piers, there are steps leading up to a platform, part of which is probably the old pulpit. A miḥrâb has been hollowed out of the S. wall of the S. aisle. The whole of the interior is plastered and whitewashed; there is no decoration of any kind. In spite of its basilical form, this church, like Mâr Tahmazgerd, retains the characteristics of Sasanian architecture, the massive simple construction, the graceless proportions, the absence in a word, of that soul of beauty which the builders of N. Mesopotamia inherited from their Hellenistic masters [205].

The churches in the Ṭûr 'Abdîn, at Ṣalaḥ, Arnâs, Kefr Zeh and Ḥâkh, are too closely related in style to differ widely from one another in date. Mâr Gabriel is connected with the others only by its architectural scheme, a scheme which may go back here to the early 5th century, since, according to the legend, the church of Anastasius was built upon the foundations of a church erected during the reign of Arcadius. I have given reasons for believing that the existing church is in fact the structure which was built by order of Anastasius. As regards the other churches, the evidence which can be drawn from history and epigraphy is scanty enough. The oldest inscription is that which dates the screen of Arnâs in the middle of the 8th century, but this screen is obviously of later workmanship than the church in which it stands. Between Arnâs and the church of the Virgin at Ḥâkh there are resemblances so close that it is not improbable that the same stone-cutters may have been employed upon the decorations of both, but the form of the acanthus, the frequent occurrence of interwoven motives, the fantastic capitals in the apse of Ḥâkh, and the running moulding upon the tambour, points to a date not earlier than the late 5th or early 6th century. The finely dressed masonry of Ḥâkh finds its counterpart at Sâlâh where the dedication of the church would seem to fit a terminus ante quem in the beginning of the 6th century. The Mohammadan invasion of the Ṭûr 'Abdîn took place in AD 640 (Caetani, *Annali dell'Islam*, vol. 4, p. 165), and it may fairly be assumed that this group of churches had all been built prior to that period. On the whole, the early part of the 6th century accords best with the character of the architecture and with such meagre facts as we have at our disposal [206].

Monastery of Mâr Ibrahîm[207].

It is now a year since this paper was written, although its publication has been delayed by circumstances beyond my control. During the course of the past year I have had opportunity to reconsider the views I had expressed and to examine some fresh material which bears, directly or indirectly, upon the churches of the Ṭûr 'Abdîn. Of this fresh material perhaps the most important item is a communication which Dr. Walther Hinrichs has been so kind as to make to me. Dr. Hinrichs travelled along the southern spurs of the Ṭûr 'Abdîn in 1911, shortly before my last visit to the country. Coming from Djeziret ibn 'Umar he reached Kinike, a village in the plain to the S.W. of Qal'at Ḥâtem Tayy, on the 14th of March (Kinike is marked in Kiepert's map, *Kleinasien* C VI). He marched westward to Sheikh Ḥassan (possibly Kiepert's Gir Ḥassan); after 2¼ hours he turned north into the mountains and reached, after a stiff climb, the Monastery of Mâr Ibrahîm. From Mâr Ibrahîm he rejoined his Caravan, and a descent of 2½ hours brought him to Mâr Bâb (Kiepert, *Kleinasien* D VI). Dr. Hinrichs has sent me the following notes and photographs[208]:

Mittwoch, 15. März 1911. Wir brechen um 6.27 früh von Kinike auf und reiten zuerst nach Westen an den Vorbergen des Ṭûr 'Abdîn entlang bis Sheikh Ḥassan; dann nach 2½ Stunden biegen wir nördlich ins Gebirge ab. Der Pfad wird sehr eng and steinig, grosse und kleine Felsblöcke erschweren das Vorwärtskommen. Um 11.15 Uhr lasse ich meine Karawane zurück und klettere mit dem Diener und einem Zaptieh allein weiter bergauf. Wir kommen an einem kleinen Höhlendorf vorbei, wo ich einen Kurden finde, der uns in

¾ Stunden auf sehr steilem Pfade nach Mâr Ibrahîm hinaufführt (Pl. 219). Dieser liegt etwas unterhalb des höchsten Gipfels und gewährt einen prächtigen Ausblick auf die weite Ebene (In these respects its position is exactly similar to that of Mâr Awgên, [Fig. 1]). Das Kloster wird von acht Mönchen und zwei Dienern bewohnt. Die Kirche ist, nach Aussage der Mönche, vor nicht langer Zeit wiederhergestellt und dabei vollständig umgebaut worden. Sie ist mit einer Tonne (erneuert) überdeckt und nur sehr spärlich beleuchtet. In Kämpferhohe sind Teile eines Ornamentstreifens und einiger weitausladender Konsolen erkennbar. Der reichornamentierte Triumphbogen ist scheinbar noch gut erhalten, kann aber wegen der Höhe und Dunkelheit der Kirche von mir bei dem Mangel an Zeit nicht aufgenommen werden. Die Kirche misst rund 6 zu 17 m und ist bis zum Kampfer schon hoher als breit. Das etwas erhöhte 5 m breite runde Chor (etwa 4 m tief) liegt an der östlichen Schmalseite (Orientierung = 285°) und ist aus der Achse ganz nach Süden verrückt. Früher standen in ihm im Halbkreise zehn Säulen, von denen noch geringe Spuren eines Gebälks und alle Basen erhalten sind. Diese sind 66 cm hoch und werden heute von den Mönchen als Sitzplätze verwandt (Fig. 50). Vom Chor aus zugänglich liegen auf beiden Seiten kleine tonnengewölbte niedrige Märtyrergräber. An der nördlichen Kirchenwand beim Chore ist eine flache Nische, die an der Westseite von einer kleinen Säule mit reichem Kapitell eingefasst wird (Pl.220). Nach Süden hat die Kirche einen Eingangsraum, von dem aus noch ein anderer östlich davon gelegener Raum zugänglich ist. In der Nähe des Einganges finde ich das photographierte Architekturstück (Pl. 221). Die Mönche wohnen neben der Kirche in Höhlen, vor denen jetzt noch viel Schnee liegt. Für den Besuch dieses Klosters steht mir nur eine halbe Stunde zur Verfügung. Nach schwierigem Abstieg erreichen wir, nach Wiedervereinigung mit der Karawane, in 2½ Stunden das christliche Dorf Mâr Bâb.

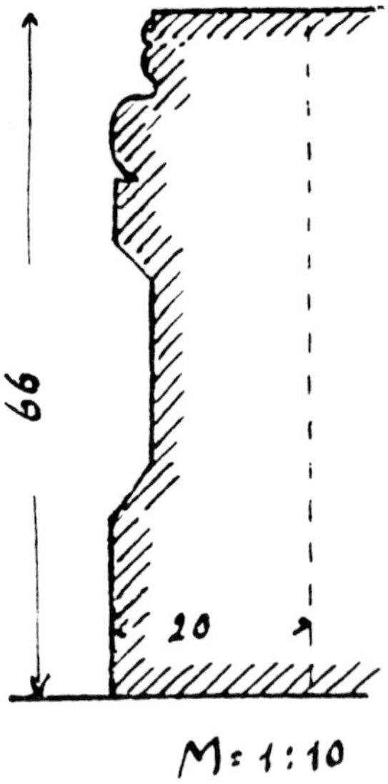

Fig. 50. Mar Ibrahim, profile and column base in apse (drawing Hinrichs)

It is clear even from this brief description that we have here an important building. In my opinion Dr. Hinrichs has solved the problem discussed on p. 37[209] and his Mâr Ibrahîm is no other than the famous monastery founded by Mâr Ibrahîm of Kashkâr in the middle of the 6th century[210]. His account places the site in exactly the position where I conjectured that it might lie.

Although the church has been rebuilt, it may be taken for certain that the original plan has been preserved[211]. The west wall seems to consist mainly of the original masonry, and to have retained part of an old stringcourse below the window (Pl. 219). The apse, according to Dr. Hinrichs, shows umistakable traces of old work, but without further examination it is impossible to determine why it was placed to the S. of the main axis of the church. In its principal features the plan seems to resemble the plan of Kefr Zeh and Arnâs, i.e. it belongs to the type which I have called the parochial church[212]. It is to be noted that Mâr Augên is another exception to the general rule which I have laid down. As at Mâr Augên, the cells of the monks are rock-cut[213], but from a photograph giving a distant view of the monastery – I do not reproduce it on account of the smallness of the scale – it is apparent that there were other buildings round the church, occupying the artificial platform cut out of the hillside on which it stands. In this respect also Mâr Ibrahîm resembles Mâr Augên (Pl. 199). In Pl. 219 small windows, with a square-headed moulding round them, can be seen in the S. wall above the low narthex. These windows must be part of the original building; they can be paralleled exactly at Kefr Zeh. At Mâr Ibrahîm the superstructure, with its shallow arched niches, is clearly modern, and the narthex seems to have been entirely rebuilt. The most interesting point in the account given by Dr. Hinrichs is the presence of 10 column bases standing round the semi-circle of the apse. It is possible that there may have been here niches containing sedilia similar to those at Ḥâkh (Figs. 38–39). The profile of these bases (Fig. 50) is not unlike those at Ḥâkh. The richly ornamented chancel arch of Mâr Ibrahîm is to be found in all the churches of the Ṭûr 'Abdîn. The decorative band of carving, and the consoles in the nave are not present at Arnâs and Keft Zeh (compare however Niṣîbîn, [Pl. 79] and Deir ez Za'ferân [Pls. 194–197]). I cannot hazard any conjecture as to the character of these ornaments since Dr. Hinrichs had not time to photograph them. Fortunately, he has supplied us with the photograph of a single capital which stands on the W. side of a small niche in the N. wall of the church near the chancel (Pl.220). It is a garlanded acanthus capital. The lower part is occupied by a row of broadly serrated acanthus leaves. On the upper register there is, in the centre of the capital, a garland enclosing the bust of a bearded man. On either side is some object, now totally defaced, supported in each case by a hand and arm. The bodies to which these arms belong are hidden on one side by plaster and on the other side by a curtain. The emblems upon the upper register of the capital are separated from the acanthus leaves of the lower register by a curving, twisted stalk or band. It must be admitted that this capital is wholly unlike any other known to me in the Ṭûr 'Abdîn. The cutting of the acanthus is closely allied to Byzantine work of the V and VI centuries (see Wulff, *Altchristliche und mittelalterliche Bildwerke*, Teil I. pp. 55 and 56) [214], it is totally different from the acanthus at Ḥâkh and Kefr Zeh, Arnâs or Ṣalaḥ.

And here I should like to review the opinion which I have expressed as to the date of these four churches. During a recent visit to Berlin I took occasion to study with care the architectural fragments exhibited in the Mshatta room of the Kaiser Friedrich Museum, and the Mshatta façade itself, which I had not seen since I visited it in the Syrian desert in the year 1900. The close relationship between the work in that façade and in the Ṭûba fragments with the decoration of the Ṭûr 'Abdîn churches is most striking. Notably the acanthus blossom and the fir cone of the Ṣalaḥ pilasters occur almost without variation both at Mshatta and at Ṭûba. The castle of Ṭûba is certainly early Mohammadan; I do not doubt that Mshatta belongs to the same period[215]. I am therefore forced to the conclusion that it is possible to date the pilasters at Ṣalaḥ, and with them the whole church, at least as late as 700 AD. I have already given reasons for believing that the church of the 'Adhra at Ḥâkh and of Mâr Cyriacus at Arnâs must be placed at about the same date as Ṣalaḥ[216]. Mâr Azizael at Kefr Zeh may be somewhat later – the chancel arch and the capitals beneath it are coarser in workmanship than the decoration of the other buildings. It follows therefore that this group of churches may belong to the end of the seventh or the beginning of the eighth centuries, that is to say that they were erected during the period of the Umayyad khalifs. (The same reasoning does not apply to Mâr Gabriel, and I see no ground for doubting that it is a sixth century church.)

The Umayyad period (661–750) is beginning to emerge from the obscurity into which it was thrown by the deliberate falsifications of the Abbâsid chroniclers. The brilliant studies of the R.P. Lammens in the Mélanges de la Faculté orientale de Beyreuth, have thrown new light upon the reigns of the first two khalifs of the dynasty[217]; the exploration of the Syrian desert has provided us with material for a more correct appreciation of Umayyad architecture and arts, and this information can now be controlled by a comparison with the civilisation of the early Abbâsid period, as revealed by the excavations at Sâmarrâ[218]. For a detailed enquiry into the administrative system of the Umayyad khalifs we must await the eleventh and subsequent volumes of Prince Teano's great history[219]; in the light of his researches we shall be able to judge whether the prosperity and the internal security of the Mohammadan dominions during the latter half of the 7th and the earlier half of the 8th centuries were sufficient to justify the assumption that a Christian community could show such proof of peaceful development as that which would be attested by the churches of the Ṭûr 'Abdîn. Meantime, I wish to call attention to the following considerations.

In the 5th volume of the *Annali* which appeared recently, Prince Teano has laid stress upon the fact that there is no breach of continuity between the administrative and fiscal systems of the Sasanian and Byzantine monarchs on the one hand and the Mohammadan khalifs on the other. The older organisation was adopted by the new rulers from 'Umar onwards, and for the subject populations, the Arab invasion implied, not a fundamental revolution, but merely a change of masters. It is indeed probable that the subject populations benefited by the substitution, for the exhausted institutions of Persia and Byzantium, of a fresh and vigorous administration. There was no doubt a period of disastrous confusion before the new order was established; we have evidence of this period in the irretrievable decay of the Christian villages of the Ḥaurân and North Syria during the early 7th century[220]. The reorganisation, or rather the adaptation of the old organisation, begun by ‘Umar, was perfected by Mu‘âwiyah, the first Umayyad khalif (Lammens, *Mélanges*, vol. 1, p. 66) and continued by his son Yazîd (Lammens, *op. cit.* vol. 5, p. 118). Both Prince Teano and the R.P. Lammens insist upon the large measure of toleration which was extended by the new rulers to their non-Moslem subjects in Syria; ecclesiastical domains remained in the hands of their original owners (*Annali*, Vol. V, p. 439), and Christians were numbered among the counsellors of the Umayyad khalifs. (See the account of the influence enjoyed by the Banu Sarjûn, *Mélanges*, Vol. III, fasc. I, p. 252. Sarjûn was able to build at least one church after the Conquest.) Such facts as these point to the conclusion that a condition of considerable prosperity may well have existed in the Ṭûr ‘Abdîn during the second half of the 7th century, and that it would be reasonable to suppose that the Christian communities were not excluded from it[221].

As regards the churches at Mayâfârqîn I have nothing to add except to notice a pair of Coptic grave stelai in the Kaiser Friedrich Museum (Wulff, *op. cit.* Teil II. Zweiter Nachtrag, Nos. 2244 and 2245), whereon the lozenge-shaped entrelac of the capitals that crown the western piers of the ‘Adhra (Pl. 62) is reproduced almost exactly. According to Wulff's catalogue these stelai belong to the V–VII century, a date which agrees well with that which I have assigned to the church. Dr. Herzfeld points out to me that in the apse of the basilica at Mayâfârqîn (Pl. 42) the curious pitting of the few remaining stones of the semi-dome is not to be attributed to natural decay. There are reasons for believing that it is artificial and that it indicates the original presence of mosaic. A similar pitting of the stone occurs in the wall of the apse, but it is clear, from the rivet holes which are scattered over the surface of the stones, that the apse must have been adorned up to the cornice with marble slabs.

NOTES TO PAGES 1- 83

By Marlia Mundell Mango

1 Monastery of Mar Awgen: see catalogue of sites, p. 135 below.

2 Cf. p. 81 above.

3 On Awgen see Vööbus, *Asceticism*, I, 217-220; J.M. Fiey, "Aonès, Awun et Awgin (Eugène); aux origines du monachism mésopotamien", *AB*, 80 (1962), 52- 81; *idem. Jalons,* 100f.

4 The East Syrians (Nestorians) held the monastery until at least A.D. 1838 and the West Syrians (Jacobites) held it from at least 1842 (Brock,"Notes"; cf. Fiey, *Nisibe*, 139 and note 36).

5 An epitaph of A.D. 1109 (?).

6 An inscription in the vault dates it to A.D. 1209 (Brock, "Notes", Mar Awgen, no. 2).

6a The scale given for this church plan in the original edition was incorrect.

6b The capital in Pl. 202 was described by Bell as being under the dome in the chamber east of the south court (*Amida*, 229, fig. 148), whereas it is clearly a capital in the north court, visible in Pl. 203. Similarly, Pl. 201 is of the NW, not the NE, corner.

7 On the Mar Awgen capitals see also Sarre and Herzfeld, *Reise*, II, 102. On the Ibn Tulun capitals see Kautzsch, 164, no. 524 and Creswell, II, pl. 122. See also the following note.

8 Two-zone plaited capitals are considered to be of the sixth century, the earliest dated example (A.D. 514-523) being in S. Clemente in Rome (E. Kitzinger, "The Horse and Lion Tapestry at Dumbarton Oaks", *DOP*, 3 [1946], 17-19, no. 85, fig. 115).

9 Legendary accounts hold that the relics of Awgen and ten disciples were transferred from the Mar Awgen monastery to Deir Za'faran (Fiey, *Nisibe*, 137f.).

10 See preceding note.

11 A refoundation by Abraham of M'arre (Marin on the map below p. 185; now called Eskihisar) is known in *ca.* A.D. 700 (*ibid.*, 135). A manuscript note recording a rebuilding of the church during two months in A.D. 1271 by the monks together with seventy men from M'arre (*ibid.*, 135), has recently been fully translated (Brock, "Notes", Mar Awgen) along with several building inscriptions in houses of M'arre dated to the twelfth to thirteenth centuries (*ibid.*, M'arre, nos. 1-6). Fiey (*Nisibe*, 135) has corrected to A.D. 1838 the date of A.D. 745 given by Jarry (236, no. 61) to a commemorative inscription found in the monastery of Mar Awgen.

12 Monastery of Mar Yoḥannan: see catalogue of sites, p. 141 below.

13 In the earliest known *Life* of John (*Book of Chastity* by Isho Denah, no. 46) he is not a disciple of Awgen but a hermit from the Lakhmid capital of Hira (hence the title Bedouin or Arab, *Ṭayaya*), who after attending the School of Nisibis, was a shepherd in the Singar Mountains and ended his days alone in a grotto above M'arre. In the ninth century the monastery, founded after (?) his death, was known as that "of the grotto of Mar John the Bedouin" (Fiey, *Nisibe*, 154f.). Another *Life* seems to combine features of both traditions making John both a native of Hira and a spiritual disciple of Awgen (see Brock, "Notes", Mar Ioḥannan, translation). A different and later (?) *Life* places John *ca.* A.D. 500 (Fiey, *Nisibe*, 155f.).

14 Pl. 226 illustrates the tower mentioned in Bell, *Amurath*, 312f. It resembles in its masonry other towers published here: Pls. 106, 149. There is a building inscription of the twelfth to thirteenth century in a small vaulted chamber in the monastery (Brock, "Notes", Mar Ioḥannan, no. 2). The *Life of Mar Sallara* claims that this monk (joint abbot of this monastery and that of Mar Awgen A.D. 643-664) converted a cave here into a kitchen (*ibid., Life of Mar Sallara*, translation).

15 Bell, *Ukhaidir*, 15, fig. 3 and, e.g., pl. 36 fig. 1 (mid-eighth century, *ibid.*, 161-168; after A.D. 775/6, according to Creswell, II, 98).

16 Monastery of Mar Gabriel: see catalogue of sites, p. 137 below.

17 Cf. p. 31 and Fig. 19.

18 See the following note and p. 137 below.

19 For the history of the monastery see Nau, "Notice" and Krüger, *Mönchtum* I.

20 Main church: see catalogue of sites, p. 137 below.

21 Pognon, 40; this is the same life published by Nau (where see "Notice", 58, 102). The text says the porticoes surrounded the church, not the atrium, on three sides (cf. p. 10 above).

21a Other examples include the churches of the monasteries of Deir Ṣaliba (p. 131 below), Mar Cyriacus (p. 135 below), Mar Ya'qub at Kaishum (Guyer, "Surp Hagop"), Mar Abai at Killit (Pognon, 186), and, perhaps, Mar Lazarus at Ḥabsenas (p. 110 below).

22 See also Monneret de Villard, 18-27; cf. Sarre and Herzfeld, *Reise*, II, 298 note 4, 346. See p. 56 and note 153 below.

23 I.e. *opus sectile*. A description and photographs of this pavement are published in Hawkins and Mundell, "Mosaics", 282, 292, figs. 47-49.

24 The lateral tympana of the sanctuary are also decorated with mosaic. On the mosaics see here p. 33 and n. 93f. See also note 26 below.

25 The wording here has misled some scholars (e.g. Strzygowski, *Syrie*, 54f. and C. Ihm, *Die Programme der christlichen Apsismalerei von vierten Jahrhundert bis zur Mitte des achten Jahrhunderts* [Wiesbaden, 1960], 209) into thinking there is a cross on the apse conch which, however, bears only faint traces of a foliate design (Hawkins and Mundell, "Mosaics", 283). Bell is referring here to the crosses in medallion in mosaic in the centre and east and west sides of the vault above the apse (*ibid.*, 282,286, figs. 18-21).

26 There are traces of mosaic in this burial chamber (*ibid.*, 283).

27 Church of the Virgin: see catalogue of sites, p. 138 below.

28 Church of the Forty Martyrs: see catalogue of sites, p. 137 below.

29 The octagon: see catalogue of sites, p. 139 below, and note 17 above. The plan of the octagon given in Figs. 5 and 19 has been corrected by Leroy (see below). A photograph of the interior of this octagon is published in Hawkins and Mundell, "Mosaics", fig. 5.

30 The last figure is undoubtedly meant to be 0.03 m. These bricks are of the same size as those of the arcades of Mar Sovo at Ḥaḥ (Bell, RGS Notes: see note 59 below). See also the following note. Constantinopolitan bricks measure 0.35–0.38 m square x 0.035–0.06 m (Mango, 11); those at Qaṣr Ibn Wardan are 0.30 x 0.34 x 0.035 and 0.34 x 0.37 x 0.04 m (Butler, *Architecture*, II, B. 33). All these are thinner than Persian bricks of the Sasanian (Qaṣr-i-Shirin 0.37 x 0.41 x 0.08–0.09 m; Bell, RGS Notes) and Abbasid (e.g. Samarra 0.25–0.29 m square x 0.07 m; K.A.C. Creswell: *A Short Account of Early Muslim Architecture* [London, 1958], 274, 283) periods.

31 One measurement of the bricks of the octagon should be ca. 0.40 m (Leroy, "Baptistères", 2).

32 This is the madrasa of Mustanzir (AD 1233), converted to a customs building, the Khan el Ortmah, in 1823; see Sarre and Herzfeld, *Reise*, II, 187–196.

33 Leroy suggests that this octagon was a baptistery of the Constantinian period (*ibid*, 6, Fig. 1). The inscription on the large block, now in the nave of the main church, is dated AD 777 (Pognon, 42), see below, p. 139.

34 Monastery of Mar Ya'qub, Ṣalaḥ: see catalogue of sites, p. 147 below.

35 Pognon referred to the ruins to the north (Pl. 241) as the patriarchal, not episcopal, palace, which he dated to the fourteenth century when Mar Ya'qub was the seat of the schismatic patriarch of the Ṭur 'Abdin (Pognon, 62 f.). The other buildings at the monastery include a church of Mar Bar Ḥadbshabo at the south-east corner of Mar Ya'qub (*ibid*, 62) and various burial chambers (*ibid*, 69), see p. 147 below.

36 Cf. p. 39.

37 See also p. 41.

38 Cf. Preusser, pl. 47.

39 The wreath rests between the antlers of a stag. This composition at Ṣalaḥ has been identified by N. Thierry as a symbol of St. Eustathius; see "Mentalité et formulation iconoclastes en Anatolie", *Journal des Savants* (1976), 87, fig. 5.

40 Church of Mar 'Azaziel, Kefr Zeh: see catalogue of sites, p. 120 below.

41 The inscription of AD 934/5 in the *beth ṣlotha* mentions a pastor ("head of church") rather than an abbot, see note 43 below.

42 These are known as *beth ṣlotha*, "house of prayer", see the remarks made p. x above, in the Introduction and the Glossary p. 165 below.

43 Pognon, 91–94, no. 51, in Jarry, 232, no. 55: the location given for the inscription is confused. The inscription starts: "The structure of this *beth ṣlotha* (= house of prayer) was built [in] the year AG 1246", i.e. AD 934/5.

44 Pl. 157 shows a small cross on the cornice, not the large one on the conch of the exedra at Kefr Zeh. The *beth ṣlotha* at Heshterek may be dated 772, see p. 118 below.

45 See Fig. 29 for the corrected plan.

46 Cf. p. 46 below. As reported by Leroy, this screen and that at Arnas have vanished (*CRAI* 1968, 485). Both have been replaced by modern screens, that at Kefr Zeh being dated to AD 1936 by an inscription (Jarry, 234, no. 55) which runs across the top of the screen (what Jarry refers to as "un arc récént"). It reads in part: "The roof of the church and the door of the sanctuary and the Holy of Holies were built ... in AD 1936". The "door of the sanctuary" is the screen and "the Holy of Holies" refers to the large modern tabernacle enclosing the altar (see also note 49 below). "The roof of the church" evidently alludes to a restoration of the nave vault after a collapse (Leroy, *CRAI* 1968, 485) which probably occurred around either 1915 or 1926 (Brock, "Fenqitho"). On this damage see *changes since 1911*, p. 120 below.

47 See also p. 45 and Fig. 31.

48 Cf. pp. 45 and 120.

49 Church of Mar Cyriacus, Arnas: see catalogue of sites, p. 99 below. Concerning the epigraphic evidence published by Jarry, it should be noted that the locations given for nos. 1–4 (pp. 207–209) are inaccurate and could lead to misinterpretation of the dates of building phases. Nos. 1–2 are not, as Jarry states, to the right and left "de l'entrée de l'église" but flank the apse on the lateral walls of the new altar screen. Both inscriptions record the building of "the Holy of Holies and the door of the sanctuary" in AD 1939 and clearly refer to the new tabernacle enveloping the altar ("the Holy of Holies") and to the new altar screen ("the door of the sanctuary") and not to the apse of the church itself, or to "ce bâtiment" (i.e. the church), as Jarry interpolates (no. 2). Similarly, nos. 3–4 are on the apse of the tabernacle of 1939 and not that of the church proper.

50 AD 1591/2. The contents of this inscription may be contradicted by the presence on the same vault of what appears to be a raised plaster inscription which is dated AD 1089 and which records a restoration (Jarry, 208 f, no. 5, pl. LV). Another restoration inscription is on a stone set into the west wall and is dated AD 1696 (*ibid.*, 210, no. 9). In 1693 buildings at Ṣalaḥ (Mar Ya'qub and elsewhere in the area were plundered (Bar Hebraeus, Appendix, p. liif.). Work was carried out in churches in Diyarbakır in 1689 and 1692/3 (see notes 73, 78 and 80 here) and at Deir Za'faran in 1689 and 1697 (see p. 134 below). Other inscriptions at Arnas include: 1) one recording a revetment (?) ("overlaid" or "covered" = *qram*) in AD 1014 (Jarry, 210, no. 8), which may have been carried out in the church or elsewhere; and 2) another (Bell negative R 207) on a stone (in situ?) in the façade of the left hand *beth ṣlotha* (Pl. 98) south of the church which states that one Gabriel "made this altar [or sanctuary = *madbha*]" in AD 1207 (Pognon, 95, 100, no. 54). For work done this century at Arnas, see note 49 above.

51 See also p. 50 here. This screen has disappeared (Leroy, *CRAI* 1968, 485) and been replaced by one of 1939 (Jarry, 207–209, nos. 1–4). See above, note 49.

52 The south room has an apse, see p. 48 and Fig. 34.

53 There is a room to the east of the main apse, see p. 48.

54 Church of Mar Sovo, Ḥaḥ: see catalogue of sites, p. 112 below.

54a This must be a typographical error: the length of the Arnas nave is 16.65 m (Bell, RGS Notes, and Fig. 9 above), and not 13.65 m.

55 See p. 112 below under *changes since 1911*.

56 The Corinthian capitals had garlands and were therefore similar to those at Diyarbakır (Pls. 9, 20–21), Mayafarqin (Pls. 42–43, 45) and Nisibis (Pl. 80).

57 There is also the foot of a large carved cross remaining on the apse conch (Pl. 121) of the type found at Kefr Zeh, Arnas and in the el ʻAdhra church at Ḥaḥ (Mundell, "Decoration", 65f., fig. 9).

58 The sculpture of the apse cornice and archivolt has been grouped with that of Diyarbakır, Nisibis, Mayafarqin, Dara, Urfa (Edessa), Deir Zaʻfaran and Rusafa (Guyer, "Amida" and Mundell, "Deir Zaʻfaran"), see p. 134 below.

59 Bell, RGS Notes, states: "The bricks used in these piers measure 0,41 x 0,41 x 0,03 m"; see also note 30 above.

60 Pognon, 121–125, nos. 65–71.

60a Tower by the church of Mar Sovo, Ḥaḥ: see catalogue of sites, p. 117 below.

61 Church of Mar Philoxenus, Midyat: see catalogue of sites, p. 131 below.

62 Church of el ʻAdhra, Ḥaḥ: see catalogue of sites, p. 114 below.

63 See also p. 54 here, and Pl. 131. A Karshuni inscription of AD 1903 by the church entrance apparently records this renovation: "construction de cette port et de la coupole" (Jarry, 222, no. 30). For more recent alterations to the roof see below p. 114 under *changes since 1911*. For inscriptions referring to work done in 1728 and 1883 see note 147 below.

64 See also p. 54 and Pl. 136.

65 See also p. 55 and Pls. 137–138.

66 See p. 54 and note 147.

67 On the dome see also below p. 54 and Fig. 38.

68 These rinceaux are compared with those at Arnas (pp. 50, 82) and at Deir Ṣaliba (p. 132).

69 The east apse conch also has a large cross carved in relief (S. Guyer, "Vom Wesen der byzantinischen Kunst", *Münchner Jahrbuch der bildenden Kunst*, N.F., Bd. 8 [1931], fig. 9) as at Mar Sovo at Ḥaḥ (Pl. 121) and at Arnas and Kefr Zeh (Pls. 99, 158).

70 See also p. 55.

71 W. Ramsay and G. Bell, *The Thousand and One Churches* (London, 1909), 440–442.

72 Church of Mar Cosmas, Diyarbakır: see catalogue of sites, p. 106 below.

73 *Amida*, fig. 90 shows the interior stonework of the apse, see p. 106 below. A Syriac manuscript note reports a destruction of this church in AD 1213 (*Amida*, pp. 165, 167) and a Greek inscription on the apse conch states that "... the Church of Cosmas and Damian was renewed in ... AD 1689..." (*ibid*, 171f., Fig. 90). Restorations occurred in other churches and monasteries at this period: el ʻAdhra, Diyarbakır (see notes 78, 80), Deir Zaʻfaran (below p. 134) and Arnas (above note 50).

74 See also *Amida*, fig. 115.

75 On both types of capitals see above p. xi.

76 Church of el ʻAdhra, Diyarbakır: see catalogue of sites, p. 107 below.

77 On these bases see p. 108 below.

78 There are two Arabic inscriptions (one Karshuni) in the narthex wall recording that "this church was restored" in AD 1533 and 1688/9 or 1692/3 (Pognon in *Amida*, 195 f, nos. I–II). Restorations may have been necessary ca. AD 1693 when Rustem Bey "took ... Amida (and) he spoiled (it)" (Bar Hebraeus, Appendix, p. lii). Reconstructions about this date are also recorded at Deir Za'faran (p. 134 below) and Arnas (note 50 above). See also note 73 above. A Syriac inscription on the wall separating the choir and nave (visible in *Amida*, fig. 109, upper right) states that "the holy church of Mary the Theotokos was restored in AG 2030" (=AD 1710) (*ibid*, 196, no. III).

79 On the sculpture of this church see p. 134 below. Pl. 19 shows one of four marble window mullions (see p. 108 below).

80 An inscription above the entrance notes that "... this church was restored in ... AD 1692/3(?)" (*Amida*, p. 197 and note 1; cf. Jarry, 220, no. 25). On events in 1693 see above note 78).

81 Above pp. 1–26.

82 For the studies published by Guyer see the bibliography p. 170 below, and Leroy, *CRAI* 1968, 479, note 1.

83 Tower Tomb, Fafi: see catalogue of sites, p. 109 below.

84 There is said to be another such tower tomb at Qaṣr el Banat in the Tektek Mountains, see p. 149 below.

85 The inscription is in ten lines and illegible; it may be in hexameter verse. In line three one can make out the first word DEIMAME(N)OS, "who has built".

86 Bell, UN Journal 1911, 22 April adds: "Between the big bit of the S. wall and the S.W. bastion I saw the foundation of a bit of wall of good masonry that looked like the same age as the tower".

87 Bell negatives R 146–147.

88 Shrine, Kersifan: see catalogue of sites, p. 122 below.

89 Shrine, Kermati: see catalogue of sites, p. 122 below.

90 Monastery of Mar Gabriel: see pp. 6–10 above and p. 137 below.

91 See Fig. 5 above.

92 Cf. p. 6 above.

93 On the mosaics see also pp. 8f above and most recently, Hawkins and Mundell, "Mosaics", esp. figs. 7, 34 and 41. For the vine trellis and amphorae see *ibid*, 284f., figs. 7–10, 14–17.

94 *Ibid*, 285–287, fig. 18. There are two other crosses in medallion within the vine-covered central field of mosaic: one over the apse and one over the door into the nave, *ibid*, 285–287, figs. 19–21.

95 There are seven colours in the forked or chevron pattern, see note 99 below. On all the border patterns see Hawkins and Mundell, "Mosaics", 287–289, figs. A, 28–30, 38.

96 *Ibid*, 289 f, figs. A, 33–39. At the base of this mosaic is the fragment of a Greek inscription ("Egeneto i mousoma ..." = "The mosaic work was done ...") taken to be

sixth century, see C. Mango, "A Note on the Greek Inscription" in Hawkins and Mundell, "Mosaics", 296, fig. 39.

97 *Ibid*, 289, 290 f, figs. B, 40–46.

98 *Ibid*, 282, figs. 47–49.

99 Although the mosaics are still not cleaned, Hawkins was able during his examination of them to wipe off small areas. His report reveals, rather, a wide range of colours: at least seventeen colours are noted throughout the sanctuary (*ibid*, 283–291, figs. A–B), e.g. the chevron pattern alone is composed of seven different colours (*ibid*, 287).

100 For the motif at Galla Placidia see F.W. Deichmann, *Bauten und Mosaiken von Ravenna* (Baden-Baden, 1958), pls. 16–17 and at San Vitale see G. Bovini, *San Vitale di Ravenna* (Milan, 1955), pl. 32.

101 M. van Berchem, "The Mosaics of the Dome of the Rock in Jerusalem and of the Great Mosque in Damascus", in Creswell, I, 292 ff.

102 For the mosaics of 1027 see *ibid.*, 300–308, Figs. 367–369. Al Malik al Ẓahir is the Mamluk Sulṭan Baybars (1260–1277) and the madrasah is his mausoleum, now the National Library; on the mosaics of 1279, see C. Watzinger and K. Wulzinger, *Damaskus, die antike Stadt* (Berlin, 1921), pls. V–VI.

103 Monastery of Mar Ibrahim and Mar Ubil, Midyat: see catalogue of sites, p. 131 below.

104 On Pl. 183 the inscription begins at the bottom of the jamb, ܥܒܕ ܬܪܥܐ ܗܢܐ "(He) made this door ...". The remainder, which continues around the door (Pl. 182), is illegible. Further writing is on the top central stone carved with a cross and an inscription also runs along the course of stones on top of the door. The inscriptions are in Serta characters in relief. Raised letters are a feature of twelfth and thirteenth century inscriptions at M'arre and the Mar Yoḥannan monastery, see Brock, "Notes".

105 On Awgen see notes 1, 3 above.

106 On this Ibrahim (Abraham) see Krüger, "Mönchtum" II, 8 f.

107 On the monastery of Abraham of Kashkar, see pp. 79, 139, Fig. 50 and Pls. 219–221.

108 Monastery of Mar Malka: see catalogue of sites, p. 140 below.

108a Brock has suggested that Athanasius of Balad did not study at this monastery but at one near Antioch (Brock, "Notes", Mar Melke).

109 On the history of Malka see Fiey, *Nisibe*, 141 f. Cf. Krüger, "Mönchtum" II, 28–31.

110 Monastery of Mar Ya'qub Ḥabisha, Ṣalaḥ: see also above pp. 10–13 and p. 147 below.

111 See also above pp. 10 f (for narthex vault) and p. 11 (for nave vault).

112 See also Preusser, pl. 44.

113 See also above p. 12 and Fig. 7.

114 See also Sarre and Herzfeld, *Reise*, II, 139–145, figs. 185–188; III, pls. XLV–XLVI a–d.

115 This is a different Ya'qub; the one commemorated at Ṣalaḥ died in AD 421 (Fiey, *Nisibe*, 205). See also below p. 147 for the *Life* of Jacob the Recluse.

116 For the inscriptions see Pognon, 62–71, nos. 22–33.

117 To the left of this inscription, on the second voussoir of the north stone arch of the

vault is painted in Esṭranghelo: ܬܐܘܦܝܠܐ ܪܝܫܕܝܪܐ "Theophilos abbot", vertically flanking a cross. At the summit of this arch is another cross in medallion surrounded by another painted Esṭranghelo inscription by a different hand, which is fragmentary and composed of five lines of which only the last word of the first line, ܟܬܐܒܐ (for ܟܬܒܐ), i.e. "inscription", is legible.

118 Monastery of Mar Cyriacus: see catalogue of sites below p. 135.

119 Church of Mar 'Azaziel, Kefr Zeh: see also pp. 13–15 above and p. 120 below.

120 There is a Karshuni commemorative inscription of AD 1832 "sur le mur est du narthex à droite" of the church entrance (Jarry, 234, no. 59).

121 See p. 15 above.

122 This *bema* is indicated on the plan given by Pognon (p. 92). Like the chancel screen, this pulpit or *bema* and low wall have disappeared (Leroy, *CRAI* 1968, 485). A wooden trellis, running north to south, now divides the nave in half. On the Syrian *bema* see the recent study by R.F. Taft, "Some Notes on the Bema in the East and West Syrian Traditions", *Orientalia Christiana Periodica*, 34 (1968), 326–359, which gives a bibliography on the subject (326 note 1) and on p. 349 and note 1 refers to the type of *bema* in the Ṭur 'Abdin.

123 See also above pp. 14 f. and note 46.

124 Cf. p. 14 above where the date is correctly given as AD 934/5.

125 Chapel of the Virgin, Kefr Zeh: see catalogue of sites, p. 121 below.

126 Chapel of Mar Yoḥannan, Kefr Zeh: see catalogue of sites, p. 121 below.

127 Church of Mar Cyriacus, Arnas: see also pp. 15–17 above and p. 99 below.

128 A chamber similarly placed exists at Deir Za'faran, see Fig. 53.

129 The vault and wall above the apse arch are now painted over, see p. 99 below.

130 See above p. 15 and note 50.

131 See also p. 16 above.

132 The capital at Arnas visible in Pl. 100 resembles somewhat that at Kefr Zeh visible in Pl. 162 which Bell considered early.

133 Cf. p. 82 here.

134 This rinceau may be compared with that at Deir Saliba, see Pls. 185–187 and p. 132 below.

135 See also Deir Saliba, Pl. 187.

136 Church of Mar Philoxenus, Midyat: see also pp. 19 f. above, p. 131 below.

137 See p. 18 above.

138 On Philoxenus of Mabbug see A. de Halleux, *Philoxène de Mabbog. Sa vie, ses écrits, sa théologie* (Louvain, 1963).

139 Church of Mar Sovo, Ḥaḥ: see also pp. 18 f above and p. 112 below.

140 Church of Mar Dodo, Ba Sebrina: see catalogue of sites, p. 100 below.

141 AD 1199, Pognon, 116, no. 62. Actually, this inscription states that "this church was restored" (ethhadtath 'idta hade) in that year, not built. The church was destroyed and again rebuilt in AD 1474 by two architects from Mardin (see p. 100 below). There is a commemorative inscription of AD 1146/7 inside the *beth ṣlotha* (Jarry, 213, no. 16) and an unpublished inscription on the outermost moulding of its

archivolt (Pl. 105) of which only the word *qadishtha*, i.e. "holy", on the upper right can be made out.

142 Church of Mar Stephanus and Mar Yoḥannan, Kefr Beh: see catalogue of sites, p. 119 below.

142a I failed to find either the text or location of this inscription published anywhere; see also below, p. 119.

143 Church of Mar Addai, Heshterek: see catalogue of sites, p. 118 below.

144 Church of Mar Symeon, Ḥabsenas: see catalogue of sites, p. 109 below.

145 Monastery of Mar Lazarus, Ḥabsenas: see catalogue of sites, p.110.

146 Church of el'Adhra, Ḥaḥ: see also pp. 20–23 above and p. 114 below.

147 The Karshuni inscription quoted above (note 63) gives the date in Arabic for both door and dome as 1903, not 1907. An inscription of AD 1728 to the right of the outer door may record the addition of some part of this porch: "these beams *(qariatha)* were set in place" (Jarry, 224 f, no. 36). The courtyard gate was restored, according to a Karshuni inscription, in AD 1883 (*ibid*, 222, no. 31).

148 See also above pp. 20 f and note 63.

149 See also G. Forsyth, "Architectural Notes on a Trip through Cilicia", *DOP*, 11 (1957), 230 f.

150 See also the bases in the apse at the monastery of Mar Ibrahim below pp.81,140 and Fig. 50.

151 These flasks could be compared with the amphora-shaped bosses on the interior cornice at Deir Za'faran (Pl. 194).

152 Bell expanded on Pognon's distinction (p. 91, note 2) between two types of sanctuaries which he associated with monastery and village churches respectively, to include the entire architectural plan, especially the layout of the nave. Cf. p. 81 for the exceptions made for the monasteries of Mar Awgen and of Mar Ibrahim (to which should be added that of Mar Yoḥannan, Fig. 3).

152a See above note 22.

153 On *bit hilani* see also more recently H. Frankfort, *The Art and Architecture of the Ancient Orient* (London, 1954), 147, 167–175.

154 For Turmanin see H. Beyer, *Der Syrische Kirchenbau* (Berlin, 1925), fig. 37 and for other Syrian examples, *ibid*, Figs. 36, 38. For Binbirkilisse, see Ramsay and Bell, *Churches* (*supra* note 71), 311–313. For twin-tower facades see also Krautheimer, 164 f, 339.

155 For a recent study of Deir Ya'qub near Edessa see Deichmann and Peschlow, *Ruinenstätten*, 41–63, pls. 16–24.

156 On Deir el Qira (the monastery of Mar Cyriacus) see above p. 48 and below p. 135.

157 In *Amida*, fig. 210. See also Guyer, "Surp Hagop".

158 See catalogue of sites, p. 107 below. On centralised churches in northern Mesopotamia and Syria see the recent study by Kleinbauer, "Tetraconch Churches", cited in the bibliography, p. 171 below.

159 Basilica, Mayafarqin: see catalogue of sites, p. 124 below.

160 On this mosque, the Ulu Cami (Bell negatives S 122–157, 159–167), which has

been rebuilt since 1911, see Gabriel, 221–228, who disagrees with Bell's assessment of the building phases as published in *Ukhaidir*, 159 f. (see p. 125 below).

161 This is the Eleona, not the Ascension Church. For bibliography and plan see A. Ovadiah, *Corpus of the Byzantine Churches in the Holy Land* (Bonn, 1970), 82 f. and pl. 33, where the apse exterior is polygonal. On the other churches catalogued in the Ovadiah book, only that at Qalat el Hisn is really comparable to the Mayafarqin church in type (basilica), size, and in its externally projecting rectangular apse without pastophoria (*ibid*, 174 f, pl. 69). This form of east end is unusual and one is tempted to see at Mayafarqin, in the doors in both the apse and the east end of the south aisle (p. 59, Fig. 40), as well as in the beam holes on the apse facade (Pl. 40), the evidence for at least one pastophorion, although Bell denies its existence.

162 It should be noted that there is a variation in the widths of the south aisle (Fig. 40) which are given as 6.85 m at the east end and 6.23 m at the west, in Bell, RGS Notes.

162a There were garlands on the western capitals also; see Pls. 43, 45.

163 On the cornice moulding see Guyer, "Amida", 209–212, fig. 9 and Mundell "Deir Za'faran".

164 On the capitals of northern Mesopotamia see Kautzsch, 215–223.

165 Bell's dating of this church is given above, p. 65.

166 Church of el 'Adhra, Mayafarqin: see catalogue of sites, p. 126 below.

167 On St. Sophia, Salonika, see M. Kalligas, *Die Hagia Sophia von Thessalonike* (Würzburg, 1935); Buchwald, *Sige* (see below p. 126), 37 note 180, pp. 43, 61 f.; Krautheimer, 309–312, figs. 255–257.

168 For St. James (Mar Ya'qub), Nisibis, see pp. 70ff. and p. 143.

169 For Dara see p. 102 below. On these capitals see Kautzsch, 231 f.

170 *Ibid*, 225–229, pls. 46–47.

171 Kitzinger, "Tapestry" (note 8 above), figs. 75, 86, 88 f., 197, 111 f., 114–119, 121. See also above pp. 3 f. where this type of capital is said to be found at Mar Awgen. This type of capital may be compared to the basket ornament at Deir Za'faran, see Mundell, "Deir Za'faran".

172 AD 641/2 – 661/2, the church of Zvart'notz at Vagharshapat, see J. Strzygowski, *Die Baukunst der Armenier und Europa* (Vienna, 1918), figs. 453–454.

173 Urfa, capital: see catalogue of sites, p. 154 below.

174 At Ksedjbeh.

175 While the el 'Adhra capitals may be later than the seventh century and be influenced from Armenia, the reverse general trend is more likely. The earliest Armenian examples of plaited capitals are early seventh century, while the Byzantine are at least early sixth and, as Bell herself has pointed out, there are early fifth century examples known in Syria (see preceding note); see Kleinbauer, "Zvartnotz" (below p. 126), 256–262.

176 Butler, *Architecture,* II, B, 26–34, 42 ff., Buchwald, *Sige*, 44, 46 f., 54 f., Krautheimer, 261–263, 278, figs. 203–207; Mango, 151, figs. 154–160.

177 Procopius, *Buildings*, III.ii.10–14.

178 This passage in Bar Hebraeus (Abul Faraj) was mistranslated by Pococke, see Buchwald, *Sige*, 48 note 219 and Fiey, "Martyropolis", 30. On the sculpture of el 'Adhra see above note 75, below p. 127 and the slab carved with an eagle in a niche (Pl. 51), published here for the first time, which may have been photographed in this church (p. 127 below). See also the carved slab from an unidentified church at Mayafarqin, and now in the British Museum (Pls. 52–53, p. 128 below).

179 The site of Tigranokerta is still debated, Dillemann, 254–257, 262–265; cf. Gabriel, 45.

180 On Marutha see Fiey, "Mārūṯā" (below p. 123), 35 f where a bibliography is given.

181 Citadel buildings, Diyarbakır: see catalogue of sites, p. 108 below.

182 Deir Za'faran, near Mardin: see catalogue of sites, p. 132 below.

183 On these basket-shaped ornaments see Mundell, "Deir Za'faran".

184 These niches are on the facade of the chapel which lies east of the south court (Pl. 188, Fig. 53). The whole doorway is illustrated in Parry, opp. p. 109. On this chapel see below p. 134.

185 Church of Mar Ya'qub, Nisibis: see catalogue of sites, p. 143 below.

186 Herzfeld corrected the building phases distinguished by both Bell and Preusser, see below p. 143. The most recent phase is that recorded by the Karshuni inscription over the south door in the west facade (Preusser, pl. 49, 1) which is dated AD 1872 (Jarry, 242, no. 73; see also Fiey, *Nisibe*, 120–121). See below p. 145.

187 Cf. Sarre and Herzfeld, *Reise*, II, 341.

188 In fact the quality of these capitals (see also B. Brenk, *Spätantike und frühchristliche Kunst*, Berlin, 1975, Pl. 245a) is higher than that of the capitals at e.g. Diyarbakır (Pls. 9, 20–21), Deir Za'faran (Pls. 194–197) etc.

189 A good reproduction of the interior ornament is available in *ibid*, pl. 245b. On these mouldings see Guyer, "Amida", 205 f. figs. 5–6; and Mundell, "Deir Za'faran".

190 The decorated jambs could be compared with those at Ṣalaḥ (Fig. 28), although the format and motifs used are different.

191 See the cross section in Preusser, pl. 49.

192 The sarcophagus is white marble tinged with rose and yellow (Fiey, *Nisibe*, 123).

193 Neither Bell nor Preusser was aware of the Greek inscription of AD 359 designating the building a baptistery and mentioning the patron, bishop Volagesos. See p. 143 below.

194 Fiey has pointed out that this work was probably started AD 713 (see p. 144). Herzfeld has connected this date with additions to the baptistery, notably what is now the north church, see below p. 143.

195 For descriptions given by travellers see Sarre and Herzfeld, *Reise*, II, 336 f. and Fiey, *Nisibe*, 114–127.

196 As just mentioned (note 193) this part of the building is dated 359. The technique of the sculpture at Deir Za'faran has more in common with sixth-century work at Rusafa, Dara, etc. See Mundell, "Deir Za'faran".

197 Monastery of Mar Tahmazgerd, Kerkuk: see catalogue of sites, p. 121 below.

198 This is said to have happened ca. 470 (Fiey, 'Karka' [see p. 121 below], 216 f.).

199 See preceding note.
200 Bell, *Ukhaidir*, e.g. pls. 9, *1*, 31, *3*, 34.
201 *Ibid*, pl. 62
202 *Ibid*, pl. 31, fig. 1 (Ukhaidir); Sarre and Herzfeld, *Reise*, I, 222–224; III, pl. XXX, 2 (Tagrit).
203 Bell, *Ukhaidir*, 18, pl. 20.
204 Mariamana Jami, Kerkuk: see catalogue of sites, p. 122 below.
205 On the indigenous features of Persian churches see Reuther, 560–566; and Monneret de Villard, 9–44.
206 See pp. 82–83 below for a revision of this dating to the period after this Arab conquest.
207 Monastery of Mar Ibrahim: see catalogue of sites, p. 139 below.
208 Hinrichs published his account of this trip in Hinrichs, *PM*, 191, pl. 33.
209 See here above.
210 On the history of the monastery which was founded ca. 571, see Fiey, *Nisibe*, 144–150 and Vööbus, *School* (p. 139 below), 206.
211 An undated Karshuni inscription records a restoration of the monastery (Jarry, 240f., no. 70). The monastery was pillaged in 1926, and is now totally abandoned (see p. 139 below).
212 For the parochial and monastic church types see pp. 8, 56 and note 152 above, and the introduction pp. viii –x.
213 A *Life* of Mar Sallara recently translated attributes to this monk (abbot AD 643–664?) the building of twenty cells at Mar Awgen (Brock, "Notes", Mar Sallara, translation).
214 See comments p. 140 below.
215 For Mshatta and Tuba see Creswell, 578–643.
216 See above pp. 50, 78f., 81.
217 A bibliography of Lammens' work is given in *Mélanges de l'Université Saint Joseph*, 21 (1937–38), 340–355.
218 For Umayyad and Abbasid architecture and decoration see Creswell.
219 L. Caetani de Teano, *Chronographica Islamica* (Milan, 1905–1926).
220 For an appraisal of the impact of events of the sixth and early seventh centuries on life in the limestone massif of northern Syria, see Tchalenko, *Villages*, I, 426–438.
221 See the remarks made in the Introduction (pp. v–vii), the Preliminary List of Dated Monuments (below p. 162), and the works by Hage, Honigmann (*Barṣauma*), Kawerau and Tritton cited in the Bibliography (pp. 169ff.).

CATALOGUE OF SITES AND MONUMENTS

By Marlia Mundell Mango

The arrangement of names of places and monuments adopted here, while imperfect, attempts to include those alternative names used by Gertrude Bell and other scholars, without pedantically giving all the other possibilities in every case. The current Turkish name is that given in italics; the first name is that used by Gertrude Bell; where differences are merely those of variant spellings used in different periods, they are separated by commas; otherwise by semicolons.

Lesser known names, such as Antoninopolis for Constantina/ Tella/Viranşehir are not included due to a lack of space, and for that reason also the language of each name has not been indicated.

Where known, the present name of each site is indicated by italics; the names of the villages are taken from the census published in 1973 (Devlet Istatistik Enstitüsü of Turkey, *Genel Sayımı idari bölünüş*, [Ankara, 1973]). Distances are given according to the U.S. Air Force map of 1975 upon which the map p. 185 *infra* is based.

AMIDA see DIYARBAKIR

ANASTASIOPOLIS see DARA

ARNAS ('URDNAS), *(BAĞLARBAŞI)*

Arnas, a village 8 km north-east of Midyat, is mentioned in an inscription at the Mar Gabriel monastery dated AD 777 (Pognon, 42), as well as in medieval manuscript notes, e.g. Zotenberg, *Catalogue*, 12.

Church of Mar Cyriacus (Quriaqos) pp. vii–xi, 13, 14, 15–17, 18, 47–50, 78–79, 81–82; Figs. 9, 34–35; Pls. 97–104. On the patron saint see p. 47f.

Bibliography: Parry, 204, 329, 333; Pognon, 95–100, nos. 52–54; Guyer, "Surp Hagop", 499 f; *idem*, "Amida", 216 f; Reuther, 563 f; Monneret de Villard, 45, 47 f, fig. 38; Strzygowski, *Syrie*, 160 f, fig. 96; Dillemann, 234; Leroy, *CRAI* 1968, 485; Jarry, 207–213, nos. 1–15 (concerning which see n. 49); Deichmann and Peschlow, *Ruinenstätten*, 26 f. Bell negatives: M 196–201, R 202–204, 207.
Dates: Inscriptions: church restored 1014 (note 50), 1591/2 *(ibid.)*, 1696 *(ibid.)*; *beth qadisha* renovated 1089 *(ibid.)*; church furniture provided ca. 750 (p. 50), 1207 (note 50), 1939 (note 49).
Changes since 1911: As Leroy has noted, the templon screen of ca. 750 has been replaced (*CRAI* 1968, 485) by one of 1939 (Jarry, 207 f, nos. 1–2), and a large tabernacle added to the sanctuary at the same date (*ibid.*, see note 49 above). The interior of the church has received a coat of white paint which has covered the figural wallpaintings on the apse conch. The apse archivolt has suffered further damage, particularly at the top. Outside, the south porch has been given a new archway.

The date of this "parochial" church is unsettled. Although there is a fair amount of epigraphic evidence here (pp. 15–17, 48–50, notes 49–50), some of it is contradictory. Bell noted remains of an earlier brick vault and she considered the south wall and arcade to be original (p. 49); the north arcade and present stone vault, however, she designated as later, a fact supported by inscription (pp. 15f., 50f.). The original masonry was ashlar, as is still visible at the east end outside (p. 49). Bell's photographs provide a valuable record of the eighth-century templon screen at Arnas (pp. 16, 50, note 46) which, like the earlier screen at Kefr Zeh, has disappeared. The problems of the barrel vault and lateral arcades are discussed above (pp. viiif.). Bell associated the sculpture of this church with the decoration of churches at Kefr Zeh and Ḥaḥ (el 'Adhra), all of which she dated before 640 (p. 78f.), but she soon after reconsidered their resemblance to Umayyad Mshatta and placed them, accordingly, later (pp. 82f.). The *beth ṣlotha* at Deir Ṣaliba could be added to this group (p. 132).

BA SEBRINA (BETH SEVERINA), *(HABERLI)*
This village, ca. 25 km south-east of Midyat and 8½ km east of Mar Gabriel monastery, is mentioned among the villages attacked throughout the fifteenth century (Bar Hebraeus, Appendix xxxviii, xli, xliv–xlv) and it figures in notes dated to the fifteenth to seventeenth centuries in manuscripts in the British Museum (Wright, *Catalogue*, 10, 305, 851, 881, 899). Pognon referred to twenty odd "churches" in the village (p. 116); Bell described the many "monasteries" like "small forts upon the hills" (*Amurath*, 304); Fiey counted twenty-four "small chapels" encircling the village (*Jalons*, 109 f); and Anschütz records the remains of twenty-five churches or chapels and two monasteries ("Ortschaften", 180). Whatever they are called, it is clear that there are many structures in and round this village.

Church of Mar Dodo (Dada) pp. ix, 52; Pl. 105

Bell decided that this was not a monastery (p. 53) although Krüger accepted it as such on the basis of her original statement (*Amurath*, 304) and that of Pognon. The story related below indicates that it was a parish church in 1474. On Dodo, a disciple of Mar Awgen, see Fiey, *Jalons*, 108.

Bibliography: Pognon, 116, no. 62; Bell, UN Journal 1909; *idem, Amurath*, 303–305; Preusser, 30; Krüger, "Mönchtum" II, 40 f; Jarry, 213, no. 16. Bell negatives: M 107–109.
Dates: Inscriptions: church rebuilt 1199 (note 141); Text: church rebuilt 1474 (p. 164).
Changes since 1911: not known.

The church (Bell negative M 107) is of the "parochial" type and there is a *beth ṣlotha* (Pl. 105). Bell described the former in *Amurath* (303–305) as having a single nave with four engaged piers on either side, and a narthex on the south side. The *beth ṣlotha* is on the east side of the courtyard south of the church. Her Journal adds the following details, namely that the apse is covered with a barrel vault, not a semi-dome and that "the corners of the wall are roughly built in to simulate the half circle"; there is a porch over the narthex door (UN Journal 1909, 17 May).
According to an inscription (see p. 52 and note 141) the church was restored in AD 1199. In AD 1474, the church was destroyed and rebuilt by two architects from Mardin, who worked for two months (cf. the account above n. 11 where over seventy men took two months to rebuild the church of Mar Awgen in 1271). Due to a "disagreement", "the framework of the timbers (or beams) under the roof" was not properly supported ("they had placed no pillars under it to take the weight") and it collapsed, killing several people. The sanctuary walls then burst open revealing the relics of Mar Dodo, Mar Asya and Mar Aḥa in great coffins of "white stone" and "black wood". There was also a silver coffer. The presence of the relics and the life story of Mar Dodo were hitherto unknown to the congregation of this church (Bar Hebraeus, Appendix xlv–xlvii). It would seem that the "framework of the timbers under the roof" referred to a pitched wooden roof over the nave rather than an exterior tiled wooden roof over a masonry barrel vault. The only other possibility is that it referred to the centering for constructing

a vault. Unfortunately, Bell did not record the measurements of this church, so it is not known whether this account bears out the suggestion made above (p. viii) that the timbers locally available for roofing were not sufficiently large enough to securely span the church naves of ca. 9 m across. The addition of the "pillars" for support, as related above here, probably alludes to the construction of internal arcades which was an established practise in the Ṭur 'Abdin well before the fifteenth century. The roof was presumably rebuilt following this incident and the present arcade (Bell negative M 107) may have been inserted then to provide the required support, although it now bears a barrel vault.
The *beth ṣlotha* has a commemorative inscription of AD 1146/7 inside (note 141) and the remains of another unpublished one on its archivolt (Pl. 105; note 141). The form of this oratory is similar to others, i.e. in addition to the cross in its conch, it has the vertical lateral frames on its façade and a profiled archivolt on capitals (uncut acanthus here) and columns. See also the remarks on the *beth ṣlotha* above, p. x.

Monastery of Mar Barṣauma Pl. 106

This monastery does not appear among those dedicated to Barṣauma in Krüger, "Mönchtum" II, 14 f.

Bibliography: Bell, UN Journal 1909; *idem, Amurath*, 303 note 1, 304. Bell negative: M 104.

In *Amurath* (p. 304) Bell mentions only the high tapering rectangular tower (Pl. 106) and the fact that the church and other rooms were "rudely built". Her Journal adds the following details: "There is the usual central court with the cistern, rooms to the N, the tower to the E, then you enter the monastic buildings, a single chamber which leads into the church which lies to the S of it. The church is again an aisleless chapel with an engaged pier on either side. Vaulted and very roughly built. (All these buildings are of rough fieldstone.) Through the monastic chambers to the E you pass into other vaulted rooms, totally dark and with pools of water on the floor" (UN Journal 1909, 17 May).
Although she does not specify so, it would seem that this church is a small version of the "parochial" type (although it lies south, not north of the courtyard) and must be similar to the chapels at Kefr Zeh (see Fig. 33). The tower resembles in its masonry one at Ḥaḥ (Pl. 149; p. 117).

Monastery of Miriam el 'Adhra (= The Virgin) Pl. 107

This monastery does not appear in Krüger, "Mönchtum" II.

Bibliography: Bell, UN Journal 1909. Bell negatives: M 105–106.

Bell recorded in her Journal the following about this monastery: "A tiny chapel to the N of the court with one engaged pier on either side, very rude–traces of rude frescoes–angels; monastic chambers to the W of the court. Curious stone-built rests in the court on which the priest lays the holy book when he celebrates the

feast of the monastery" (Bell, UN Journal 1909, 17 May).
This church seems to resemble in plan the preceding (see also Fig. 33), although it lies like most "parochial" churches to the north of the court, unlike the latter. Although the masonry is rough and of an indeterminate period, the lower courses east of the entrance in the south wall of the church (Pl. 107) are of large, ashlar blocks which may represent an early construction. Bell describes the book rests as "curious" only because she was at the beginning of her first trip to the Ṭur 'Abdin where these tables (called *guda*) are in fact common (*supra* p. 14). (See the Glossary *infra* p. 165 and Pognon, 42, 93.)

CONSTANTINA see VIRANŞEHIR

DARA (ANASTASIOPOLIS), *(OĞUZ)* pp. iii–vii, x, xi, 48, 64, 65; Pls. 1–8, 67a–b

Built by the Emperor Anastasius AD 505–507, it was refortified by Justinian ca. 530. It was the seat of the Dux of Mesopotamia 507–532, 540– 573, metropolitan bishopric with dependant bishops at Theodosiopolis (Resh'aina), Turabdion (= Ṭur 'Abdin, Rhabdios?), and Mnasubion or (?) Banasymeon (= Mar Gabriel?) (see *supra* p. iv). The city was under Persian control 573–591, 606–629, and fell to the Arabs 639.
The only published photographic survey of Dara is that of Preusser (44–49, pls. 53–61, fig. 12). Recent photographs appear in Mango (24, 39, figs. 9, 23, 38–41). In addition to the remains of the city published here, there are two massive subterranean chambers (Preusser, 46 f, pls. 57–58) which were probably cisterns (one of which may have stood under a basilical church [Guyer, "Amida", 213]); and a building partially standing to a considerable height of which four joined arches remain (Poidebard, *La trace*, pl. CXXXII) and which has a monolithic baptismal font nearby (Mundell, "Dara", 219). Both Anastasius and Justinian are credited with building the Great Church (i.e. cathedral) and the church of St. Bartholomew (*ibid.*, 218 f). On the village today see Anschütz, "Ortschaften", 185.

Bibliography: Stein, *Histoire*, II, 101 note 1 for bibliography on the foundation; on which see also C. Capizzi, "L'imperatore Anastasio I (491–518)", *Orientalia Christiana Analecta*, 184 (1969), 216–221. Bell negatives: R 106–129, 132–133.

Circuit Walls Pls. 1, 3

Bibliography: Procopius, *Buildings*, II.i.4–iii.25; *idem, Wars*, II.xiii. 16–19; Sachau, *Reise*, 394–398; Chapot, 313–317, figs. 13–14; Preusser, 44 f, pls. 54–56, 1; D. van Berchem, "Recherches", 262–267; Gabriel, 106 note 3, 107, 176 note 1; Oates, *Studies*, 97–106; Mango, 24, 39, figs. 9, 38–40. Bell negatives: R 106, 108–113, 132–133.

Dates: Text: walls built 505–507 (p. 102); walls rebuilt ca. 530 (*ibid.*).

Changes since 1911: The north half of the U-shaped tower in the centre of Pl. 3a has collapsed (Mango, fig. 39 showing interior) and the top part of the wall above the south sluices (Pl. 1) has fallen (Mango, fig. 9).

In Pls. 3 a–b can be seen much of the north-east circuit wall which preserves the three projecting U-shaped towers shown here with one or two rectangular buttresses in between. On the right of Pl. 3 b can be seen two of the five sluices through which the stream, descending from Kordis (Yardere) on the hill to the north of Dara, entered the city, crossed it under the bridge (Pl. 2) and flowed out through another set of sluices in the south circuit wall (Pl. 1), all of which is described by Procopius in *Buildings*, II.ii.1–iii.25 and *Wars*, VIII.vii.8–9. In the foreground of Pls. 3 a–b to the left and right of the right hand tower are visible the few courses that remain of the *proteichisma* or forward wall. While there is work of later period evident on the lower front of the middle tower (in addition to the newer structure on top of it and the left tower), the rest of this section of wall preserves on the outside the original sixth-century masonry which is double-faced ashlar with a rubble core clearly seen where the outer facing of stone is now missing. The tower and curtain wall on the right, above the sluices, display the cellular technique of construction where header blocks run through the rubble core.

Slightly projecting towers and the second, forward wall are characteristics of the land walls of Constantinople (AD 413) (Mango, 49, 53, fig. 57) as well as of the walls of such eastern cities as Diyarbakır and Dara. While the *proteichismata* of Dara are known to be sixth century, those of Diyarbakır could be either fourth or sixth (see *infra* p. 105) and it is of some importance to date all such walls in order to determine whether this feature developed in response to military tactics in the east or whether it can be attributed to the capital. Recently double walls have been identified at Singar which are undoubtedly fourth century (Oates, *Studies*, 97–106).

Bridge Pl. 2

Bibliography: Preusser, 45, pl. 56, 2; A. Poidebard, *La trace de Rome dans le désert de Syrie* (Paris, 1934), pl. CXXXII, 4; Dillemann, 130, pl. XI, b. Bell negative: R 107.

Changes since 1911: none.

The bridge, which is in the south part of the town, has three arches, the central one of which measures ca. 5 m across. The bridge spans the stream which flows through the city (see circuit walls above). This bridge is similar to those at Nisibis (Pl. 69) and Urfa (Pl. 85).

Horreum (Granary) Pl. 4

Bibliography: Preusser, 45 f, pl. 57, 1; Mango, fig. 41. Bell negatives: R 115–116.

Dates: Text: granary built 505–507 (infra).

Changes since 1911: large sections of the walls and vaults (Pl. 4; Preusser pl. 57, 1) have fallen (Mango, fig. 41).

Although usually described as a cistern, it is more likely that this is the granary mentioned in several sources (see Dillemann, 227 note 2, where he suggests, however, that the granary is to be identified as the deep subterranean rock-cut structure [Preusser, 46, pls. 57, 3 – 58, 3–4] which is probably a cistern; see also Capizzi,

219). The building here, Pl. 4, stands at present only 2 m above ground. It is composed of ten parallel vaulted chambers (each 4 x 25 m) of which the lower half is hewn from solid rock (0.60 m thick) and the upper half is built of several alternating courses of brick and roughly squared stones and terminates in a barrel vault (0.40 m thick). Comparisons could be made between this *horreum* and those at Masada (BC 37–31), Myra and Patara (both AD 128); see G. Rickman, *Roman Granaries and Store Buildings* (Cambridge, 1971), 137–140, 153, figs. 30–31, 34. It is possible that a dove cote at Diyarbakır is built on the foundations of an ancient granary. It measures 9 x 11 m, has four long rectangular compartments, exterior buttresses and walls 0.60 m thick (Gabriel, 204f., fig. 158, pl. LXXV, 4).

Unidentified Building near Granary Pl. 5

Bibliography: unpublished. Bell negatives: R 114, 121.

Changes since 1911: this building still stands.

The walls are single-faced of ashlar. The profiles of the door resemble those, for example, at Ṣalaḥ (Pls. 235, 246), Ḥaḥ (Pl. 124), Diyarbakır (Pl. 14), and Deir Za'faran (Parry, fig. opp. p. 109). The lintels of the doors at Dara and Ṣalaḥ are flat arches while those of the other examples are monolithic. See also p. 116 *infra* and Deichmann and Peschlow, *Ruinenstätten*, 22–24, pl. 11, 2.

Capital and Column reused(?) in Medrese Pl. 6

Bibliography: unpublished. Bell negatives: R 122–123.

Changes since 1911: none known.

This column capital with rings suspended from its upper uncut acanthus leaves could be considered a variant of the garlanded acanthus type frequently found among the monuments in this book, both cut (e.g. Pl. 20) and uncut (e.g. Pl. 246) and most closely resembles the capitals of el 'Adhra at Ḥaḥ where the garlands have assumed a more circular shape (Pls. 139, 141, 145).

Loose Pier Capital Pl. 7

Bibliography: unpublished. Bell negatives: R 118–119.

Changes since 1911: whereabouts unknown.

This capital is similar to fifth-century capitals found all over the Byzantine Empire, but its very flat and sharply cut surface could be compared with some examples excavated at Antioch (*Antioch-on-the-Orontes*, III, pl. 34, nos. 45, 71, pp. 154; pl. 35, no. 82, p. 158; this last forms the back of a capital with a plaited boss [compared elsewhere with the basket cornice bosses at Deir Za'faran, see Mundell, "Deir Za'faran", fig. 10] with box monogram which is said to be either of Anastasius or Justinian). The closest parallels with the Dara capital may be drawn, however, with the capitals of the four marble window mullions reused as chancel posts in the church of el 'Adhra, Diyarbakır (Pl. 19) which also have the raised dot between the lowest leaf tips. The flat surface and sharp cutting have been noted as characteristics of some carving at Rusafa *(ibid.)*.

In addition to these two capitals at Dara (Pls. 6–7) and the two published *supra* (p. 64; Pls. 67 a–b), two further capitals of different styles were found in the city in 1972 and are still unpublished. Further loose pieces of sculpture found at Dara–cornice fragments, a niche head–have been published (Guyer, "Amida", 212 f, fig. 213–214; Mundell, "Dara", figs. 6–7); their ornament resembles that on a large rock-cut tomb in the necropolis (*ibid.*, figs. 1–3; Preusser, pl. 61) and elsewhere in Mesopotamia (see *infra* p. 134).

Quarry Necropolis Pl. 8

Bibliography: Preusser, 47–49, pls. 59–61; Mango, 39, fig. 23; Mundell, "Dara". Bell negatives: R 126–129.

This limestone quarry stretches for some distance from the west gate of the city. Innumerable tombs have been cut into the quarry, many with Greek and Syriac inscriptions (Mundell, "Dara", 210, 213) and various ornamental reliefs (Preusser, 47–49, pls. 59–61; Mundell, "Dara", figs. 4–5). One façade has a life-size figural relief of Ezekiel in the Valley of the Dry Bones (*ibid.*, 209–217, figs. 1–3). The compositions of some tomb façades–arched entrances flanked by columns and the whole façade defined by vertical frames–could be compared with those of the *beth ṣlothe* of the Ṭur 'Abdin (see above p. x). A similar comparison is made below with the entrance of Mar Addai at Heshterek (p. 118; Pl. 151).

DEIR EL QIRA see MONASTERY OF MAR CYRIACUS, nr. ZARGEL

DEIR EL 'UMAR see MONASTERY OF MAR GABRIEL, nr. KARTMIN

DEIR ṢALIBA see MONASTERY OF DEIR ṢALIBA

DEIR ZA 'FARAN see MONASTERY OF DEIR ZA 'FARAN

DIYARBAKIR, **(AMID, AMIDA)** pp. iii–vii, 1, 22, 24, 26, 58, 60, 74

Amida was the capital and metropolitan bishopric of Mesopotamia. It was fortified by Constantius II in 349, conquered by Shapur II in 359 and retaken by Julian the Apostate in 363, the year in which it received refugees from Nisibis. It is thought the present circuit walls (*Amida*, 6–42, 277–297) (exclusive of Islamic medieval restorations and additions) date to this period (Gabriel, I, 95–182; Oates, *Studies*, 103–106) or to that of Justinian (D. van Berchem, "Recherches", 265–267) who is said to have rebuilt the walls (Procopius, *Buildings*, II.iii.27–28). (Bell negatives of the walls are: N 41–44, 48–51, 53–71, T 6–14, 118–132.) In 502 the city was taken by Kavad, but returned to Byzantium three years later. The buildings of the city were restored by Anastasius. Many stories related by John of Ephesus in his *Lives of the Eastern Saints* are set in and round his native sixth-century Amida. In 602 Amida fell to Chosroes II, was liberated by Heraclius in 628 when he built the church of St. Thomas there; the city came under the Arabs in 639. The Byzantines failed to reconquer it in the tenth century for more than a short time. The city came under the Marwanids (ca. 990–1096) and then the Ortokids until the thirteenth century. It was the seat of the Jacobite Patriarch of Antioch temporarily in the medieval period (Honigmann, *Barṣauma*, 113).

Apart from the monuments included below and the circuit walls mentioned above, the following are relevant to this book and have been published: 1) the Ulu Cami (Bell negatives N 74, 77–98, T 36–117) in *Amida*, 43–69, 136–163, 207–218, 298–334, figs. 23–25, 57–59, pls. VIII–XVI, XX; Guyer, "Amida"; Bell, *Ukhaidir* (*supra* note 15), 158 f, pls. 90, 93-1; Gabriel, 100; M. Rogers, "A Renaissance of Classical Antiquity in North Syria 11th–12th centuries ", *Annales archéologiques arabes syriennes*, 21 (1971), 347–356; 2) three marble capitals and columns found in the courtyard of the Armenian church by J. Strzygowski, "Les vestiges d'art chrétien primitif près de l'église arménienne de Diarbékir et leur décoration irano-nordique", *Mélanges Charles Diehl*, II (Paris, 1930), 197–205, figs. 2–3. There are said to have been five monasteries inside the city before the Arab conquest (Voobus, *Asceticism*, II, 233). Six churches of the sixteenth and seventeenth centuries are indicated on the plan, fig. 1 in *Amida*.

Bibliography: in addition to the references cited above, see the art. "Diyār Bakr" by J. Sourdel-Thomine in *EI* (1965).

Church of Mar Cosmas pp. vii, x, 23–24, 26; Fig. 13; Pls. 9–12.

Bibliography: Pognon, 57 note 3; *Amida*, 167–173 (from which the contribution by G. Bell [pp. 167–169] reprinted here [pp. 23–24] has been extracted), figs. 89–91, 115; Guyer, "Surp Hagop", 501; Leroy *CRAI* 1968, 479 f. Bell negatives: N 99–101, T 34–35.

Dates: Inscriptions: church restored 1689 (note 73); Text: church restored 1213 *(ibid.)*.

Changes since 1911: Nothing of the church now remains (Leroy, *CRAI* 1968, 479; Kleinbauer, "Tetraconch Churches", 106 note 85).

Bell's description and plan of this church seem to diverge in some details from those of Beylié as quoted by Strzygowski (*Amida*, 169–173, figs. 89–91), where the apse conch is said to rest on squinches (*ibid.*, 170, although these are not visible in Fig. 90). Both Beylié and Bell refer to the brick work of the "semi-dome of the apse" but the former's photograph (*Amida*, fig. 90) reveals that "über dem Kranzgesimse folgt die in Quadern aufgerichtete Wölbung" as Strzygowski puts it (*ibid.*, 171). On the apse conch is a "barbaric" Greek inscription commemorating a restoration of AD 1689 (see note 73). Below, on the apse wall, the contours of marble revetment are visible through the white wash (*Amida*, 170, fig. 90). The tomb altar seen in Pl. 11 (and *Amida*, fig. 91) (which Strzygowski refers to successively as that of St. Cosmas and that of St. Thomas, *ibid.*, 172) is faced with a marble slab, carved with a lozenge, which matches two slabs incorporated into the modern iconostasis (*ibid.*, Fig. 89). The three probably derive from a chancel screen.

Guyer suggested that originally this was a column basilica ("Surp Hagop", 501), in which connection it should be noted that the arch over the north window (Pl. 11) once continued on its west side into another arch. These may have formed part of an aisle arcade. Concerning the basilica in northern Mesopotamia see p. viii above and p. 125 below.

Church of el 'Adhra (= The Virgin), (Mariamana = Mary the Mother) pp. vii, x, xi, 24–26, 58, 68; Figs. 14, 51; Pls. 13–24

Bibliography: Pognon in *Amida*, 195–197; *Amida*, 187–195 (from which the contribution by G. Bell [pp. 193–195] reprinted here has been extracted), figs. 108–113, pl. XXII, 1–2; Guyer, "Amida", 212, fig. 11; *idem*, "Surp Hagop", 501 and note 56; *idem* in Sarre and Herzfeld, *Reise*, II, 32, fig. 149; A. Grabar, *Martyrium* (Paris, 1943–46) I, 115, 189 f.; E.B. Smith, *The Dome* (Princeton, 1950), 119 f, fig. 185; Jarry, 219–222, nos. 24–29; Kleinbauer, "Tetraconch Churches", 104–107, figs. 12–13; Deichmann, *BZ*, 121; Krautheimer, 500 note 9; Mundell, "Deir Za'faran". Bell negatives: N 102–109, T 28–33.

Dates: Inscriptions: church restored 1553 (note 78), 1688/9 or 1692/3 *(ibid.)*, 1710 *(ibid.)*; chapel restored 1692/3 (note 80).

Changes since 1911: None known.

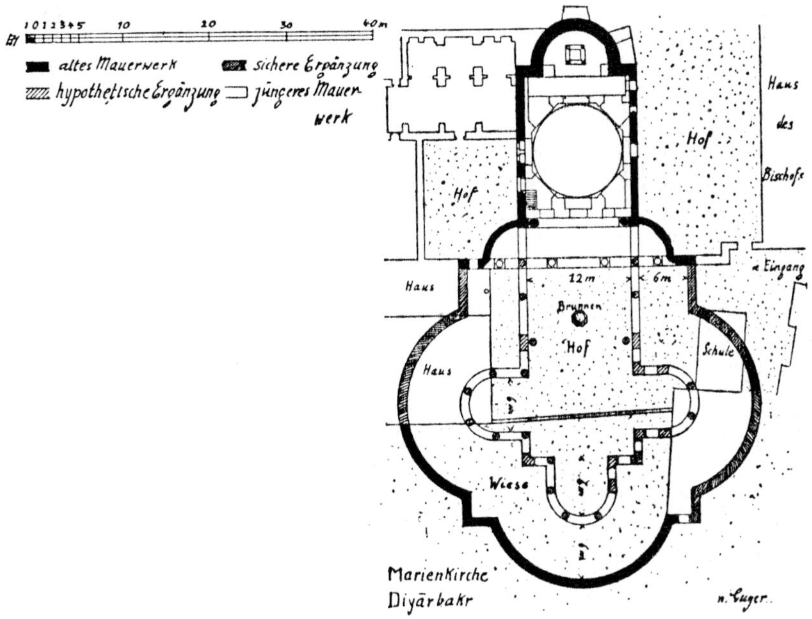

Fig. 51. Diyarbakır, el 'Adhra, plan of church by Guyer in Sarre and Herzfeld, *Reise*, II, fig. 149 (cf. Fig. 14 above)

Guyer re-examined the site of this church and by discovering further traces of outer walls was able to correct Bell's plan (Fig. 14) from a circle to a lobed plan (Fig. 51). The system of internal supports which one would expect was not found and remains conjectural, e.g. an internal octagon on massive piers like that at Viranşehir (Fig. 58), or an internal trefoil or quatrefoil with columnar exedras, like that at Rusafa (i.e. an aisled tetraconch, see Kleinbauer, "Tetraconch Churches", 104, fig. 5). The plan of the outer walls of el 'Adhra resembles that of the church at Apamea (*ibid.*, fig. 6). Smith proposed a dome over the nave which Kleinbauer rejects (*ibid.*, 104). Guyer has pointed out ("Surp Hagop", 501 note 56) that Bell's plan (Fig. 14) fails to distinguish between the medieval supports of the dome over the present nave (former chancel) and the original wall construction. Fiey discovered the traces of a bishop's throne (in a *synthronon*) in the apse (Fiey, *Mossoul*, 96). Published here for the first time are Bell's photographs of the blocked south door (Pl. 17), one of the marble column bases reused in the narthex (Pl. 22) (which Guyer compared to bases at the Ulu Cami , Diyarbakır, "Amida", 227), and one of the four marble window mullions reused as chancel posts (Pl. 19). (See also *Amida*, fig. 109.) Similar but smaller (ht. 0.44 m) mullions in limestone have been excavated at Antioch (*Antioch-on-the-Orontes*, III, pl. 37, nos. 72 a–c) which have been compared (*ibid.*, 157) to examples at Gerasa dated 531 (C. Kraeling, *Gerasa* [New Haven, 1938], pl. XLVI, p. 244). The same sort of mullions are to be found, e.g. at Qalb Loseh (Mango, fig. 149). The capitals of the Diyarbakır mullions are very close in execution to a loose capital at Dara (Pl. 7) (see comments *supra* p. 104). The mullions and column bases of the el 'Adhra church may derive from the original nave.

Kleinbauer suggests that this church and the fifth to sixth-century aisled tetraconch churches of Syria were Melkite cathedrals of the Patriarchate of Antioch.

Silver Book Covers in the el 'Adhra church Pls. 23–24

The front cover (Pl. 23) is decorated with a Resurrection of western iconography, and the back with the Crucifixion (Pl. 24) (*Amida*, fig. 109), under which is a four line inscription which is illegible in the photograph. Both sides are bordered by figures: at the centre top, the Virgin and Child on one, and the Pantocrator, the other; the four Evangelist at the corners; and martyrs (?) holding symbols, in between. Such covers were manufactured until recent times by Armenians in Mardin (Leroy, *Manuscrits*, 105 note 3). On the cloth below the covers are plaques in various styles: twelve single Apostles (?) in a Sasanian-Georgian style (and possibly inscribed) and several scenes (Adoration of the Magi, etc.) in a post-Renaissance Western style. Cf. the book cover at Ḥaḥ: Pl. 146 and p. 23 above.

Citadel Buildings pp. vii, 66–69, Figs. 43–45; Pls. 25–30

Bibliography: *Amida*, 173 ff, Guyer, "Surp Hagop", 501; J. Strzygowski, "Die sasanidische Kirche und ihre Ausstattung", *Monatsheft für Kunstwissenschaft* (1915), 349–365; Sarre and Herzfeld, *Reise*, II, 94; Gabriel, 156 and note 4; Reuther, 561 and note 6; Monneret de Villard, 30 f, 50. Bell negatives: T 12, 15–27.

Changes since 1911: These buildings are no longer used for military storage. There has been a certain amount of dilapidation as well as clearing. The roofing of the east building, including the metal sheathing of the dome, has been removed, exposing the brickwork. The west dome has sustained further damage, but has been given a tiled roof over its centre. The ground to the north has been excavated freeing part of the four blocked doors and windows above, which are under the brick arches in the north wall of the east building. Above them, four windows have been let into the wall. Two doors have been opened in the north wall of the west building. The wooden gallery and staircase inside the east building have been removed and the large door leading into the chamber south of the sanctuary blocked.

Strzygowski considered the east building to be pre-Islamic, while Herzfeld thought it to be entirely Islamic. Reuther suggested that the lower part of the nave arcade and aisle vaults may be pre-Islamic and that the later dome may replace an earlier one. He also compares the plan with that of the Sasanian palace of Sarvistan where one finds the same combination of vault and dome on squinches.

EDESSA see URFA

FAFI (FAFA; SINA)

Fafi has been identified with the *limes* fort of Sina (Dillemann, 230 f).

Bibliography: Pognon, 42 f; Dillemann, 51, 210 and note 2, 222, 230–232, fig. XXVIII.

Circuit Walls pp. v, 29; Pls. 113–114

Bibliography: Bell, UN Journal 1911. Bell negatives: R 181–183.

See above note 86 for Bell's remarks (UN Journal) about the remains of fortification walls apparently contemporary with the tower tomb.

Tower Tomb pp. 28–29; Pls. 108–112

Bibliography: Pognon, 16 note 1; Bell, UN Journal 1911. Bell negatives: R 174–180.

Changes since 1911: not known.

Bell's Journal adds the following information about the tomb: "Fragments of column, one with an Attic base. There had been a pediment over the first storey. Inside much ruined. Traces of an arch or vault" (UN Journal 1911, 22 April).

ḤABSENAS (ḤAFSINAS, ḤABSUS), *(MERCIMEKLI)*

Ḥabsenas, a village 7 km north-west of Midyat, is mentioned in the *Life* of Mar Gabriel of Qarṭamin (AD 593–667) (Nau, "Notice", 66) and in that of Symeon d-Zayte (= " of the olives") (+ 734), a native of Ḥabsenas, who was a monk of the Mar Gabriel monastery and in AD 700 became bishop of Harran. In addition to the church of St. Symeon below, he renovated and built a number of other churches, monasteries, mills and villages. See Brock, "Fenqitho", Appendix; Sachau, *Verzeichnis*, 93, 759f.; Fiey, *Nisibe*, 72 note 381; see also

p. vi above and p. 137 below. The village also figures in a medieval inscription at Ṣalaḥ (Pognon, 65 no. 26).

Church of Mar Symeon pp. vi, ix, 53

This church is named after Symeon d-Zayte, see below.

Bibliography: Pognon, 66 note 1; Bell, UN Journal 1911 and references given above. Bell negatives: none.

Dates: Text: church built or renovated 700–734 (infra).

Changes since 1911: not known.

Bell's Journal entry on Ḥabsenas says: "Saw two churches, one parochial, a close imitation of Arnas but the decoration round the apse arch [has] quite flat palmettes and entrelac, no modelling on the acanthus capital on the S side of the apse. Dedicated to Simon Peter" (UN Journal 1911, 27 April).
It is interesting that Bell's mention of Simon Peter finds its parallel in the *Life* of Symeon d-Zayte (see above) where it is related that Symeon returns to his native village of Ḥabsenas and renovates the church there which had "formerly been dedicated to Simon Peter, but from that time on was called after Symeon of the olives" (Brock, "Fenqitho", trans. of p. 151). This visit occurred between AD 700–734. The account in the Berlin manuscript Syriac 247 (Sachau, *Verzeichnis*, 760) says that Symeon founded, not renovated, the church at Ḥabsenas. If there is any eighth-century work left here, it would, of course, be important in evaluating the date of other Ṭur ʻAbdin churches, particularly since Bell describes it as a close imitation of Arnas (see also above p. ix).

Monastery of Mar Lazarus (Ḥabsusiatha) pp. vi, ix, 53–54; Pl. 115

On the titular saint see below and on names connected with this monastery see Krüger.

Bibliography: Pognon, 66 note 1; Krüger, "Mönchtum" II, 23 f. Bell negative: S 6.

Dates: Text: tower built 700–734 (infra).

Changes since 1911: not known.

Recently two slightly conflicting accounts of the foundation of this monastery have been published. At first, a *Life* of Mar Lazarus of Harran (preserved in a manuscript of AD 1463/4 written in this monastery), recounts the story of the young Lazarus, born in the "pays d'Urfa", becoming a monk and later specializing in the destruction of pagan temples. The monastery he founded at Ḥabsenas grew after his death and the monks there dedicated themselves to preserving his memory. See A. Vööbus, "Découverte d'un panégyrique sur Lazare de Harrān", *AB* 96 (1978), 105–107. The other account is contained in the *Life* of Symeon d-Zayte, native of Ḥabsenas (see above); it claims that some time between 700 and 734 Symeon went south of the village to a monastery "built of hewn stone" where he dedicated the church to Mar Lazarus whose relics he brought from the monastery of Lazarus near Harran (Brock, "Fenqitho", trans. of p. 152). A monastery of Mar Lazarus is mentioned in an inscription among the remains of a monastery at Qasr el-Banat in the Tektek Mountains between Harran and Viranşehir (see below p. 149). The *Life* of Symeon furthermore mentions that he built at the monastery at Ḥabsenas "a column (*esṭona* [i.e. *stylos*]) for recluses", also referred to as a "tower (*borga* [i.e. *pyrgos*])" *(ibid.)*. This must refer to the "round tower on a square base" described and illustrated by Bell (p. 53; Pl. 115). Its base resembles that of the column of St. Symeon the Younger Stylite on the Wondrous Mountain (J. Lafontaine-Dosogne, *Itinéraires archéologiques dans la région d'Antioche* [Brussels, 1967], Figs. 45–47 bis.). Bell claimed as unique for the area the round tower at Ḥabsenas. Perhaps the intention of the design was to combine the appearance of the stylite's column *(esṭona)* with the function of the tower *(borga)* of recluses of the sort mentioned in the *Life* of Jacob the Recluse (Nau, "Resume", 4f.).

Another monastery mentioned in the *Life* of Symeon as being near Ḥabsenas, the monastery of Mar Zbina (Brock, "Fenqitho", Appendix, trans. of p. 152) (= Derizbin, now called Acırlı) is situated ca. 4 km south-west of Ḥabsenas (Socin, 265 no. 98) and may perhaps be identified with the monastery of Zebinus of Mesopotamia restored by Justinian, according to Procopius (above p. v).

ḤAḤ (KHAKH, ḤAKH) (ḤAḤTA = PLUM), *(ANITLI)*

Ḥaḥ, a village ca. 21 km north-east of Midyat, called Ḥaḥta in the history of the Mar Gabriel monastery (Nau, "Notice", 48), appears to have been relatively large and important, particularly between the sixth and ninth century, for it contains at least six churches from that period. Furthermore, it is possible that Ḥaḥ was an early bishopric–that of "Turabdion"–(on sixth-century bishoprics of the Ṭur 'Abdin see p. iv; p. 146) and the church of Mar Sovo (early sixth century), its cathedral (see p. 112). Such village bishoprics are known to have existed elsewhere at this time (Jones, *LRE*, II, 877–879). From 1089/90 Ḥaḥ was the seat of the bishop of the Ṭur 'Abdin (Honigmann, *Barṣauma*, 140, 153). A bishop of Ḥaḥ appears in the twelfth century (*ibid.*, 127) and the village is mentioned in notes of medieval manuscripts, e.g. Zotenberg, *Catalogue*, 40. The martyrology of Rabban Ṣliba was written by a native of Ḥaḥ (which figures prominently therein) in the thirteenth century (Peeters, "Martyrologe", 130f.).

The new Turkish name of Ḥaḥ, Anıtlı = "full of monuments", is well chosen. In addition to the monuments listed below (four churches–one now dated AD 740–, two towers and one unidentified building), the following are also known: a monastery of SS. Sergius and Bacchus (Krüger, "Mönchtum" II, 32–34) whose church is dated AD 691 (Jarry, 230, no. 47); a chapel of Mar Samuel north of Mar Sovo with a highly ornamented doorway (Bell, UN Journal 1909, 23 May); and a church of Mar Musa (Moses) (Fiey, *Jalons*, 109). Parry reported "twenty or more" old buildings (p. 202) and Socin further mentions another monastery church and a "castellartiger ... Bau", in which connection it should be mentioned that Ḥaḥ, like other villages, was also known, at least in the medieval period, as "Qasṭra Ḥaḥ" (Socin, 247–249). On the village today see Anschütz, "Ortschaften", 184 f.

Church of Mar Sovo (Saba) pp. viii, ix, xi, 18–19, 51, 52, 53; Fig. 10; Pls. 116–128

The full title of the patron saints of this church is given in the thirteenth century martyrology of Rabban Ṣliba (of Ḥaḥ) as, "sanctus Sabai (patronus) ecclesiae maioris Hachensis atque duodecim milia martyrum eius sociorum" on 23 January and commemorated also 16 April and 16 August; see Peeters, "Martyrologe", 173 f, 192 note 1 and Nau, "Resumé", 10 note 1.

Bibliography: Pognon, 121–125, nos. 65–71; Bell, *Amurath*, 319; Guyer, "Amida", 215, 225; *idem*, "Surp Hagop", 499; Strzygowski, *Syrie*, 29 f, fig. 13; Monneret de Villard, 26, 45 f, 61, fig. 41; Mundell, "Deir Za'faran". Bell negatives: N 1–22.

Changes since 1911: One stage of the rebuilding of this church may be elucidated by the recent uncovering, by parties unknown, of part of a chancel barrier on the south side of the apse built against the north face of the eastern pier of the south arcade. This unpublished discovery reveals two thick slabs (one *in situ*) carved with crosses and rosettes. The pier against which the barrier is built has been half dismantled since 1911 so that the south garlanded capital of the apse and the ornamented archivolt above it are better visible. On the north side of the nave the easternmost arch shown in Pl. 121 has fallen.

This is probably "the Great Church" (*'idta rabtha* i.e. cathedral) mentioned at Ḥaḥ in the history of the Mar Gabriel monastery (Nau, "Notice", 48 and above). Considering its size (27.30 x 11.10 m, noted by Bell, above p. 18), a designation as cathedral is not unlikely. Furthermore, the presence of so many churches of an early period at Ḥaḥ would seem to indicate that it was a place of relative importance then (see p. 111). Three suffragan bishoprics under Dara are known in the sixth century (see above, p. iv). Of these, it is unlikely that the bishopric of Turabdion was situated in the small hilltop fort of Qal'at Ḥatem Ṭay (identified with Rhabdios, see p. 146); it should be sought elsewhere in the Ṭur 'Abdin, possibly at Ḥaḥ. The possibility of Mar Sovo possessing such official status could have some bearing on the question of its architecture providing a model for other, somewhat smaller, village churches; Bell suggested that it was the prototype of the "parochial" church of the Ṭur 'Abdin. An illuminated manuscript was produced for this church in AD 1226 (Leroy, *Manuscrits*, 329).
The sculpture of Mar Sovo has figured in two articles on north Mesopotamian carving (Guyer, "Amida" and Mundell, "Deir Za'Faran") and it is clear from the capitals, archivolt and cornice of the apse that this church is probably a sixth-century building (see p. 134). It is also of local interest that the large cross in relief on the conch found elsewhere in the Ṭur 'Abdin (see above p. xi) appears at an early date at Mar Sovo. The stages of renovation of the church–the addition of nave arcades and aisles–are still to be clarified (on the bricks used see notes 30, 59), but as observed above, Bell deduced that Mar Sovo was originally a wooden-roofed hall church and that it was the probable forerunner of "parochial" churches which, unlike Guyer, she believed were originally built with barrel vaults (see also p. 120). The newly revealed east wall south of the apse (see *changes* above) apparently has no trace of the respond of an arcade. I have suggested tentatively above (p. viii) that this church, being the largest (known) church in the Ṭur 'Abdin, was important

and, being important (i.e. a cathedral?), may have justified the expense of long imported timbers which could not be afforded for the ordinary village churches (Arnas etc.) wherein was introduced the expedient of internal arcades supporting the local, smaller timbers.

Unidentified Building p. ix; Fig. 52; Pls. 129–130

Bibliography: Bell, RGS Notes; *idem*, UN Journal 1909. Bell negatives: N 23–24.

Changes since 1911: not known.

The only statements recorded by Bell about this building are: "A small later chapel further W" (UN Journal 1909, 23 May) and "below toward the west" (RGS Notes). To my knowledge it has not been previously published. The plan in the RGS Notes is given here (Fig. 52) in a redrawn form.

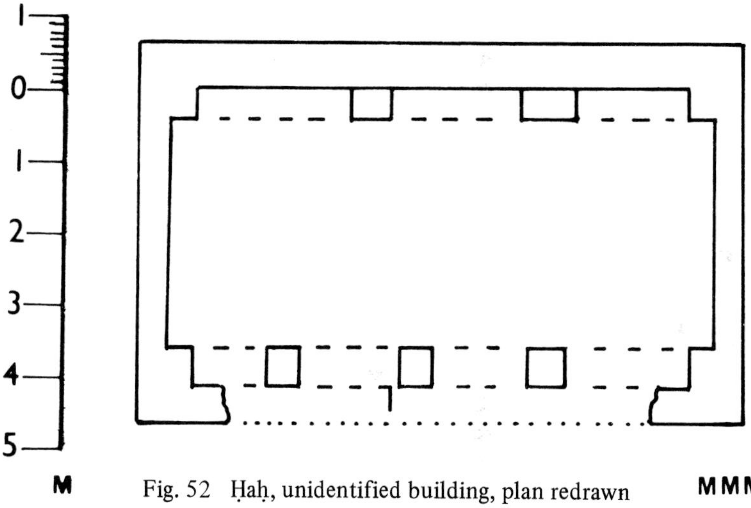

Fig. 52 Ḥaḥ, unidentified building, plan redrawn from Bell, RGS Notes

The only comment appended to this plan is "arches are horse shoe". It would seem that this building was a timber roof chamber with two interior lateral arcades. There is no evidence left on the inside of the gable (Pl. 130) that a masonry vault had been built against it. Although Bell's plan roughly indicates the missing south wall, it did not include a door. The arcades were obviously not bonded to the lateral walls; her plan does not show this and it has been corrected in our Fig. 52. Equally, one cannot confirm from Pl. 130 whether or not the arcades were bonded at the east and west ends. If it was all of a piece, however, this little building could be related to the large "parochial" churches at Kefr Zeh and Arnas as regards the presence of arcades (see above p. ix). In masonry and size the building at Ḥaḥ resembles somewhat the small building at Sha'ib Shahr in the Tektek Mountains (Pls. 254–256, p. 151). The masonry, cyma cornice and, to a lesser extent, the arcuated unprofiled window, are typical of both the Ṭur 'Abdin and northern Syria.

According to Bell's plan the arcades rest on piers rather than columns. The formation of the arches is typical of that found in northern Syria from the end of the fourth to the sixth century (C. Strube, "Baudekoration in den Kirchen des nordsyrischen Kalksteinmassivs", *Archäologischer Anzeiger* [1978], 581, fig. 26). Except for a plain rectangular abacus visible under the far arch in the centre, nothing can be seen here of the carving of the capitals. The two visible in the foreground faced the wall and were undecorated on this side. Although this building is oriented, its function is unclear.

Church of El 'Adhra (= The Virgin) pp. ix–xi, 20–23, 24, 39, 50, 54–58, 70, 73, 78, 81, 82; Figs. 12, 37–39; Pls. 131–146

The original dedication of this church is open to question. Although known as el 'Adhra (= the Virgin) to Bell and others, what may be the only documented mention of a name, the Yaldath Alaha (=Theotokos), is in an inscription of 1939 AD (Jarry, no. 33). Since the ruined church at Ḥaḥ, now known as Mar Yoḥannan, was originally called Yaldath Alaha (in 740 AD) (p. 115 below), the el 'Adhra church probably once had a different name.

Bibliography: Parry, 202, 327–333; Socin, 248; Bell, *Amurath*, 317–319, figs. 200–213; Guyer, "Surp Hagop", 501; *idem*, "Amida", 216 f, Sarre and Herzfeld, *Reise*, II, 345 f; Guyer, "Le rôle", 62, fig. 1; Reuther, 562, 566; Monneret de Villard, 58 f, 97, fig. 61; Leroy, *CRAI*, 484 f; Jarry, 222–225, nos. 30–36; Krautheimer, 320, 516 note 8, fig. 263; Mango, 184, pls. 211–213. Bell negatives: M 215–254, S 2–5.

Dates: Inscriptions: church restored 1728 (note 147), 1903 (note 63), 1939 (supra). Courtyard entrance restored 1883 (note 147).

Changes since 1911: As Leroy has reported, the new exterior dome (Pl. 135) was masked by a second elevation of niches and topped with a tiled roof in 1939 (Jarry, 222 f, nos. 32–34) (cf. Krautheimer, fig. 263 and p. 516 note 8, where these are incorrectly described as being done in 1907). The bell tower at the southwest corner of the roof was probably added at the same time. The narthex roof has been paved and structures built against the north and south façades. Inside, a half-vault in the southwest corner of the narthex is now visible (see below) and the damaged lintel of the central door leading into the nave (Pl. 139) has been heavy-handedly restored.

Bell called this church "the crowning glory of the Tur 'Abdin" (p. 20) and suggests that it may be the earliest example of a domed transept (Kuppelquerschiff) church (p. 22). On the basis of its carving, Bell associated el 'Adhra church with those at Ṣalaḥ and Arnas and attributed them all to the early sixth century (p. 79), but later reconsidered their dating to be in the period around AD 700 (p. 82). The date of 1907 which Bell gave for the reconstruction of the outside of the dome (pages 20f., 54f.) is contradicted by a Karshuni inscription which places it in 1903 (see note 63).

Herzfeld considered the dome a later modification. He compared the square plan, antechamber and a reconstructed pyramidal wooden roof of the el 'Adhra with the baptistery of Nisibis (Figs. 46, 55), and he related the transversal layout of its nave to the "monastic" plan of the Ṭur 'Abdin. The el 'Adhra architecture has also been associated with that of the Deir Za'faran church (Fig. 53 and p. 134) and St. Sophia at Edessa (p. 134). The ornamentation of the exterior of el 'Adhra, especially the pilasters, has been compared with that of antique funerary buildings, such as Fafi (Pls. 108–112). Guyer published a reconstruction of the el 'Adhra ("Le rôle", fig. 1), which is in part incorrect, for he has eliminated the porch in front of the narthex. The porch is clearly contemporary with the church, as can be seen in Pls. 135–136 where to the right of the fourth and westernmost pilaster the north wall slopes down to meet the lower cornice still visible on the west façade (Pl. 134). Furthermore, the open narthex postulated by Guyer *(ibid.)* is also incorrect in that the arched openings of the narthex are, as Bell showed them, of varying lengths (Fig. 37). There is some evidence for an opening through the arch (which Bell considered a niche, p. 54) in the south half of the west façade, for in the south-west corner of the narthex (Fig. 37) there is now uncovered behind the north-south arch an ashlar half-vault springing from the west.

Since Bell's publication, this church has been variously dated sixth to eighth century. As Bell suggests (p. 81), the church of Mar Ibrahim monastery shares with the Ḥaḥ church certain features such as the engaged columns round the apse (a sculptural feature she overlooked at Ḥaḥ is the cross on the apse, see note 69). As Mar Ibrahim was a foundation of ca. 571, further investigation of the church could yield important criteria for dating the el 'Adhra church. If Mar Ibrahim, with its earlier sculpture style, provides a *terminus post quem* of 571 for el 'Adhra, then the sculpture of Mar Symeon at Ḥabsenas may offer a *terminus ante* (or *ad*) *quem* of 700–734 AD (see p. 110 above). Another monument which should be considered in comparison with the Ḥaḥ church is Deir Ṣaliba, on which see the hitherto unpublished photographs of its *beth ṣlotha* (Pls. 185–187) and the remarks p. 132.

Church of the Theotokos (= Yaldath Alaha), (Mar Yoḥannan) pp. ix, xi; Pl. 147

On the dedication of this church, which is not to be confused with that of the Virgin (el 'Adhra) at Ḥaḥ, see below.

Bibliography: Bell, UN Journal 1909; Jarry, 225 f, 231, nos. 37, 51. Bell negative: N 26.

Dates: Inscription: church built 740 (p. 116).

Changes since 1911: not known.

Although known now as Mar Yoḥannan, both the original name and date (AD 740) of this church are given in the inscription on the doorway (Pl. 147) which has been published by Jarry (225 f, no. 37). More of the text is preserved by Bell's photograph so that from Pl. 147 I have emended somewhat the reading by Jarry and have given the full date below.

(right jamb) ܐܬܫܬܠܡ + ܘܥܒܕ ܕܝܢ ܗܝܟܠܐ ܗܢܐ ܕܒܝܬ ܝܠܕܬ

(lintel, above) ܐܠܗܐ ܒ....... ܡܢ ܦܘܠܚܢܗ... ܕܥܒܪܗ... ܕ

What follows (ܐܠܗܐ ܕܡܛܠܬܗ ܥܒܕܗ ܢܫܘܐ ܠܗ
(ܠܡܠܟܘܬܐ ܕܫܡܝܐ ܘ ܠܥܘ(ܒܐ) ܕܐܒܪܗܡ in Jarry) is in deep shadow here (Pl. 147) and unreadable.

(lintel below) ..... ܘܚܡܫܝܢ ܘܚܕܐ ܕܐܠܟܣܢܕܪܘܣ ܒܝܘ̈ܡܝ ܩܕܝܫܐ
ܐܬܢܣܝܘܣ ⊕ ܦܛܪܝܪܟܐ ܘܡܝܩܪܐ ܡܪܝ ܠܥܙܪ ܐܦܝܣܩܘ(ܦܐ)

What follows (ܘܒܝܦܠܘܬܐ in Jarry) is in darkness and unreadable.

"+ G .... [patron] used diligence and made, then, this church of the Theotokos, through the service of ... who aided him ... May (God for whose name's sake he did this make him worthy of the kingdom of heaven and the bosom of Abraham) .... and fifty one of Alexander in the days of the holy Athanasius † Patriarch and the venerable Mar Lazarus bishop (and by the care.......)"
It is unclear whether or not the phrase "For the sake of Our Lord, pray for him and for ..." which is "sur le montant droit de l'entrée vers le bas" (Jarry, 231, no. 51) is part of this inscription.
If correctly read, this inscription indicates that the church was originally dedicated to the Theotokos. The date –51 of the Seleucid era would yield –40 AD. The only Patriarch Athanasius whose dates would include a year –40 would be Athanasius III (724–740), and Lazarus bishop of the Ṭur ʿAbdin is mentioned at a synod of 735/6 (Hage, 106). The date of this church would therefore be AD 740.
Bell's Journal records only "Mar Yoḥannan of the same date I should say as the church N of Mar Saba–a decorated door which I photographed" (UN Journal, 1909, 23 May). The "church N of Mar Saba" is that of Mar Samuel; its decorated door, which is unpublished, is carved with the motifs used at Arnas and in the el ʿAdhra at Ḥaḥ. It is different, therefore, from the door shown here.
The original masonry of the Theotokos church is ashlar, as visible in the arcade behind the doorway and the far wall opposite (Pl. 147); the rough masonry round the door is probably a later refacing or rebuilding. Above the door is a shallow brick relieving arch. The door itself leads into the nave and not "à l'entrée de l'abside" as Jarry states (p. 225). The profiles of the door frame are basically the same as others in northern Mesopotamia, e.g. at Dara (Pl. 5), but at Ḥaḥ they are mostly flat with sharp edges; the lintel of the Theotokos church is monolithic as at Mar Sovo and elsewhere (see p. 104). The cross and rinceau likewise repeat earlier conventions. The rinceau derives from the undulating scroll (e.g. at Deir Zaʿfaran, Pls. 194–195), but there is a shift in design: the grapes and leaf appear together within the same curve of the vine, rather than alternating separately. The style has changed also: the vine is deeply grooved and somewhat slack (on the lintel)and the leaves are reduced to three chip-carved lobes; the grapes are flat and those on the lintel resemble pine cones. Comparisons for this vine are not easy to find but two capitals, at Dara (Pl. 67 b) and Nisibis (Sarre and Herzfeld, *Reise*, II, 351; IV, pl. CXL–8), are covered with a vine scroll which is similarly grooved and which seems to have some chip-carved tendrils in addition to vine leaves. This building ought, of course, to be included among those of the Ṭur ʿAbdin meriting close examination.

Church of St. Mary Magdalen Pl. 148

Bibliography: Bell, UN Journal 1909; Jarry, 226, no. 38. Bell negative: N 27.

Changes since 1911: none known.

Bell's Journal notes concerning this church, which she did not publish, "To the E [of Ḥaḥ] Miriam Aghathiatha with a tower, late, a dome on squinches" (UN Journal 1909, 23 May). The name intended must be Mary Magdalen from near which church Jarry has published an epitaph (226, no. 38). Pl. 148 shows one of the squinches mentioned by Bell and a series of niches. A Maltese cross is carved on a stone on the left side. The masonry recalls both late Sasanian (Qasr-i-Shirin: Bell, *Ukhaidir* [above, note 15], e.g. pl. 69) and medieval (Ḥasan Keyf: *ibid.*, pl. 68) stonework. These upper walls rest, on the east side, upon an earlier ashlar arcade with uncut acanthus capitals, beyond which are three closed sanctuary chambers, also of ashlar masonry. The sill of the doorway into the central chamber is a reused decorated lintel similar to that of the Theotokos church (Pl. 147).

Tower by Church of St. Mary Magdalen Pl. 149

Bibliography: Socin, 248; see also preceding monument. Bell negative: N25.

Changes since 1911: none.

For a reference to this tower see entry from Bell's Journal above. Whether or not this tower is also the "castellartiger grosser Bau mit Gitterfenstern" mentioned by Socin is not known. The general aspect and masonry of this tower resemble those of the tower of the monastery of Mar Barṣauma at Ba Sebrina (Pl. 106); see also the comments on the masonry of the preceding monument (Pl. 148) and the tower below.

Tower by Church of Mar Sovo pp. 19, 53; Pl. 126

Bibliography: *Amida*, 333, fig. 282. Bell negatives: N 15, 22, 22 x.

Changes since 1911: none, apparently.

This tower stands south-east of Mar Sovo. Evidently this tower has never been examined as to the fabric of its masonry, its interior, or the contents of its inscription. The masonry, which is ashlar, differs from that of the preceding tower. See also the comments on the tower at Ḥabsenas (p. 111 above).

ḤARABEH 'ALEH (HARAPALI; KEFR 'ALA ?), *(ÜÇKÖY)*

This village which is ca. 12 km south-west of the Mar Gabriel monastery, may figure as Kefr 'Ala among villages which, according to tradition, belonged to that monastery from the sixth century (Krüger, *Mönchtum* I, 43). This site has also been identified with Arkah where Mar Malka (on whose monastery see below p. 140) chased a demon (Fiey, *Nisibe*, 141 note 49).

Church of Mar Theodore (?) Pl. 150

Bibliography: Socin, 255; Bell, *Amurath*, 314. Bell negative: M 145.

Changes since 1911: not known.

The name of the church given by Socin, assuming it is the same church, is Doras which may be a corrupt form of Theodoros (see Fiey, "Martyropolis", 29). On the far right of Pl. 150 is visible a standing ashlar arch and some masonry at its base.

HESHTEREK (ASHTARKA, ASHTARAK), *(ORTACA)*

This village lies 17 km north-east of Midyat and 5 km west of Ḥaḥ. There are several references to Ashtarka in the fifteenth and sixteenth centuries: as attacked by the Turks in 1454 (Bar Hebraeus, Appendix, p. xlii); and in manuscript notes of 1405 (Wright, *Catalogue*, I, 165) and of 1535 and 1555 (F. Rosen and J. Forshall, *Catalogus codicum manuscriptorum orientalium qui in Museo Britannico asservantur. Pars I. Codices syriacos et carshunicos amplectans* [London, 1838], 37). "Ashtarak" is Armenian for "tower" (Dillemann, 232).

Church of Mar Addai pp. ix, x, 53; Pl. 151

Socin and Pognon provide the name of the church, which is mentioned in the third manuscript note cited above and by Peeters, "Martyrologe", 165 note 13.

Bibliography: Socin, 250, 268 no. 146; Pognon, 191–202, nos. 95–116. Bell, UN Journal 1911. Bell negative: S 9.

Dates: Inscription: church and/or *beth ṣlotha* built 772 (infra).

Changes since 1911: not known.

Bell's unpublished papers lack any information about this site beyond the note that "There is a church here of later date, ruined" (UN Journal 1911, 26 April). The church (Pl. 151, on left) is of the "parochial" type (p. 53 above) with its entrance on the south. The continuation of the archivolt moulding may be compared to mouldings round the three windows above the entrance into the main church at Deir Za'faran (Pl. 188); round the windows at Kefr Zeh (Pl. 154); and on certain tomb façades at Dara (Preusser, pl. 59 below [where the columns are also similar] and 61), as well as to some building façades in northern Syria, e.g., Qal'at Sem'an (Mango, fig. 153). In the *beth ṣlotha* at Heshterek (Pl. 151, on right) there are about thirty dated commemorative inscriptions from AD 913 to 1294, many honouring a "head of the church", indicating a parochial church. A further inscription, said to be in its original place in the same *beth ṣlotha*, is dated AD 772. It states that "this church *('idta)* was erected" (Pognon, no. 96), whereas at Kefr Zeh the building inscription of the *beth ṣlotha* dated AD 934/5 uses the term *beth ṣlotha* (see above, note 41). There is, therefore, some room for uncertainty as to which structure at Heshterek the inscription refers. Furthermore, the *beth ṣlotha* and the church may not be contemporary, as they differ in ornament. The *beth ṣlotha's* archivolt is not horse-shoe shaped and it has a different set of profiles from that of the church; the archivolt of the former rests on a *cyma recta* cornice, rather than on capitals and columns as in the latter case; the continuous moulding is lacking and the entire effect is heavier than that conveyed by the church entrance. It would therefore be important to try to determine definitely to which the date 772 applies (see also above, p. ix).

ḤIRBET SHORISH (SHERISH ?)

This ruined village is probably in the vicinity of the village of Shorishba (Sorozbah, now Çavuşlu) 15 km north-west of Midyat, if it is not, in fact, to be identified with it. Ḥirbet Shorish would seem to lie off the road between Ḥabsenas and Derindib (see below) as it does not appear on the route between these two villages as given in the *Handbook of Mesopotamia* (p. 287).

Church of Mar Yoḥannan Ma'mdana (?) (= John the Baptist)

Bibliography: Bell, UN Journal 1911.

The Journal says simply: "Off [from Ḥabsenas] at 7 & rode up to Khirbet Sherish where there is a ruined village & small church of Mar Yuhanna el Ma'methan—no trace of old work—Deirindib at 8:45 ..." (27 April). "El Ma'methan" is most probably "the Baptist", in Syriac, *ma'mdana.*

KARTMIN (QARṬAMIN), *YAYVANTEPE* see MONASTERY OF MAR GABRIEL

KEFR BEH *(GÜNGÖREN)*

This village is 2 km east of the monastery of Mar Gabriel.

Church of Mar Stephanus and Mar Yoḥannan pp. ix, 53

Bibliography: Bell, UN Journal 1911; Jarry, 232, no. 54. Bell negatives: none.

Dates: Inscription: church built 1465 (p. 53).

Changes since 1911: not known.

Further information on this church of "parochial" plan (p. 53) is given in Bell's Journal, "... the usual exedra in the atrium & an aisle to the N. The priest said that this aisle was the original church & the rest had been added" (UN Journal 1911, 25 April). The inscription published by Jarry (232, no. 54) is dated AD 779 and looks in his photograph to be rather heavily incised for a graffito, as he describes it. If the stone is in its original place, the church would be considerably older than AD 1465 (the latter, the text of which is unpublished, may then refer to a restoration, a distinction Bell failed to make at Mar Dodo, note 141). As the inscription mentions "a priest of the church" rather than an "abbot" or "monk" this was a parish and not a monastery church.

KEFR ZEH (KEFERSE ?), *(ALTINTAŞ)*

This village lies ca. 8 km north-east of Midyat. Keferse is mentioned in the martyrology of Rabban Ṣliba (thirteenth century; Peeters, "Martyrologe", 174 and note 10), and Kefr Zeh features in the account of an attack by Kurds in AD 1416 (Bar Hebraeus, Appendix, p. xxxviii).

Church of Mar 'Azaziel (Azizael) pp. vii–xi, 13–15, 16–18, 33, 44–47, 49, 51, 57, 78, 81, 82–83; Figs. 8, 29–32; Pls. 152–165

On the patron saint see p. 47 and F. Macler, *Histoire de S. Azazail* (Paris, 1902).

Bibliography: Pognon, 91–94, no. 51, pl. IV left; Guyer, "Surp Hagop", 499f.; *idem*, "Amida", 217, fig. 16; Reuther, 564; Monneret de Villard, 44f., 47f., 59f., fig. 37; Dillemann, 234; Leroy, *CRAI* 1968, 485; Deichmann, *BZ*, 121; Jarry, 232–235, nos. 55–59; Krautheimer, 319f.; Deichmann and Peschlow, *Ruinenstätten*, 26f. and note 12. Bell negatives: M 202–213, R 205–206, 208–216, S 1.

Dates: Inscriptions: *beth ṣlotha* built 934/5 (note 41); vault of church repaired 1936 (note 46); church furniture provided 1936 *(ibid.)*; Text: church pillaged 1416 (supra), 1915 or 1926 (note 46).

Changes since 1911: The disappearance of the *bema* and templon screen; the addition of the modern altar screen and tabernacle; the partial collapse and restoration of the nave vault, all have been noted (note 46). The extent of the damage to the vault has yet to be determined, but much of the east bay and the lower north side remains undisturbed with the brick work still exposed. The north side of the apse conch has been repaired and the east end of the church painted white. A wooden trellis divides the east and west halves of the nave. As at Mar Gabriel and Ṣalaḥ, this church has been given a new roof, probably when the vault was repaired. Several more blocks of the raking cornice are now gone from the west gable. Both the east and west ends of the south façade have been masked by new structures.

The dates of this "parochial" church, and that at Arnas, remain unsettled; there is little epigraphic evidence at Kefr Zeh (see notes 41–44, 46, 120). In terms of decoration, Bell considered Kefr Zeh slightly later than Arnas and other churches with related sculpture; she finally placed all of them around 700 AD (p. 82f.). The main architectural problem at Kefr Zeh and Arnas concerns the nave arcades and the brick vaults they support. Bell revised her original opinion that the nave vault and the north arcade were later restorations (p. 15), at least partially when after her second visit there she decided the entire vault was original (p. 45); whether she also changed her mind about the nave arcade is unclear. After her visits, there was a partial collapse of the nave vault, possibly in either 1915 or 1926, which was repaired in 1936 (see note 46). For a general discussion of the roofing of this and related churches see p. viii above, where I have suggested that nave arcades were an original feature providing additional support for the timber roofs which were later replaced by barrel vaults.

The original ashlar masonry of the church is undoubtedly that best visible at the east end (Pl. 152; the upper wall and the gable are now obscured by modern additions) and around the west windows (Pl. 154), but I would not agree with Bell that it is likewise displayed on the south façade (p. 15). Bell's records of the bema (p. 45, Pl. 158; see also note 122) and the templon screen (Pls. 161–163) are invaluable as both are now gone. Although she had considered the screen as later than the church (p. 14), she subsequently decided it was contemporary (p. 46). The oratory of 934/5 AD at Kefr Zeh (pp. 13f., 47 ; see also notes 41–44) is very interesting because it offers proof that in the tenth century masonry in the Ṭur 'Abdin was still ashlar and, according to its inscription, such exedras were then called *beth ṣlotha.*

Chapel of the Virgin (el 'Adhra) p. 47; Fig. 33

Bibliography: Monneret de Villard, 49, fig. 42; Dauphin, 325. Bell negatives: none.

Changes since 1911: not known.

This and the following chapel probably resemble the two at Ba Sebrina (see above, p. 101).

Chapel of Mar Yoḥannan p. 47; Pl. 166

Bibliography: Jarry, 235, no. 60; Dauphin, 325. Bell negative: R 205.

Changes since 1911: not known.

On the plan of this chapel see the preceding monument.

KERKUK (KIRKUK; KARKA D-BETH SLOKH)

Kerkuk, east of the Tigris, in Iraq, is ca. 300 km south-east of Cezre and ca. 250 km north of Baghdad. It was the metropolitan bishopric of Beth Garmai. On the churches of Kerkuk see Fiey, *Assyrie*, III, 49–53.

Bibliography: J.M. Fiey, "Histoire de Karka d'Bét Sloh", *AB*, 82 (1964), 189–222; *idem, Assyrie*, III, 11–53.

Monastery of Mar Tahmazgerd pp. 74–78; Figs. 48–49; Pls. 31–37

On Tahmazgerd see Fiey, "Karka", 212–216.

Bibliography: Sarre and Herzfeld, *Reise*, II, 330–336, fig. 308; W. Bachmann, *Kirchen und Moscheen in Armenien und Kurdistan* (Leipzig, 1913), 18–22, pls. 17–19; Reuther, 563; Monneret de Villard, 29, fig. 23; Fiey, "Karka", 212–216; *idem, Assyrie,* 51.

Dates: Text: monastery founded ca. 470 (note 198).

Changes since 1911: The church was completely destroyed in 1918 by an explosion of Turkish gun powder stored there. It was rebuilt in 1923 as a smaller church of a different plan (Fiey, "Karka", 217 and note 5).

Mar Tahmazgerd is discussed in the context of Sasanian buildings, especially the churches at Ctesiphon and Hira, by Reuther (pp. 560–563).

Mariamana Camii = Mosque of Mary the Mother (Ulu Camii) p. 78

Bibliography: Sarre and Herzfeld, *Reise*, II, 329f., fig. 307; Reuther, 564f.; Monneret de Villard, 77, fig. 74; Fiey, *Assyrie*, III, 52.

Changes since 1911: not known.

A plan was produced by Sarre and Herzfeld (*Reise*, II, fig. 307) who considered the church to be no earlier than the beginning of the thirteenth century.

KERMATI, *(KAYABALI)*

This site is ca. 22 km south-east of Midyat and ca. 3 km north of Kersifan.

Bibliography: Dillemann, 51.

Shrine p. 31; Figs. 17–18.

Bibliography: none. Bell negative: R 188.

KERSIFAN (GUIRSEOUAN), *(IKITEPE)*

This site is ca. 22 km south-east of Midyat and ca. 3 km south of Kermati.

Bibliography: Dillemann, 51.

Shrine p. 30; Fig. 16; Pls. 167–168

Bibliography: none. Bell negatives: R 184–187.

KHAKH see ḤAḤ

MARDIN **(MARGDIS, MARDE)** see also DEIR ZA'FARAN

Marde is first mentioned, apparently, by Ammianus Marcellinus, as part of the Roman *limes*. It was a bishopric from the seventh century onwards and was taken by the Arabs in 640. Although little mentioned before the conquest, it was an important city thereafter. It was dominated by the Marwanids (ca. 990–1096), the Seldjuks, and was the seat of an Ortokid emir ca. 1107–1260. Ṣalaḥ al Din was unable to conquer it. On the Islamic monuments, including the citadel (Bell negatives R 130–131, 134–160), see Gabriel.

Bibliography: Art. "Mārdīn" by V. Minorsky in *EI* (1928–36); Gabriel, I, 3–82, pls. a–e, I–XXIII; Hage, 102; Dillemann, 98f., 214f., fig. XXX.

Concerning churches in Mardin, Bell's Journal notes: "... the Old Syrian church (said to be ancient but no details to go by, heavy basilica plan) & the Catholic Armenian church ditto. It has a building inscription in a stone of which I only saw the copy dating it in the 4th cent. ... I saw another church on way home, Mar [left blank], but it was equally uninteresting" (UN Journal 1911, 19 April); "So to Mar Mikhail (O. Syrian) where nothing but the plan seemed to be old ..." (20 April). This last church was restored in AD 1744 and 1816 (Jarry, 236f., nos. 62–63). See also Parry, 73–79. Fiey has published a photograph of an episcopal throne *(synthronon)* in the Jacobite cathedral of Mar Behnam and the Forty Martyrs (Fiey, *Mossoul*, 95f., fig. 1). For Deir Za'faran, see p. 132.

MAYAFARQIN (FARKIN; MARTYROPOLIS; MAIPHERQAṬ), *(SILVAN)* pp. iii, v, vii, x, xi; Pl. 38

This town (Pl. 38), the modern Silvan, lies north and east of the Tigris and has long been identified by some scholars with Tigranocerta (see note 179), an identification rejected by others. Less controversial is its identification with Martyropolis, founded ca. 410 by the bishop Marutha (see note 180) who brought there the bones of the Persian martyrs. But a large village is said to have existed there before that time in the province of Sophanene which belonged to the Romans from 297. Kavad took Martyropolis briefly in 502 after which it was refortified by both Anastasius and Justinian. The latter made it the capital in 536 of the new province of Armenia IV, although it remained a bishopric under Amida. It fell to the Persians in 589–591 and 602–622, and to the Arabs in 640. The Byzantines failed to take the city in 943. It was the capital of the Marwanid dynasty 990–1085 and was ruled by the Ortokids, 1122–1184 (from which period dates the record of monuments of AD 1176/7 published by Fiey, see below), followed by the Ayyubids, 1185–1260.

Bibliography: Art. "Maiyāfāriḳīn" by V. Minorsky in *EI* (1928–36); Gabriel, 209–230, pls. LXXVI–LXXX; Dillemann, 236, 254–257; Fiey, "Mārūṭā de Martyropolis d'après Ibn al-Azraq (+1181)", *AB*, 94 (1976); *idem*, "Martyropolis".

The circuit walls (Bell negatives S 100–116) were studied by Gabriel, but Bell's photographs document further sections of wall which have since disappeared. What must have vanished even before her arrival was the lengthy Greek inscription in the north wall recorded by C.F. Lehmann-Haupt, *Armenien einst und jetzt* (Berlin, 1910), I, 410–418. Of great value are Bell's photographs (Bell negatives S 117–157, 159–167) of the so-called mosque of Ṣalaḥ al Din (Ulu Cami ; Bell, *Ukhaidir*, 159f., pls. 84,3, 92, 93,2) which was rebuilt before Gabriel's study of it (see note 160). Fiey has recenlty published two interesting articles on a Syriac legend which was translated by Ibn al-Azraq and inserted into his history of Mayafarqin written in 1176/7. Seven churches are given by name and/or locations; four of these are described as being destroyed or in ruins; three were still in use, namely: 1. the Cathedral ("Great Church"), said to have been the oldest church in the city; 2) the church of the Jacobites; and 3) the monastery church of SS. Peter and Paul built by Marutha (died ca. 420), which stood in the Jewish quarter. Fiey suggests: 1) that the first and last of these three are the same church which would be the Melkite church and might be identified with Gertrude Bell's basilica; 2) that "the Jacobite church" might be that built (or perhaps rebuilt) by Athanasius Sandalaya in 752 and might, as the only other church still standing in the twelfth century, be Bell's el 'Adhra. See Fiey, "Martyropolis", 24–30, and the remarks concerning these suggestions made below where I have tentatively suggested that: 1) the basilica is the "Great Church" (p. 124); 2) the el 'Adhra, the "Jacobite church" (p. 126); and 3) that the "monastery church" was destroyed before 1911 (p. 130). The two churches published below have vanished. A loose slab from an unidentified church at Mayafarqin is now in the British Museum (p. 128).

Basilica pp. vii, viii, 58–60, 65; Figs. 40–41; Pls. 38–39

Bibliography: Guyer, "Surp Hagop", 501; *idem*, "Amida, 209–212, 216, figs. 9, 15; *idem, Journey*, 114–117, pl. VIII B; Strzygowski, *Syrie*, 29; Leroy, *CRAI* 1968; 480f.; Fiey, "Martyropolis", 24–30; *idem*, "Mārūṯā" (see above), Mundell, "Deir Za'faran". Bell negatives: S 168–176.

Changes since 1911: This church has now entirely disappeared (Leroy, *CRAI* 1968, 480f.). In this connection it is interesting to note that Bell's Journal records a visit to her by the local Jacobite priest who feared that the basilica would soon be converted into a medrese (UN Journal 1911, 3 May). It is possible that its stone was used in rebuilding the Ulu Camii which took place after Bell's visit.

It is clear that the basilica cannot be identified with any of the four churches designated by Ibn al-Azraq as destroyed or in ruins in 1176/7 (see above) as all are indicated as to their locations: one outside the walls, two in the northern corners and one in the south-west corner of the city. The basilica, on the contrary, stood in the centre of the city. Of the three churches still standing in the twelfth century, Fiey has apparently suggested that the basilica is to be identified as both the monastery church of SS. Peter and Paul *and* the "Great Church". I see no reason, however, why these two churches which are mentioned as separate foundations of two different people in the twelfth-century description, should be considered as one building. Of the two, I think the second is the more likely candidate for identification with the basilica. The first, according to Ibn al-Azraq, was built by Marutha (died 420) and was still standing in AD 1176/7 inside the city, in the Zuqaq al Yahud (the Jewish quarter), near the synagogue (Fiey, "Martyropolis", 27–30). The basilica stood just north of the Ulu Cami ("Ṣalaḥ al Din mosque" ; Pl. 38; cf. photograph on p. 68 of Adil Tekin, *Diyarbakır* [Istanbul, 1971]) and was presumably very close to where the *cardo* and *decumanus* crossed (Gabriel, fig. 159). This very central location was an unlikely area either for a monastery, or for the Jewish quarter, in either the early Christian period, or the medieval, for the main mosque was also first built there on the site of the Ulu Cami in early Islamic times (see below). (On the monastery church see the comments made below on p. 130 concerning the marble sarcophagus/reliquary [?] photographed [Pl. 50] in the Saray.) On the other hand, the centre of the city would have been a very appropriate situation for the "Great Church", i.e. cathedral, of the "city of the martyrs" founded by a bishop. The location, therefore, and the large size of the basilica argue in favour of its identification with the "Great Church" and, if Ibn al-Azraq attributes it to Constantine and Helena (*ibid.*, 25) on the grounds of its antiquity (it had, he reported, a cross in the middle of its altar, "un signe chez les chrêtiens pour la première église qu'on bâtit"), this is a traditional cliché. Martyropolis became a city and a bishopric under Marutha between 410 and 420 and it is likely that a cathedral was built then. The twelfth-century account apparently states that Marutha was buried in the "Great Church" (*idem*, "Mārūṯā", 43; cf. *idem*, "Martyropolis", 27f., where Fiey says he was buried in the monastery church).

On formal grounds the basilica could be dated 410–420, as its sculpture appears closer in technique to that of the baptistery at Nisibis (p. 143) than to the related examples of the sixth century (p. 134). Its large size accords well with that of a number of Syrian basilicas of the late fourth and early fifth centuries; in particular its dimensions (nave = 38.65 x 25.75 m, from Bell RGS Notes) could be compared with those of the martyrion basilica (nave = 38.50 x 23.75 m) at Dibsi Faraj, which is dated AD 429 (on the latter and Syrian basilicas see R. Harper, "Excavations at Dibsi Faraj, Northern Syria, 1972–74", *DOP*, 24 [1975], 333). This church at Mayafarqin is the only one of the group published in this book to represent the standard early Christian columnar (?) basilica with a wooden roof. It is cited by Guyer, together with the conjectural case of Mar Cosmas at Diyarbakır (p. 106) and the known cases at Rusafa and Halabiya (Zenobia), as an indication that the basilica existed in northern Mesopotamia as well as in Syria ("Surp Hagop", 501). To this list may be added the churches of Dibsi and that of St. Sergius (Qaṣr Serij) in the Singar Mountains. It is noteworthy for the question of the roofing of the Ṭur 'Abdin churches that in the latter church a mortared-rubble barrel vault replaced a timber roof at some unknown period (Oates, *Studies*, 109–111, pl. XIII c).

Concerning the columns which Bell deduced were removed from the basilica to the mosque, Fiey argues that if the basilica was still standing in 1176/7, it was unlikely to have been in ruins by 1185–93 when Ṣalaḥ al Din was said to have built his mosque alongside. Fiey suggests therefore that the mosque was built on the site of, and incorporating the remains of, buildings belonging to the monastery of SS. Peter and Paul (i.e. the basilica), of which only the decorated arch (Pl. 49) nearby remains (ibid., 27–29). It should be mentioned that Gabriel disagrees with the dates Bell assigned to the building phases of the mosque (*Ukhaidir*, 159f.,), which, he concludes, occupies the site of a mosque of the early Islamic period. The present mosque, he proposed, was built in AD 1031, its dome fell in 1152 and was replaced by the larger dome in AD 1152–1157, at which time the columns were inserted (Gabriel, 221–228). If the columns were removed from the basilica ca. 1157, then they were either replaced by piers or the church stood henceforth as a ruin. Neither possibility is likely: 1) one would expect Bell to have found some trace of piers; and 2) as shown above, the basilica cannot be identified with any of the four churches in ruins twenty years later in 1176/7. One must then agree with Fiey ("Martyropolis", 29), although for different reasons, that the mosque columns were taken from elsewhere.

On the south face of the westernmost arch of the south arcade (Pl. 43) is evidence that the basilica was restored, at least in part, at some period before its final abandonment. The upper three voussoirs of this arch had apparently been refaced so that the first and third facings were set at right angles to the existing voussoirs. A new small block inserted against the intervening voussoir linked the other two. The only pre-Palladian parallel for the type of archivolt thus created, that I have been able to find, is in the inner keep of the castle at Ḥarran whose Islamic building phases have been put as eleventh century, 1191 and 1315 (Rice, "Harran", pp. 42–7). It is interesting to note that this arch was imitated in Mayafarqin itself, in the windows of the south façade of the Ulu Cami when it was rebuilt in 1913 (Gabriel, pl. LXXVII,1). The very damaged state of the remaining arches of the basilica (Pls. 42–46), as compared with the relatively good condition of the new voussoirs (Pl.

43) would indicate perhaps that a collapse of the roof or upper walls occurred before the refacing of the arc(s?), possibly between the eleventh and fourteenth centuries.

Church of El 'Adhra (= The Virgin) pp. viii, xi, 61–65; Fig. 42; Pls. 51, 54–66

Bibliography: Bell, UN Journal 1911; *idem*, RGS Notes; Guyer, *Journey*, 118f., pls. VIII A, IX A; Strzygowski, *Syrie*, 30, 99f., 170, figs. 62, 66; Leroy, *CRAI* 1968, 480; H. Buchwald, *The Church of the Archangels in Sige near Mudania* (Vienna, 1969), 48 and notes 216–219, pp. 50–52, 59–62; W.E. Kleinbauer, "Zvartnotz and the Origins of Armenian Architecture", *Art Bulletin*, 54 (1972), 256–262; Krautheimer, 310f., 340; Fiey, "Martyropolis", 24–30. Bell negatives: S 177–199.

Dates: Inscriptions: 673 ? (p. 127); ca. 1400 ? *(ibid.)*; Text: on the date 591 proposed by Bell (p. 65) see note 178.

Changes since 1911: This church has also completely disappeared (Leroy, *CRAI* 1968, 480f.).

Like the basilica (p. 124) the church of el 'Adhra cannot be identified with any of the four churches in ruins in the twelfth century because of its location. Guyer described it as being in the south-west part of the city (*Journey*, 118). It was at some distance south of the basilica and Ulu Camii, for Pl. 38 was taken from in front of it (although there is no record of this, it is clearly the case as the walls in the foreground of both Pls. 38 and 56 are identical). Among the three churches remaining in 1176/7–the Great Church, the Jacobite church, and the monastery church–Fiey has proposed that the el 'Adhra may have been the second, which was "près de la Tour al-Zariba (= de l'enclos aux troupeaux)". He further suggested that this was the "magnificent church" built by the Jacobite bishop Athanasius Sandalaya in AD 752 (Fiey, "Martyropolis"' 24–30).

It is evident that the el 'Adhra stood near the south city wall and so could be near the al Zariba tower (whose location is otherwise unknown) and therefore identified as the Jacobite church; it may equally have stood in the Jewish quarter and therefore be identifiable as the monastery church of Peter and Paul where the black marble reliquary is said to have been placed. This reliquary may be that object Bell (Pl. 50) photographed in the Saray, which might indicate that the monastery church was destroyed by 1911 (see p. 130). And, although one might ask if the links of the el 'Adhra with Byzantine architecture (p. 61) could perhaps point to a Melkite patron, I would tentatively agree to its identification with "the Jacobite church" of al-Azraq. The further identification with the Jacobite church built in 752 should be evaluated through comparisons with the dated eighth-century buildings cited above (p. ix). It is, of course, also possible that Athanasius' church was one of the four churches in ruins in the twelfth century.

Buchwald, in a study of the cross-domed basilica within the development from the domed basilica to the inscribed cross plan, rejects (rightly) as a mistranslation the textual date of 591 for the el 'Adhra (p. 65; *Sige*, 48, note 216; see also note 178 above: cf. Krautheimer) and places it 825–850 on stylistic grounds. He postulates columns at the corners of the main piers instead of the cross piers conjectured by Bell (p. 61; Fig. 42) and he denies the possibility of a dome. The comparisons he then makes with the Kalenderhane Camii in Istanbul are no longer relevant as that church has since been redated from the early ninth century (*Sige*, 61) to the late twelfth: C.L. Striker and Y.D. Kuban, "Work at Kalenderhane Camii in Istanbul: Third and Fourth Preliminary Reports", *DOP*, 25 (1971), 258. (On the theory of the development in general, see Mango 161–180.) Buchwald finds support for a ninth-century date in the carving at Mayafarqin: while some capitals he considers Justinianic (cf. p. xi above) and reused (Pls. 62, 66), the remaining sculpture (e.g. Pls. 63–65) he likens to the example of AD 934/5 at Afyonkarahisar and to others of the late tenth century (*Sige*, 48, 50–52, 59–62).

It is apparent from Bell's account (p. 62) and the photographs that this church was restored at least once. While Bell's Journal (1–4 May 1911) adds no new information about the el 'Adhra, her RGS Notes contain this cryptic note alongside her measured plan, "Miriam el Adra, Farkin 985 (Greek)–312 = 673 AD ask Mutran Elyas; also a stone said to be built in the wall high up AD 1400 and something". The implication is that these are both inscriptions she has found and/or been informed about. Both, of course, could have been reused. Nor is it clear in what language they were written. No events are mentioned for the period around 673 in Fiey, "Martyropolis", but the date may provide a *terminus ante* (if not *ad*) *quem* for the construction of the church. It should be noted, furthermore, concerning the dates 752 and 825–50 proposed by Fiey and Buchwald respectively, that the arcades between nave and aisles have on the soffits of their voussoirs the centering bosses which are found at Dara, Deir Za'faran and other sixth-century sites (Pls. 57, 59–60). This structural detail, taken together with the late sixth-century architectural parallel of Qasr Ibn Wardan (ca. 564; cited by Bell, p. 65), could reinforce the case for a date before the Arab conquest. Although the dating 591 given by Bell is founded on a mistranslation (see note 178), the events of that period, or for example, the creation of the new province of Armenia IV in 536 AD with Martyropolis as its capital, could understandably have been commemorated by such a construction. Evidence of later restorations to the church may be offered by the carved slab (twelfth–thirteenth century ?) which follows and the fifteenth-century date noted by Bell high in the wall. In 1479 Martyropolis became a metropolis of the West Syrian (Jacobite) diocese (Fiey, "Martyropolis", 22) and some alteration to the building may have been caried out then. In 1911 this church belonged to the Jacobites (Bell, UN Journal 1911, 2 May), who used the north pastophorion (p. 62).

Carved Slab I: eagle (?) in a niche Pl. 51

Bibliography: unpublished. Bell negative: S 188.

Changes since 1911: whereabouts unknown, church destroyed.

It is not absolutely certain that this block was found inside the church, for Bell did not identify this photograph, but she numbered it within the sequence of the el 'Adhra negatives.

Although the composition of this slab is reminiscent of the niche decoration on the

outside of the dome drum at Ḥaḥ (Pl. 137), the bird in question here, with its tapering wings, resembles more closely the eagles of, for example, the walls of Diyarbakır, than the doves of the Ṭur 'Abdin (cf. Strzygowski, *Die Baukunst* [above note 172], I, 284). Another comparison could be made with a similar slab above an entrance porch of the cathedral of Ani (AD 989–1001; *ibid.*, I, fig. 20). It is the band of intersecting semi-circles, however, which allows us to place the Mayafarqin slab within the Ayyubid sphere of influence and in the twelfth to thirteenth century. This particular ornament is known in Syria and is thought to have been imported into Seldjuk architecture by a Damascene architect at Konya where the motif is found on the mosque and medrese of AD 1220/1 and 1252 respectively; it also adorns the mosque at Malatya (1247); see *Amida*, 141f., fig. 61; Gabriel, 273, pl. XCV,1). I thank Dr. J. Allan for the following information about this ornament. The earliest Syrian example of it is apparently on the mihrab of the Shabhbakhtiyya Madrassah in Aleppo of AD 1193 (E. Herzfeld, *Matériaux pour un corpus inscriptionum arabicarum*, II [Cairo, 1954], pl. CIX). The ornament itself may derive ultimately from the cusped decoration as found around the arch on the south wall of the tomb of Safawat al Molk at Damascus, dated AD 1110/1 (Institut Français de Damas, *Les monuments ayyoubides de Damas* [Paris, 1938], pl. VIII-1). As the apse and building are composed of brick and stucco, they betray Iraqi influence, which may also be the source of the cusped decoration.
The proposal concerning the origin and dating of the ornament provides a *terminus post quem* in the period 1110/1 to 1193 for a renovation of the el 'Adhra church at Mayafarqin in which the block (Pl. 51) may have been used. The city came under Ayyubid rule in 1185, after which time the ornament may have been introduced.

Carved Slab II: birds and animals in interlaced panels Pls. 52–53

This slab, said to have come from a church at Mayafarqin (*Amida*, 366), was acquired by the British Museum shortly after the photographs by Beylié were first published (*ibid.*, Fig. 317).

Bibliography: *Amida*, 366f., fig. 317; O.M. Dalton, "A Sculptured Marble Slab from Northern Mesopotamia", *Proceedings of the Society of Antiquaries of London*, 2nd series, 32 (1919–20), 54–63.
Bell negatives: none; Beylié's photographs in Bell archive in University of Newcastle-upon-Tyne.

Changes since 1911: none.

This marble slab now measures 1.27 x 0.53 m, and its reconstructed height, including the top missing panel, is 1.83 m; there are two holes in each edge. It was decorated on both sides with three interlaced panels of circular, square and diamond shapes. Side one (Pl. 52) has a series of birds and two leaves filling the interstices, while side two (Pl. 53) has animals (some ill-defined), and winged palmette motifs. Some of the figures on side two appear to have been recarved in places. The framing bands on the first side are broad with grooves along the edges; on the second they are cut down the centre by two grooves. Similar slabs have been found at Myra and Istanbul, see C.L. Striker and D. Kuban, "Work at Kalenderhane Camii in

Istanbul: Fifth Preliminary Report (1970–74)", *DOP*, 29 (1975), 314f., fig. 12, where a provisional date of tenth to eleventh century is suggested for the Istanbul slab. Grabar dates to the latter century similar slabs at St. Irene in Istanbul (A. Grabar, *Sculptures byzantines du Moyen Age II. XIe–XIVe siecle,* [Paris, 1976], pl. XVI d, no. 6); Mt. Athos (*ibid.*, pl. XXXIX a–b, no. 62); and Ohrid (*ibid.*, pl. XLII a–b, no. 69). Particularly close to the carving style of the Mayafarqin slab are examples at Prespa (ca. AD 1014; *ibid.*, pl. XXXVI a, no. 50), and Kiev (AD 1000–1037 (*ibid.*, pl. LVII a, no. 76).

In view of the strongly Byzantine character of this slab it should be noted that the Byzantines in fact failed to take and occupy this city in the medieval period.

Marble Reliquary found in the Saray Pl. 50

This receptacle is not mentioned in Bell's journals and is only identified from her photograph album where she noted simply "in serail", which must refer to the citadel seen in Pl. 38 (see below).

Bibliography: unpublished; cf. J. Ebersolt, *Mission archéologique de Constantinople* (Paris, 1921), 12–27, pls. V–XXII; R. Marcus, "The Armenian Life of Marutha of Maipherkat", *Harvard Theological Review*, 25 (1932), 47–71; Lassus, *Sanctuaires*, 163ff., pl. XXVIII; Tchalenko, *Villages*, I, 347f.; III, figs. 8–9; S. Eyice, "Reliquaires en forme de sarcophage en Anatolie et à Istanbul", *Istanbul Arkeologi Müzeleri Yilliği*, 15–16 (1969), 127–145, figs. 1–32; C. Mango, "A Newly Discovered Byzantine Imperial Sarcophagus", *ibid.*, 307–309, Fig. 1; J. Noret, "La vie grecque ancienne de S. Marūtā de Mayferqaṭ", *AB*, 91 (1973), 77–103; Fiey, "Martyropolis", 24–30. Bell negative: S 199.

Dates: Text: reliquary made ca. 410 (?), p. 130.

Changes since 1911: removed to Diyarbakır Museum in 1954.

This object is illustrated here for the first time. It is of dark purple marble and carved in the form of an antique sarcophagus with acroteria. Two small reliquaries of the same stone and of similar design were brought with it from Silvan to the museum. Its dimensions (ht. 1.08 m, l[ength] 1.25 m) are too small for a sarcophagus, which–unless it was a child's sarcophagus–should have been about 2 m long, but they nearly coincide with those of a reliquary in the form of a sarcophagus (ht. 1.08 m, l. 1.20 m) found by Tchalenko in northern Syria (*Villages*, I, 347f.; III, figs. 8–9). The latter has two small chambers excavated inside in which the relics were placed; two holes in the lid allowed oil to be poured in, flow over the relics and be collected from two openings in the front. This reliquary also has a lid with acroteria, but is further decorated with symbolic carvings both on the trough and lid. Tchalenko dates the west church at Behyo where it was found to the mid-fifth century (*ibid.*, I, 351) and the designs of its carvings have been compared with those on a slab dated AD 489 (*ibid.*, II, pl. CXLIV, no. 15; III, 17). Such large reliquaries (e.g. also at Sokhani [ht. 0.62 m, l. 1.44 m], Lassus, *Sanctuaires*, 164ff.) were popular in northern Syria where they were often placed in a south martyrial chapel and made accessible to the public. Smaller reliquaries (averaging about 0.25 m in length) in the form of a sarcophagus and generally dated fifth to seventh centuries, have recently been studied by S. Eyice ("Reliquaires") who concluded that they were placed under altars and that those found in Anatolia and Istanbul exhibited greater faithfulness to the traditional antique sarcophagus type (as does that at Mayafarqin) than did those from Syria and Africa which have additional ornamentation (*ibid.*, 142, 145).

The receptacle at Mayafarqin would seem, then, to have been a reliquary rather than a sarcophagus, although no holes for oil are visible. In its simplicity of design it is in the tradition of the porphyry imperial sarcophagi used from Constantine to Marcian (died 457), four of which still preserve their lids. Three of these are pitched with corner acroteria, but the cross ornaments are placed on the gables of the lids rather than the front of the troughs (Ebersolt, *Mission,* pls. XIII–XVI). After Marcian, imperial tombs are known to have been in *verd antique* (e.g. Zeno, Leo I) or in white marbles (Justinian, Theodora; *ibid.,* 17f.). Surviving *verd antique* sarcophagi often have crosses on the front of the trough (*ibid.*, 15f.) as does a sarcophagus discovered in 1969 near the find-spot of some of the porphyry ones, which may be that of Heraclius, said to have been "like onyx" (Mango, "Sarcophagus"). If the imperial sarcophagi set the fashion for reliquaries like that at Mayafarqin and the smaller ones mentioned above, then the cross on the front may indicate a date after 457, but I think this would be an unproven criterion.

The reliquary at Mayafarqin may be of great interest in view of the activities of Marutha at the time of the foundation of Martyropolis (see above). In the Syriac account published by Fiey, Marutha had made a "black marble reliquary" to house the glass phial containing the blood of Joshua which he had brought back from Constantinople. It is conceivable that he had it made while in the capital or at least brought the marble from there. A persuasive element in favour of identifying our reliquary with that of the story is its dark colour, so unlike all the examples published by Eyice where light marble is much more prevalent. Unfortunately, the other accounts of Marutha's assembling of relics provide no further details concerning reliquaries. Even if an ultimate connection with Marutha is not verifiable, I think it possible that this reliquary is the same mentioned in the twelfth century by Ibn al-Azraq as being in the monastery of Peter and Paul. Since Bell found the reliquary in the Saray (which must refer to the Old Palace, Qaṣr al Atik, built by the Hamdanids on the site of the old Byzantine citadel, on the hill just north-west of the mosque and basilica, Pl. 38), one could conclude that eventually the monastery church was destroyed and the reliquary moved to the qaṣr.

MIDYAT

Midyat is mentioned as a bishopric in AD 1478 (Honigmann, *Barṣauma*, 167). It is now considered the capital of the Ṭur 'Abdin. About this town, Bell's RGS Notes contain the following: "There is also a small monastery of el-Hadra near Mar Philoxenus of no architectural importance, a much worn inscription in Syriac in the south wall. In the town is Mar Shimun which was largely rebuilt and Mar Barsaum which had been completely rebuilt". In addition to these, Anschütz reports the churches of Yaldath Alaha (perhaps the same as "el-Hadra"?), built before World War I by Americans, and Mar Sharbil, built after World War II ("Ortschaften", 181f.).

Church of Mar Philoxenus pp. viii, ix, 18, 19–20, 51–52; Figs. 11, 36; Pls. 169–175

On the patron saint see note 138.

Bibliography: Bell, *Amurath*, 316; Stryzygowski, *Syrie*, fig. 69; Reuther, 564; Monneret de Villard, 45, 47, 49, fig. 39. Bell negatives: M 171–181, R 190.

Changes since 1911: It has been rebuilt.

The general remarks about the "parochial" churches made above, pp. viiif. in the Introduction, would apply here as the arcades are later additions (see Deichmann and Peschlow, *Ruinenstätten,* 26).

Monastery of Mar Ibrahim (Abraham) and Mar Ubil (Habil, Abel) pp. 8, 10, 35–38, 51; Fig. 23; Pls. 176–183

On Abraham see Krüger, "Mönchtum" II, 8f. Ubil (Habil), a stylite, is mentioned in the history of the Mar Gabriel monastery (Nau, "Notice", 46).

Bibliography: Preusser, 34, fig. 8; Bell, *Amurath*, 316 note 2; Strzygowski, *Syrie*, 29f., fig. 13; Krüger, "Mönchtum" II, 8f.; Reuther, 563f., fig. 163; Monneret de Villard, 57, fig. 56; Leroy, *CRAI* 1968, 483. Bell negatives: M 159–170, R 189.

Changes since 1911: The west gate (Pls. 182–183) has been replaced. Today the monastery is deserted but visited by pilgrims (Anschütz, "Ortschaften", 182).

The general remarks about the "monastic" churches made above, p. ix in the Introduction would apply here. See note 104 on the inscription on the gate.

(MONASTERY OF) DEIR SALIBA (= MONASTERY OF THE CROSS), *(ÇATALÇAM)* pp. x, xi; Pls. 184–187

This monastery lies ca. 30 km north-east of Midyat and ca. 13 km north of Ḥaḥ. According to Krüger (pp. 10, 35), it was founded by Mar Aḥa some time before his death in AD 556. An abbot of Deir Ṣaliba features in the *Life* of Mar Gabriel of Qarṭamin (AD 593–667; Nau, "Notice", 63). The monastery is also mentioned in notes in medieval manuscripts, e.g. at Paris, Zotenberg, *Catalogue*, 13f.

Bibliography: Socin, 266, no. 119; Parry, 200f.; Bell, UN Journal 1909; Krüger, "Mönchtum" II, 34f.; Fiey, *Mossoul*, 99.

Dates: Text: monastery founded before 556 (supra).

Changes since 1911: The church once had a *bema* like that at Kefr Zeh (Pl. 158; see Fiey, *Mossoul*, 99; see also note 122) which may have disappeared before Bell's visit as she does not mention it in her notes. Other changes not known.

Bell entirely omits this monastery from her publications. Her Journal of 1909 notes: "It belongs to the later period. The church down a long dark passage, narthex, nave crossways & 3 sanctuary chambers. No decoration in this but a late decorated apse in the court with the usual cross in its roof. At the SW corner of the outer wall some very big stones, but I

doubt whether any part belongs to the older period" (24 May).
The large ashlar stone work referred to is visible in Pl. 184 behind and to the right of the central tree. The church is apparently of the "monastic" type although it is found combined with a *beth ṣlotha* which is a "parochial" feature. It is strange that Bell calls the *beth ṣlotha* (Pls. 185–187) "late", since its scupture is so similar to that of the el 'Adhra at Ḥaḥ and of Arnas, which she originally considered early (p. 79; cf. p. 82). The cross carved on the apse at Deir Ṣaliba has bulbous terminations as in the churches at Kefr Zeh (Pl. 161) and Arnas (Pl. 99). The foot of the cross at Deir Ṣaliba rests on a large sphere and a tall base. Below the cross is a niche similar to that in the apse at Qal'at Ḥatem Ṭay (Pl. 230). The *beth ṣlotha* differs from others in the Ṭur 'Abdin in having a window and, presumably, an upper storey. The archivolt is decorated with a rinceau frieze and bead-and-reel which are repeated on the window frame which has a row of palmettes above and the fragment of a Syriac inscription (see below). The rinceau frieze is extremely close to those at el 'Adhra, Ḥaḥ (Pls. 139–141, 143) and Arnas (Pls. 101–102: see also above, p. xi), as are the forms of the palmettes and bead-and-reel. The two vases at the lower corners of the window frame at Deir Ṣaliba (Pl. 186) bear a close resemblance to those at Ḥaḥ (Pl. 143), and on either side of the *beth ṣlotha* apse is a damaged bracket carved on its underside with a dove (Pl. 187) somewhat similar to those at el 'Adhra, Ḥaḥ (Pls. 137–138) and at Arnas (Pl. 101). The capital (reused ?) set into the north wall of the *beth ṣlotha* apse (Pl. 185) is of the uncut acanthus type (see *supra* p. xi). The exedra façade is flanked by two vertical frames, as is typical of the *beth ṣlotha* (see above p. x), along which runs a band of double dentils found also at Mar Awgen (Pl. 202), Kefr Zeh (Pls. 159–160) and Nisibis (Pl. 82). The fragment of inscription on the window frame is in Estranghelo script and appears to preserve the following:

... "shall pray for ... the monastery ..."

(MONASTERY OF) DEIR ZA'FARAN (= DAIRA D–KORKAMA = THE SAFFRON MONASTERY; MAR ḤANANIA), nr. MARDIN

Deir Za'faran is ca. 5 km east of Mardin (on which see p. 122 *supra*). Its earliest history is uncertain, although it is clear on the basis of the sculpture that the main church and south chapel existed in the sixth century. The monastery was refounded in 793 as the seat of the bishop of Mardin. It fell into abandon again and was once more refounded ca. 1125 from which time it has continued to flourish until today. From the medieval period until the early twentieth century it was the seat of the Jacobite Patriarch of Antioch. North of the courtyard is the domed patriarchal throne room preserving what may be the back of the patriarchal throne *(korsi)* of Antioch, carved in the sixth century, on which see Leroy, "Deir es-Za'pharan", 324–328 with 2 figs. Until recently the monastery contained a large and important library (see *ibid.*, 321–323). In the cliffs above Deir Za'faran to the east (Pl. 188) are a number of monasteries both built and rock-cut.

Bibliography: Parry, 103–120; Pognon, 186–189, no. 93; Bell, UN Journal 1911; Preusser, 49–53, figs. 13–17, pls. 62–65; Guyer, "Amida", 212, 225, fig. 11; Krüger, "Mönchtum" II, 19–23; Gabriel, pls. XI,4, XXIV,1–2; Monneret de Villard, 46, fig. 40; A. Vööbus, "Neues Licht über das Restaurationswerk des Jōḥannān von Mardē", *Oriens Christianus*,

47 (1963), 129–139; idem, "Eine wichtige Urkunde über die Geschichte des Mār Ḥananjā Klosters", *ibid.*, 53 (1969), 246–252; Leroy, *CRAI* 1968, 486–490, figs. 1–2; Jarry, 213–217, nos. 17–20; Fiey, *Nisibe*, 137f.; Leroy, "Deir es-Ze'pharan"; Mundell, "Deir Za'faran".

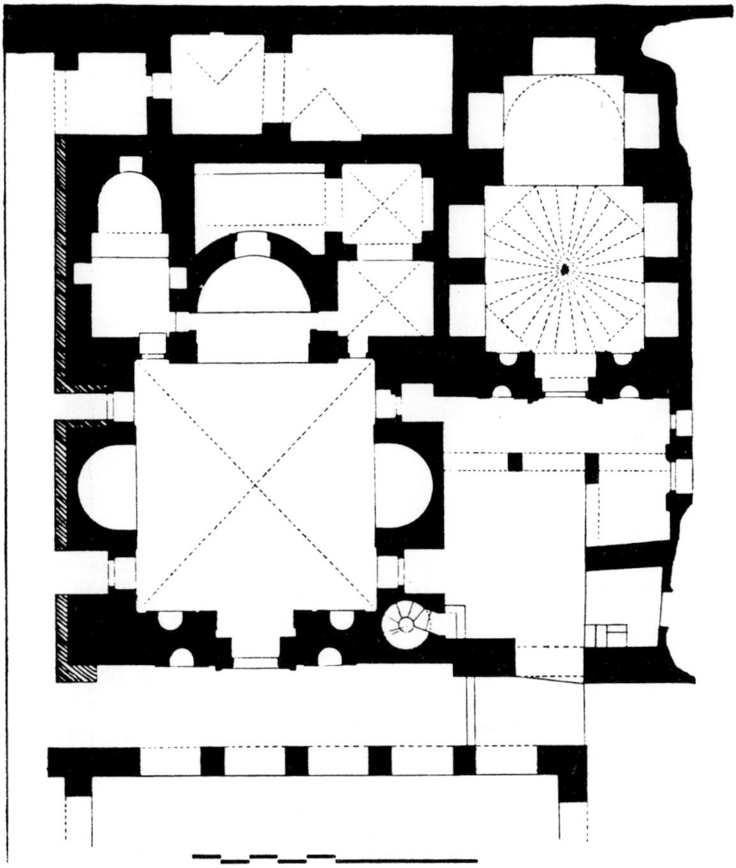

Fig. 53. Deir Za'faran, plan of main church and S chapel in Leroy, *CRAI* (1968), fig. 1

Main Church pp. ix–xi, 29, 69, 71, 73, 81; Fig. 53; Pls. 188–191, 194–198

Bibliography: included in that given above. Bell negatives: R 161–162, 165–173

Dates: Inscriptions: church and/or monastery restored 1250 (p. 134), 1697 *(ibid.)*, 1903 *(ibid.)*; church furniture provided 1903 *(ibid.)*, 1941 *(ibid.)*.
Text: monastery refounded 793 (p.132), 1125 *(ibid.)*; church and/or monastery restored 1496 (p. 134), 689 *(ibid.)*, 1873 *(ibid.)*.

Changes since 1911: Aside from the addition of wooden balconies at the interior west corners of the nave, the removal of the stucco half-columns flanking the east apse (on which see Preusser, 51), and a new coat of white paint which conceals the painted figural decoration in the east apse (*ibid.*, 52, Pl. 63), nothing worthy of note appears to have been done here. The inscription of 1903 (Jarry, 214, no. 18) is not, as Jarry states, inscribed on the iconostasis (there is and was none), but on the east wall north of the main apse. The tabernacle of 1903 was replaced by a new one in 1941.

Bell implied that the Deir Za'faran church was later than the el 'Adhra at Ḥaḥ (p. 70, "The plan is a modification ... a simplification of the 'Adhra at Hakh ...") and in her Journal she remarked: "... the church is certainly later than [others of ?] the Ṭur 'Abdin" (UN Journal 1911, 19 April). In fact, the reverse is true. Guyer showed that the sculpture of the main church is extremely close in style and motifs to carving in other north Mesopotamian monuments. Although he was at first intent on grouping this sculpture as much as possible around a conjectural seventh-century façade of the church of St. Thomas at Amida (whose decorations he suggested were reused in the Ulu Cami of that city), it is clear now that this group of sculpture dates from the fourth (Nisibis) and fifth (Mayafarqin basilica) centuries, as well as from the early sixth (el 'Adhra and Ulu Camii at Diyarbakır, Mar Sovo at Ḥaḥ, Deir Za'faran, several buildings at Rusafa, and loose pieces at Urfa and Dara, where there is also a tomb façade decorated in the same manner: see Mundell, "Deir Za'faran"). The Deir Za'faran church and chapel also share certain sculptural features with monuments in Syria, e.g. Seleucia Pieria and Qal'at Sem'an *(ibid.)*. The cross dome of the main church is not original. Elsewhere *(ibid.)* I have suggested that the trilobed plan may be a reduced version of that of the destroyed church of St. Sophia at Edessa (Urfa; p. 152 *infra*) and that the former church may, in view of its thick walls (2.35 m) have supported a masonry dome (span less than 8 m) on squinches, as did the latter. In turn, the Deir Za'faran church may have influenced somewhat the architecture of the el 'Adhra at Ḥaḥ, rather than the reverse as Bell suggested. Renovations are recorded at the monastery in ca. 1250 (Pognon, 186–189, nos. 92–93); 1496 (Mundell, "Deir Za'faran", note 61); 1689 *(ibid)*; 1697 (Jarry, 216, no. 20); 1873 (Mundell, *op. cit.*); 1903 (Jarry, 214, no. 18).

South Chapel pp. 69–70; Fig. 53; Pls. 188, 192–193

Bibliography: Parry, 108–110, fig. opp. p. 109; Bell, UN Journal 1911; Preusser, 53, fig. 17; Leroy, *CRAI* 1968, 487, 489f., fig. 1; Jarry, 215–217, nos. 19–20; Leroy, "Baptistères" 3; *idem*, "Deir es-Za'pharan". Bell negatives: R 162–164.

Dates: see supra.

Changes since 1911: Leroy has pointed out that the walls have been cleaned (*CRAI* 1968, 486f.).

The chapel, a *beth qadisha*, contemporary with the main church (Leroy detected physical evidence that the chapel was built first, "Deir es-Za'pharan" 321), was largely overlooked by Bell. Her Journal notes merely: "... the tomb chamber with a fluted dome which was certainly new" (UN Journal 1911, 19 April). Its plan was not included in Preusser's study. Leroy pointed out this oversight and published a plan (*CRAI* 1968, fig. 1), that used here (Fig. 53). This was a mortuary chapel *(beth qadisha)*, at least in modern times (Jarry, 215–217, nos. 19–20). The exterior fluted dome (Pl. 188) is of a type known in Mardin, from at least the fourteenth century, on the Sultan ʿIsa Medrese (AD 1385) and the tomb of Sultan Hamza (ca. AD 1444), where small arcades run around the base of the domes (Gabriel, 32, 39, pls. XI,3, XIV). The dolphin motif used above the door of the chapel (Preusser, 53, fig. 17; Leroy, *CRAI* 1968, 490) and beside the semi-dome, is found in the tetraconch at Rusafa (Mundell, "Deir Zaʿfaran"). The entire exterior doorway is shown in Parry, drawing opp. p. 109; on the doorway see also *supra* p. 104).

MONASTERY OF MAR ABRAHAM see MONASTERY OF MAR IBRAHIM

MONASTERY OF MAR ABRAHAM AND UBIL see MIDYAT

MONASTERY OF MAR AWGEN (EUGENIOS) pp. ix, xi, 1, 3–5, 10, 37, 38, 80–81; Fig. 2; Pls. 199–206

This monastery is ca. 18 km north-east of Nisibis and ca. 20 km south of Midyat. On Awgen, the patron saint and founder of the monastery, who is popularly credited with having brought monasticism from Egypt to Mesopotamia in the fourth century, see above p. 3, note 3.

Bibliography: Pognon, 109, note 1; Bell, *Amurath*, 310–312, fig. 194; Herzfeld, *OLZ*, 412; Guyer, "Surp Hagop", 500; Stryzgowski, *Syrie*, 29f., fig. 13; Monneret de Villard, 55, 57, 79, fig. 79; Dillemann, 234; Jarry, 236, no. 61; Fiey, *Nisibe*, 134–141; *idem, AB*, 80 (1962), 52f.; Brock, "Notes", Mar Awgen.
Bell negatives: M 120–132.

Dates: Inscriptions: vaulted chamber W of central court, built 1209 (note 6). Texts: twenty cells built 643–664 (?) (note 213); monastery refounded ca. 700 (note 11); church rebuilt 1271 *(ibid.)*.

Changes since 1911: not known.

See note 6a above concerning Bell's plan as originally published.
Unaware of the thirteenth century reconstruction date, Herzfeld and Guyer assigned this church and that of Mar Yoḥannan (below p. 141) to the eighth century. Monneret de Villard (p. 79) however, was informed of the 1271 rebuilding and considered the present construction characteristic of that period, especially the south chambers which he compared to contemporary structures at Mosul. This and the Mar Yoḥannan church differ from other "parochial" churches, not only in being monastic churches, but also in the absence of internal mural arcades. On "parochial" churches see above pp. viiif.

MONASTERY OF MAR BARṢAUMA see BA SEBRINA

MONASTERY OF MAR CYRIACUS (QURIAQOS = DEIR EL QIRA, DIRAKIRA), *(AYRANCI)* **nr. ZARGEL (ZERCIL)**, *(DANALI)* pp. 44, 58; Fig. 54

This monastery is ca. 15 km north of the Tigris, between the Batman and Redvan Rivers.

Bibliography: Bell, RGS Notes; Mingana, *Catalogue*, col. 364; Fiey, *Nisibe*, 258.
Bell negatives: none.

Dates: Text: monastery renovated 1481 (see infra).

Changes since 1911: not known.

The plan of this "monastic" church mentioned by Bell (p. 44) is reproduced here (Fig. 54) redrawn from her plan in the RGS Notes. It should be noted that the thickness of the outer east wall was not measured and that for convenience was taken to be the same as the west (0.75–0.79 m).

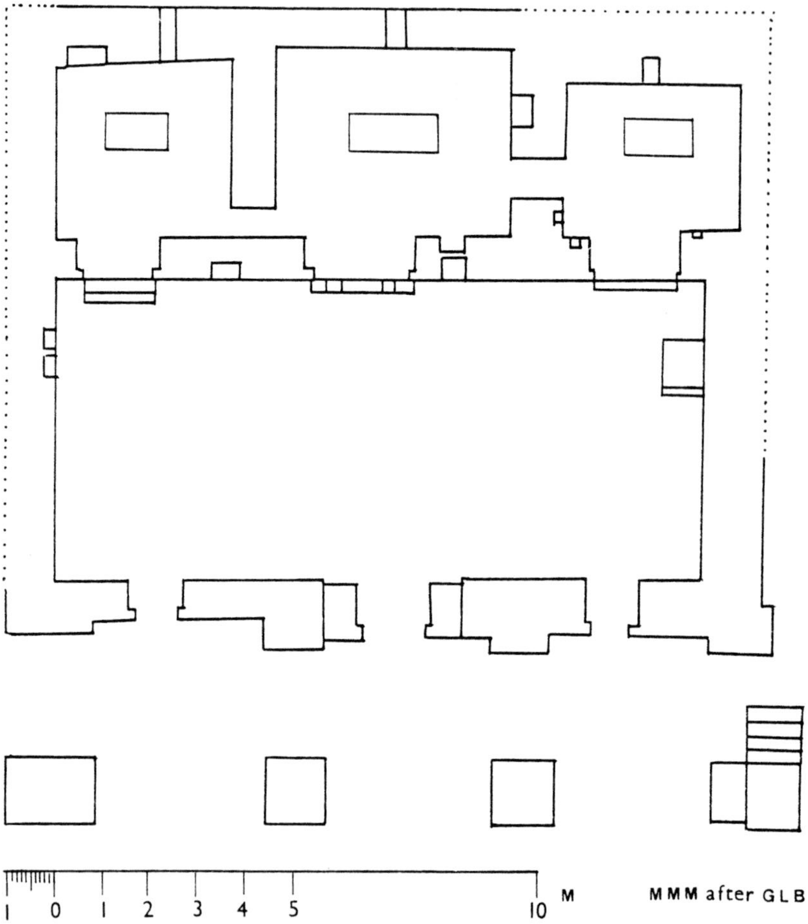

Fig. 54. Mar Cyriacus, plan of church redrawn from Bell, RGS Notes .

A colophon of AD 1483 written there mentions renovations to the monastery carried out two years previously and the fact that its monks then numbered 100 (Mingana, *Catalogue*, col. 364). On "monastic" churches see above p. ix.

MONASTERY OF MAR GABRIEL (DEIR EL 'UMAR), nr. KARTMIN (QARṬAMIN); *(YAYVANTEPE)* pp. iv–vi, 1, 6–10, 11, 31–35, 38; Figs. 4, 5, 19–22; Pls. 207–218

This monastery, ca. 18 km south-east of Midyat and 4 km north of Kartmin, and known also as that of Samuel (+ 408), Symeon (+ 433), and Gabriel (+ 667), is said to have been founded in AD 397 and to have been the recipient of imperial donations by several early Byzantine emperors including Anastasius (491–518) to whose beneficence are ascribed the main church and its mosaics. (On the history of the monastery see note 19 above.) Dillemann considered the monastery, which had Symeon as a titular saint from the fifth century (called monastery of Beth Mar Symeon; Nau, "Notice", 55, 98), to have been the *limes* fort Banasymeon refortified by Justinian (Procopius, *Buildings*, II.iv.14). In this connection it is interesting to note a rectangular tower which stands 500 m west of the monastery; see p. 6 above and M.H. Dolapönü, *Deyr-el-Umar (Mar Gabriyel).Tarihi* (Istanbul, 1971), fig. p. 32. If it was Banasymeon, the monastery may also have been a bishopric in the sixth century, for the *Notitia Antiochena* of 570 appears to list Banasymeon as a suffragan see of Dara (see above, p. iv). From ca. 614 the monastery was the residence of the bishop of the Ṭur 'Abdin until 1089/90 when it became that of the bishop of Qarṭamin, while the bishop of the Ṭur 'Abdin moved to Ḥaḥ. In 639 Mar Gabriel, abbot and bishop, after whom the monastery is now called, received a charter from the Caliph 'Umar I, which gave him authority over the Ṭur 'Abdin including the permission to build churches there (see also above p. vi). The monastery was evidently quite prosperous, owning many fields, mills, villages and other property (Nau, "Notice", 60) some of which was donated by Symeon d-Zayte (Brock, "Fenqitho", trans. of pp. 130, 138) from Ḥabsenas who was bishop of Ḥarran (700–734; see p. 117). One of these villages was Kaphar 'Ala which may be identified with Ḥarabeh 'Aleh (see p. 117).

Bibliography: Parry, 214–218; Pognon, 39–50, nos. 13–14; Nau, "Notice", 38–75; Krüger, *Mönchtum I;* Monneret de Villard, figs. 25, 52; Dillemann, 205, 225, 229, 234, 262 note 1, 318 note 2; Hage, 106; Jarry, 243–246, nos. 76–82; as well as bibliographies below. Bell negatives: M 146–158, R 194, 198–200.

Dates: Text: monastery founded 397 (supra); Banasymeon refortified ca. 530 (? supra).

Changes since 1911: A number of constructions have been added to the monastery, notably an enclosing wall on the south: see Dolapönü, *Tarihi* (see above), figs. on pp. 11, 108 and 119 (cf. Pl. 207), 122, 125f., 133, 141, 146f., 153.

In addition to the two churches and octagon, treated singly below, which have been the subject of subsequent publications, Bell describes and offers plans and/or photographs of other parts of the monastery including: the churches of the Forty Martyrs (p. 9 and p. 31 Fig 20); and of Mar Shim'un (p.6 and p.9; Pl. 209); the tomb of the Egyptian monks (p. 6, p. 10, p. 31, Figs. 4, 19; Pl. 208); and the tower mentioned above. See also Pls. 207, 210, 212 for other views.

Main Church pp. vi, ix, x, 6, 8–11,16,19,31–35; Figs. 5, 19, 21–22; Pls. 211, 213–218

Bibliography: In addition to the relevant parts of references given above: Preusser, 31–34, pls. 42–43; Guyer, "Surp Hagop", 498f., 505; Baumstark, "Alterskriterium", 117–120; Strzygowski, *Syrie*, 54f.; Reuther, 564f.; Monneret de Villard, 55–60,

77, fig. 53; Leroy, "Le décor", 75–81; Grabar, "Observations", 83–91; *idem*, *CRAI* 1968, 488f., 490–494; Hawkins and Mundell, "Mosaics", 279–296, figs. 1–49. Bell negatives: M 151–152, 155–157, R 198–200.

Dates: Text: church built and decorated 512 (infra).

Changes since 1911: In addition to the cement roof which replaces the tiled one, as mentioned by Leroy (*CRAI* 1968, 483), the following have changed (see Hawkins and Mundell, "Mosaics", fig. 4): a bell tower in the 1930's style has been added to the roof; all but one window in the south wall have been opened; a wall has been built against the west end of the south façade; and the construction with a half barrel vault against the same façade (visible in Pl. 216) has been removed leaving along the length of the wall a horizontal groove with remains of brick. Just above this groove and two courses below the lower windows is a row of ten blocks projecting from the wall. In the same wall under the south sanctuary window is a stone arch filled with brick. A tall stone altar, like those at Arnas and Kefr Zeh, has been placed in the sanctuary.

Bell describes the plan (p. 8) and masonry (p. 32) of this church, which she identifies with that built by Anastasius (pp. 8, 32) in AD 512 (see Nau, "Notice", 57f.; Hawkins and Mundell, "Mosaics"), although possibly based on the plan of an earlier church (p. 8). She gives other examples of this type of church (pp. 8f., 58; see also notes 21a, 152–155), which she calls "monastic" (p. 56), and traces its prototype to Babylonian latitudinal palace and temple chambers (pp. 8, 56) and, in turn, to the earlier Hittite *bît hilani* (pp. 56–57).
A sixth-century date for this church has not yet been seriously challenged although Guyer and Baumstark dated it seventh and ninth century respectively, on the basis of its resemblance to the church at Kaishum (Keysun; AD 818–845) west of the Euphrates. Guyer saw in the Mar Gabriel church the disseminating source in the Ṭur 'Abdin of the "monastic" church type which he and Herzfeld (Sarre and Herzfeld, *Reise*, II, 345) said was brought to Mesopotamia from Egypt, the home of monasticism. On the "monastic" church see p. ix above.
The recently exposed south façade (see above under *changes*) should perhaps be examined in the light of the passage in the history of the monastery where it states: "And all the church was built on the small stone which the angel and Mar Symeon posed and the foundations were not hidden in the earth and on the south side the masons allowed these to be seen and noticed without laying on them plaster (lime) or iron" (Nau, "Notice", 58f., 102f.). The projecting blocks in the south wall may be the remains of a portico on that side of the church, as mentioned in the history of the monastery, and which was sought by Bell (see pp. 8, 10, and note 21). The decorations of the sanctuary described by Bell—the *opus sectile* pavement (p. 8) and the vault mosaics (pp. 8f., 33f.)—have recently been studied (see notes 23; and 24–26, 93–102, respectively), and a Greek dedicatory inscription was discovered on the former (see note 96).

Church of el 'Adhra (= The Virgin) pp. 6, 9, 31; Figs. 5, 19

Bibliography: Monneret de Villard, 77, fig. 73. Bell negatives: none.

Changes since 1911: none known.

Bell describes this church as of a type known in the region of Mosul (p. 9). Monneret de Villard, relying on Herzfeld (Sarre and Herzfeld, *Reise* II 289f.) places these latter churches in the eleventh century (cf. Fiey, *Mossoul*) and suggests, therefore, a construction date after the pillage of the Mar Gabriel monastery by the Turks in AD 1075.

Main Octagon pp. 6, 9–10; Figs. 5, 19; Pl. 212

Bibliography: Monneret de Villard, 57f.; Hawkins and Mundell, "Mosaics", fig. 5; Leroy, *CRAI* 1968, 490, 492f., fig. 3; *idem*, "Baptistères", 1-4,6; figs. 1–2. Bell negative: R 194.

Dates: Inscription & Text: furniture provided 777 (note 33 and infra).

Changes since 1911: it has been cleaned out (cf. p. 9).

Leroy has pointed out that Bell's plan is incorrect. He has published a new plan and section (*CRAI* 1968, fig. 3 and "Baptistères", figs. 1–2) and suggests that the building was a baptistery of the Constantinian period (*ibid.*, 6, fig. 1). Attention may be drawn also to a similar, although smaller (diam. 7 m, as opposed to 10.50 m) octagon at Circesium, said to be Byzantine (Sarre and Herzfeld, *Reise*, I, 173, fig. 79). The stone and brick construction of the octagon at Mar Gabriel could be compared with that of the granary at Dara (Pl. 4) and the church of el ʻAdhra at Diyarbakır (Pl. 15), which are presumably ca. 500 AD, as well as with that of the later interior arcades of Mar Sovo at Ḥaḥ (Pl. 120) and Mar Philoxenus at Midyat (Pl. 175). Bell compared the size of the bricks of the octagon with those of Mar Shimʻun at Mar Gabriel (p. 9f; see also note 30) and of Mar Sovo at Ḥaḥ (see note 59). Bell's attribution of the octagon to the thirteenth century (p. 10) disregards the evidence for an earlier date offered by the history of the monastery which states that the stone block bearing the inscription of AD 777 was placed in the octagon in the eighth century (Pognon, 43f.; Nau, "Notice", 64f., 108f.).

MONASTERY OF MAR ḤANANIA see (MONASTERY OF) DEIR ZAʻFARAN

MONASTERY OF MAR IBRAHIM (ABRAHAM OF KASHKAR) pp. ix, xi, 37–38, 79; Fig. 50; Pls. 219–221

This monastery lies ca. 30 km north-east of Nisibis.
On the patron saint and founder, Abraham of Kashkar, see p. 37 and Fiey, *Nisibe*, 144.

Bibliography: Hinrichs, *PM*, 191, pl. 33; Monneret de Villard, 59; Dillemann, 234; Vööbus, *School*, 206; Leroy, *CRAI* 1968, 482; Jarry, 240f., no. 70; Fiey, *Nisibe*, 144–150. Bell negatives: none.

Dates: Text: monastery founded ca. 571 (note 210).

Changes since 1911: The monastery was pillaged in 1926.
(Fiey, *Nisibe*, 150 note 98).

As mentioned above (pp. 81, 115), the older remains of this church may have a bearing on the church of el ‘Adhra at Ḥaḥ. Bell has drawn further possible parallels at Deir Za‘faran and Nisibis for the decorated cornices and consoles (p. 81). The block with dentils (Pl. 221) could be similar to the mouldings at Salah (Pls. 240, 244, 247). As the foundation date, ca. 571, is known, any sculpture at Mar Ibrahim could help date other sculptures in this book. The capital shown (Pl.220) is, as Bell remarked (p. 81), unusual for the area and appears to be in the mainstream of Byzantine work. As far as can be determined from the photograph, this capital may be one of the two-zone Byzantine capitals with “Theodosian” *(feingezahnten)* acanthus leaves which Kitzinger dates generally to the second half of the fifth century and which he distinguishes from the type of capital known in the first half of the sixth century, where the zones are more clearly demarcated and of which the capital with plaited bottom at Mar Awgen is said, by Bell, to be an example (pp. 3f.); see Kitzinger, “Tapestry” (note 8 above), 17–19. The leaf style at Mar Ibrahim may resemble some of the “Thedodosian” types, e.g. *ibid.*, Figs. 55, 59, 64, 66–68, but it is difficult to be sure from the photograph reproduced here (Pl. 220). A few examples of fine-toothed acanthus have been found at Antioch and in the tetraconch at Seleucia Pieria (*Antioch-on-the-Orontes*, III, 150, pl. 34, nos. 26, 78, pp. 152, 158). Fifth to sixth century Byzantine two-zone capitals rarely have human figures on them. Examples may be cited from the neighbourhood of Antioch: 1) pilaster revetment capitals found in the tetraconch at Seleucia Pieria portray single standing angels and possibly an Annunciation among the acanthus leaves (*Antioch-on-the-Orontes*, III, pl. 26, nos. 461–472, pp. 146f.); and 2) genre (?) scenes set in rinceaux fill the upper zone of capitals in the Trinity church of the monastery of St. Symeon the Younger Stylite on the Wondrous Mountain (Djobadze in *Istanbuler Mitteilungen*, 15 [1965], 232f., pl. 53, 2). For a composition closer to that at Mar Ibrahim, one may turn to the *imago clipeata* type of Roman capital, e..g. that at Trier, dated perhaps AD 325 (E. von Mercklin, *Antike Figuralkapitelle* [Berlin, 1962], no. 346, fig. 645), an earlier type of which may be the second-century example in Augst (*ibid.*, no. 345 a, fig. 647).

MONASTERY OF MAR IBRAHIM AND MAR UBIL see MIDYAT

MONASTERY OF MAR KYRIAKOS see MONASTERY OF MAR CYRIACUS

MONASTERY OF MAR LAZARUS see ḤABSENAS

MONASTERY OF MAR MALKA (MELKE), nr. ḤARABEH ‘ALEH pp. 8, 38–39; Fig. 24; Pl. 222

The monastery is ca. 2 km from Ḥarabeh ‘Aleh (on which see p. 117). On the patron saint and history of the monastery see Fiey, *Nisibe*, 141–143.

Bibliography: Bell, *Amurath*, 312f.; Krüger, “Mönchtum” II, 28–31; Reuther, 564; Monneret de Villard, 57, fig. 55; Dillemann, 234; Fiey, *Nisibe*, 141–143; Brock, “Notes”, Mar Melke. Bell negatives: M 140–144.

Changes since 1911: The church was destroyed ca. 1926 and rebuilt in 1955 (Fiey, *Nisibe*, 143). The monastery was restored again in 1973 and is inhabited now by one monk and two nuns (Brock, “Notes”, Mar Melke).

On "monastic" churches see above p. ix.

MONASTERY OF MAR SHIM'UN (SYMEON), nr. BA SEBRINA

This ruined monastery is 5 km east of Ba Sebrina (*Handbook*, 278) on which see p. 100 above. Krüger merely quotes Bell on this monastery and has nothing of historical interest to add.

Bibliography: Bell, UN Journal 1909; *idem, Amurath*, 303f.; *Handbook*, 278; Krüger, "Mönchtum" II, 45. Bell negatives: none.

Changes since 1911: not known.

In *Amurath* Bell says only that the monastery was "of little architectural interest". Her Journal continues: "The church is a chapel without aisles, 2 engaged piers on either side of the nave, very high walls and a vault. The half caps. of the piers are built and plastered–no decoration. To the S of it lies a kind of vaulted narthex separating it from the central court of the monastery in which is a vaulted cistern or spring. The monastic buildings are vaulted chambers on the N, W, S of the court" (UN Journal 1909, 17 May). It sounds as if this monastery chapel was also, as in the case of the two monastery chapels at Ba Sebrina (p. 100), of the "parochial" type, i.e. a vaulted single-naved building with a vaulted narthex to the south and a court beyond that, although the *beth ṣlotha* is apparently lacking here. On "parochial" churches see above p. viii.

MONASTERY OF MAR TAHMAZGERD see KERKUK

MONASTERY OF MAR YA 'QUB see ṢALAḤ

MONASTERY OF MAR YOḤANNAN ṬAYAYA (= JOHN THE BEDOUIN OR THE ARAB)
pp. ix, 5f.; Fig. 3; Pls. 223–226

This monastery lies about 3 km north-east of the monastery of Mar Awgen (see p. 135). On the patron saint and history of the monastery see note 13.

Bibliography: Bell, *Amurath*, 312f.; Herzfeld, *OLZ*, 412; Guyer, "Surp Hagop", 500f.; Monneret de Villard, 78f., fig. 78; Fiey, *Nisibe*, 154–157, Brock, "Notes", Mar Ioḥannan. Bell negatives: M 133–139.

Dates: Inscription: vaulted chamber built 12th–13th century (note 14); Text: monastery founded ca. 500 (?), note 13; kitchen installed 643–664 (?), note 14.

Changes since 1911: There are no guardians at the monastery at present and the church has suffered damage inflicted by the Kurds (Brock, "Notes", Mar Ioḥannan).

Herzfeld and Guyer considered the narthex dome on squinches to be eighth-century and dated accordingly both this church and that of Mar Awgen, although the latter is now known to have been rebuilt in 1271 (see p. 135). Monneret de Villard thought the church of Mar Yoḥannan no earlier than the eleventh century. Both this and the church of Mar Awgen lack the interior mural arcades which characterize the "parochial" churches of the Ṭur 'Abdin (see above p. viii). The tower illustrated here (Pl. 226) has the same small, rough stone construction as the towers at Ba Sebrina (Pl. 106) and Ḥaḥ (Pl. 149) but does not taper at the top as they do.

MONASTERY OF MIRIAM EL 'ADHRA see BA SEBRINA

NISIBIS (NISIBIN, *NUSAYBIN*) pp. iii, iv, vi, vii, 1, 37

Known from the beginning of the first millenium, Nisibis was a Seleucid provincial capital under the name of Antioch on the Mygdonius. It was Roman 68–58 BC, then mostly Parthian until AD 165. The Sasanians unsuccessfully besieged the city in 338, 346, and 350. It was ceded to the Persians in 363 by Jovian's treaty on condition that its population could emigrate to Roman territory. Many of its people moved then to Amida (see above p. 105) and Edessa (see below p. 152). While in Roman territory Nisibis was a bishopric under Amida; under Persian rule it became the metropolitan bishopric of Beth 'Arabaye. Among the refugees to Edessa in 363 were St. Ephrem and those scholars who were to found and staff what was known as the School of the Persians at Edessa. Because of its Nestorian bias, the School was closed by the Byzantine Emperor in 457 and its personnel removed themselves to Nisibis where a School was founded in 489. Nisibis figured in the sixth-century wars between Byzantium and Persia and was considered a gateway between the two states. This status was lost after the Arab conquest and from 640 it declined in importance, although Christian building continued there (see p. 162 below). Hamdanid rule was briefly interrupted in 943 and 972 when the Byzantines took the city. At the end of the tenth century the Marwanids were in control of Nisibis and from ca. 1106, the Ortokids. In 1182 it fell to Ṣalaḥ al Din. On the Christian monuments of Nisibis see Fiey, *Nisibe*; concerning *ibid.*, p. 126, it should be pointed out that the church of St. Febronia restored by Symeon d-Zayte (see p. 109), who built and rebuilt a number of churches in Nisibis (AD 700–734), is not the church illustrated by S. Guyer in *Meine Tigrisfahrt*, pl. IV B. The latter is located in Nizib (Nizip) west of the Euphrates and not in Nisibis.

Bibliography: Dillemann, 80f. and see index; Vööbus, *School*; Fiey, *Nisibe*, 1–133; art. "Naṣībīn" by E. Honigmann in *EI* (1928–36).

Bridge p. vii; Pl. 69

Bibliography: Oppenheim, *Mittelmeer*, 31; Dillemann, 81, 130. Bell negative: R 86.

Changes since 1911: not known.

The bridge is to the south outside the town over the Djaghjagh (Mygdonius, Hirmas, Masaq or Maskas) River. It has twelve arches. It was said by Yakut (AD 1179–1229) to have been "built by the Greeks" (Dillemann, 130). This bridge could be compared to the smaller bridges at Dara (Pl. 2) and Urfa (Pl. 85).

Colonnade Pl. 68

Bibliography: Parry, 225 and fig. opp. p. 223; Oppenheim, *Mittelmeer*, 31; Preusser, 39f., fig. 10; Dillemann, 81. Bell negative: R 105.

Changes since 1911: not known.

This colonnade is in the south-west part of the city near the south gate. Two columns bear a section of architrave and stand at right angles to the other three. The front of the architrave has three fascias (Preusser, fig. 10) and the three remaining capitals are Corinthian.

Church of Mar Ya'qub (Ya'kup = Jacob of Nisibis) pp. vii–ix, xi, 1, 64, 70–73, 81; Fig. 55; Pls. 70–83

On the patron saint, Mar Ya'qub of Nisibis, see Fiey, *Nisibe*, 21–26.

Bibliography: Parry, 225–227, 329–335; Preusser, 40–44, figs. 10–11, pls. 49–52; Guyer, "Amida", 205f., figs. 5–6; Sarre and Herzfeld, *Reise*, II, 336–346, figs. 314–317; IV, pls. CXXXVIII–CXXXIX; Strzygowski, *Syrie* 9, 30, 147, 161, 171, figs. 3, 87; Monneret de Villard, 57–60, fig. 57; A. Grabar, *Martyrium*, I (Paris, 1945), 79, 86, 195, 196, 337, 446, 586, fig. 12; Khatchatrian, "Le baptistère de Nisibe", *Actes du Ve Congrès international d'archéologie chrétienne. Aix-en-Provence 1954*, Studi di antiquità cristiana, 22 (Vatican, 1957), 407–421; Jarry, 242f., nos. 73–75; Krautheimer, 317, 517 note 6; Fiey, *Nisibe*, 23, 29f., 75–77, 130f. Bell negatives: R 87–104.

Dates: Inscriptions: baptistery built 359 (note 193 & infra) ; church restored 1872 (note 186). Text: church rebuilt 713–758 (p. 144), 1562 (p. 145)

Changes since 1911: none known.

Bell's two great failings as regards this church were pointed out and corrected by Herzfeld. Neither Bell nor Preusser properly distinguished the several phases of construction, the most noticeable and important of which are three: 1) the south church which was a baptistery dated by inscription to AD 359; 2) the north church added 713–758; 3) a reconstruction, particularly of the south-west section and of the north wall and arcade of the north church, dated by inscription to AD 1872. The three types of masonry (large ashlar blocks, smaller ashlar blocks and small well worked blocks) are clearly visible. A fourth type of small rough stones probably represents another modern phase. Furthermore, Bell's reasoning about the present dome over the south church was found to be deficient: the present dome is sufficiently supported because the three large windows in the east wall were filled. Undoubtedly the church is further buttressed now that it is buried in earth on three sides. Herzfeld offers a reconstruction of the baptistery with a pyramidal wooden roof and an open porch (*Reise*, II, fig. 317) and he links its architectural form to antique funerary buildings of Syria. Moreover, he saw in the original baptistery the prototype of the church of el 'Adhra at Ḥaḥ whose dome he also considered a later addition; the reconstruction of the latter church produced by Guyer ("Le rôle", fig. 1) resembles that by Herzfeld of the Nisibis building. The type of construction of the eastern windows of the baptistery (Pls. 70, 78) of a lintel resting on two monolithic uprights is compared below with some windows remaining at Sha'ib Shahr in the Tektek Mountains and with those of some fourth century churches in northern Syria, notably that at Fafertin (AD 372), see below p. 151.
The north church of Mar Ya'qub may throw some light on the problems of the "parochial" churches of the Ṭur 'Abdin, as it is a dated example (713–758) of a

hall church with lateral arcades (see above p. ix).
The Greek inscription of 359 is still in situ on a moulded string course between the two central doors of the south façade (Pl. 74). It was first noticed by Ainsworth in 1837 and was successfully deciphered in Sarre and Herzfeld, *Reise*, II, 337f., and recently republished by Jarry (242f., no. 74). It records the construction of the baptistery by the bishop Volagesos in 359, four years before Nisibis was ceded to the Persians. The cathedral to which the baptistery belonged was built between 312–320 by the bishop Mar Ya'qub (Chronicle of Elias of Nisibis, written AD 1019, see Fiey, *Nisibe*, 23) whose tomb is said to be that in the crypt of the south church. This cathedral has disappeared and its remains may lie under the mound adjacent to the present church (*ibid.*, 30). Fiey has pointed out that the building of the north church, which was completed in 758, was started in 713 (*ibid.*, 71f., 76f., 130f.).

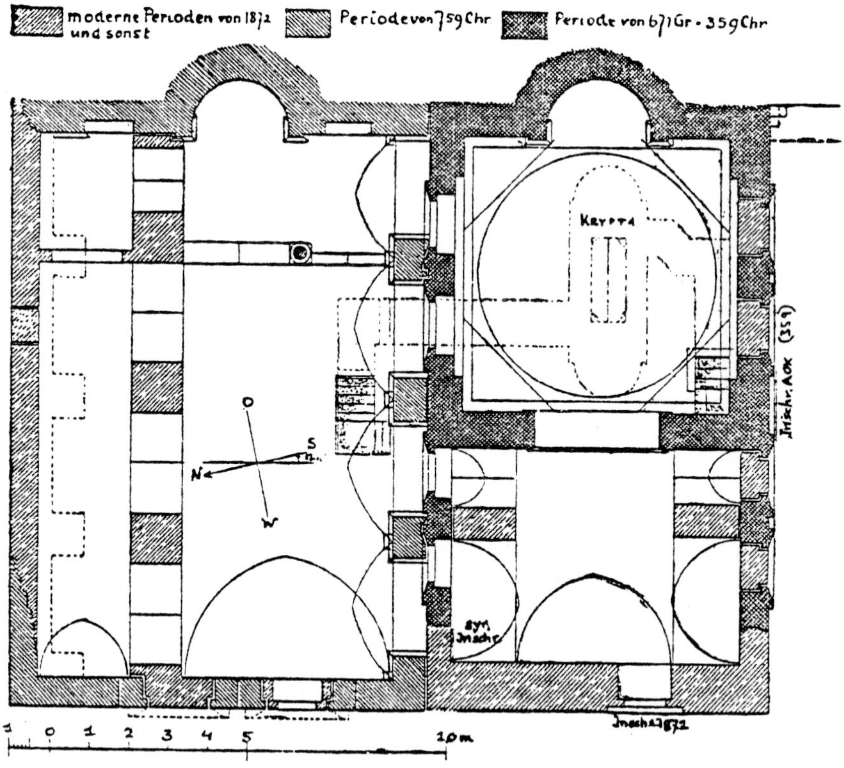

Fig. 55. Nisibin, Mar Ya'qub, plan of church in Sarre and Herzfeld, *Reise*, II, 315 (cf. Fig. 46 above)

Another reconstruction of the church is noted in AD 1562 (*ibid.*, 112); see the summary of the history of the cathedral *ibid.*, 130–132. A Syriac inscription to the left inside the present entrance is indicated on Herzfeld's plan and is probably the same as the one mentioned by Fiey (*ibid.*, 120 note 644) who gives its dimensions (50 x 50 cm), but no text. On the sculpture of the church see pp. xf., 70f., above.

QAL'AT ḤATEM ṬAY (RHABDIOS, TOU RHABDIOU, TURABDION ?) pp. iv, v, 38, 79; Fig. 56; Pls. 228–231

This site, ca. 40 km north-east of Nisibis and ca. 5km north of Serwan, was planned by Taylor (Fig. 56). Bell identified it with the *limes* fort Rhabdios which was said to be situated on a large rock surrounded by "the Field of the Romans" *(Rhomaios agros)*. The general aspect of Qal 'at Ḥatem Ṭay (Pl. 228; Map) would seem to accord with this description.

Bibliography: Procopius, *Buildings*, II.iv.1–13; Nau, "Resumé", 7; Taylor, *JRGS*, 35 (1865), 52f., fig. no. 3; Bell, *Amurath*, 306–308, fig. 193; *idem*, UN Journal 1909; Dillemann, 37, 62, 84, 100, 104, 108, 220, 223, 225, 239. Bell negatives: M 113–118.

Dates: Inscription: fort rebuilt (?) 1232/3 (infra) ; Texts: fort built ca. 349 (*ibid.*); fort rebuilt ca. 530 *(ibid.)*.

Changes since 1911: not known.

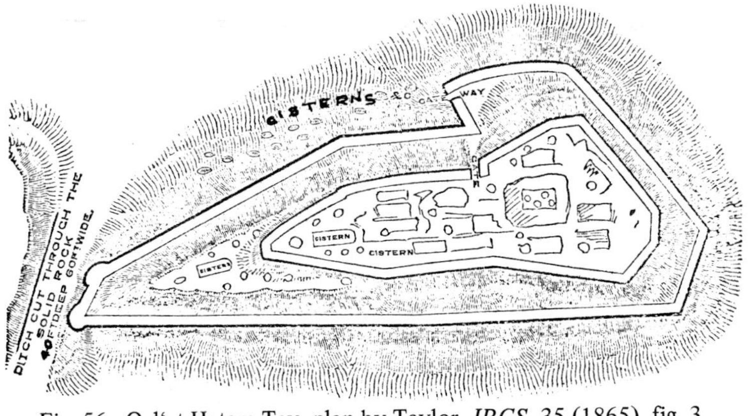

Fig. 56. Qal'at Ḥatem Ṭay, plan by Taylor, *JRGS* 35 (1865), fig. 3

In *Amurath* (306–308) Bell commented: "The summit of the hill is enclosed in a double line of fortification following the contours of the slopes. The lower ring is provided with towers at the angles of the wall and with round bastions of very slight projection. Within the inner enclosure stands the citadel, now completely ruined and bearing evidence of frequent reconstruction. The oldest parts are unmistakenly Byzantine masonry and contain a chapel of which the apse is well preserved" (Pl. 230). She further notes an Arabic inscription (which gives only the date AD 1232/3; Pl. 229) whose reuse in the walls of the citadel would imply two medieval rebuildings; smaller cisterns between the two walls and a large one inside the citadel. The vault of Pl. 231 may be that referred to in Bell's UN Journal 1909 as "a vault partly of bricks laid slanting against the mur de tête" (18 May). She concludes about the constructions: "... the ruins, therefore, exhibit Yezidi or Arab work (or both) upon Byzantine foundations and ... that the castle of Hatem Tay is that of Rhabdion ..." (*Amurath*, 308).

On the double line of walls which is an essential feature in discussions of late Roman and early Byzantine fortification see above p. 103. The niche in the apse (Pl. 230) resembles both a *mihrab* and a niche in the wall of the *beth ṣlotha* of Mar Dodo at Ba Sebrina (Pl. 105).

The eact relationship between the names Rhabdios, tou Rhabdiou (Greek *Rhabdion* = "a small rod") and the Syriac *Ṭur 'Abdin* (= "mountain of the servants [of God]", which is not a mixture of Arabic and Syriac as Dillemann states, p. 31) is not clear. Procopius says that the fort Rhabdios was (re-?)fortified by Justinian and that it protected the flat, fertile fields round it, the Field of the Romans, which were, in fact, surrounded by Persian territory (*Buildings*, II.iv.1–13). This account has been matched (Dillemann, 31, 104) to that given in the *Life* of Ya'qub Ḥabisha (on whose monastery at Ṣalaḥ see below p. 147) in which the Emperor Constantius, after having fortified Amida (AD 349), built two large castles to protect the lands which were next to the Persians; it specifies that "the Ṭur 'Abdin was in the middle of this land". One fortress was on "the frontier of Beth 'Arabaye on the top of the mountain", and the other was Ḥasan Keyf on the Tigris (Nau, "Resumê", 7). Dillemann (fig. XXXIII: copied onto the map below p. 185) does not equate the Field of the Romans with the Ṭur 'Abdin, although this is a possible interpretation. A suffragan bishopric of Turabdion is listed under Dara in the *Notitia Antiochena* of 570 (see above p. iv). Whether this is to be identified with the fort Rhabdios (and, therefore, with Qal'at Ḥatem Ṭay), or whether it is to be sought elsewhere in the Ṭur 'Abdin, is open to question. From 614 the bishop of the Ṭur 'Abdin was resident at the Mar Gabriel monastery (Honigmann, *Barṣauma*, 140). The latter has been identified as the *limes* fort Banasymeon (Dillemann, 229), and Banasymeon is apparently also listed as a suffragan bishop of Dara in the same *Notitia* as Turabdion (Honigmann, *BZ*, 75, 83f.; see also above p. iv). It is suggested above that Ḥaḥ may also have been a bishopric in the sixth century (above p. 111), and perhaps this was the seat of the bishop of Turabdion.

Qal'at Ḥatem Ṭay is mentioned repeatedly in the accounts of the Mongol period and beyond (AD 1394–1474; Bar Hebraeus, Appendix). Although a place of refuge for Christian villagers of the Ṭur 'Abdin during the Mongol attack of 1394 (*ibid.*, p. xxxiv), it was apparently in the fifteenth century more often a source of hardship for them at the hands of its Turkish lord (*ibid*, p. xliv).

QAL'AT EL JEDID p.38 ; Pl. 227

The fort is situated ca. 23 km north-east of Nisibis.

Bibliography: Bell, *Amurath*, 309 note 1. Bell negative: M 119.

Changes since 1911: not known.

Bell was unable to ascend and inspect this site but she proposed that it be identified with the Persian fort of Sisarbanon, destroyed by Belisarius, although she admitted that it is farther from Qal'at Ḥatem Ṭay than the three miles that separated Sisarbanon from Rhabdios (*Amurath*, 309 note 1). On the identification of Sisarbanon with the modern Serwan see Dillemann, 60, 83, 229. Qal'at el Jedid has been identified with the "new citadel" mentioned in the fifteenth century (Bar Hebraeus, Appendix, p. xxxiv; and Socin, 239).

ṢALAḤ (ṢALIḤ, ṢALḤE, SHILLOḤ), *(BARIŞTEPE)*

This village, which lies about 5 km north-east of Midyat, is not to be confused with the Ṣalaḥ (Solachon) south of Mardin. The Syriac writer Daniel of Ṣalaḥ in the Ṭur 'Abdin flourished ca. AD 540 (J.B. Chabot, *Littérature syriaque* [Paris, 1934], 68). In the Life of Mar Ya'qub (see below) the village is called Shilloḥ (Nau, "Resumé", 9) and in medieval manuscript notes, e.g. Leroy, *Manuscrits*, 329, it appears as Ṣalaḥ. It was attacked in 1454 and 1693 (see below). On the village see also Anschütz, "Ortschaften", 182f.

Monastery of Mar Ya'qub Ḥabisha (=Jacob the Recluse; Jacob the Egyptian) pp. xi, 8, 10–13, 16, 27, 33, 39–44, 45, 78, 81, 82; Figs. 6–7, 25–28; Pls. 232–248

In the manuscript note mentioned above (Leroy, *op. cit.*) the monastery of Ṣalaḥ is called that of Mar Ya'qub the Intercessor and Mar Saba and his eleven disciples. According to his *Life*, Mar Ya'qub (also known as the Recluse and not to be confused with the Ya'qub the Recluse cited by Bell on p. 43) came from a monastery at Alexandria to Amida and then went on to the Ṭur 'Abdin where he founded a monastery at Shilloḥ (Ṣalaḥ) on the spot where his contemporary Mar Barshabba (= Saba ?), an abbot, and his ten or eleven disciples were martyred by a Persian general. Ya'qub died AD 421 and his monastery grew large and prosperous (Nau, "Resumé", 3–12). On Barshabba and Saba see *ibid.*, 10 note 1. From AD 1292 the monastery was the seat of a bishop and in the mid-fourteenth, of the schismatic patriarch of the Ṭur 'Abdin (Honigmann, *Barṣauma*, 162). In addition to the main church studied by Bell there is at its south-east corner a smaller church dedicated to Mar Bar Ḥadbshabo (Pognon, 62), i.e. Barshabba. There are burials under this building and in other buildings to the south of the main church and east of the monastery (*ibid.*, 69). What Bell and others refer to as the ruins of the patriarchal palace (see note 35), north of the main church, are illustrated in Pl. 241. A church dedicated to Mar Pinḥas was built at the monastery before 1481 (Fiey, *Nisibe*, 173 note 65).

Bibliography: Parry, 180f., 331–335; Pognon, 62–71, nos. 22–33; Preusser, 35–40, fig. 9, pls. 44–48; Bell, *Amurath*, 319; Guyer, "Surp Hagop", 498; Nau, "Resumé", 3–12; Krüger, "Mönchtum" II, 26f.; Reuther, 564; Monneret de Villard, 57, 59f., fig. 57; Strzygowski, *Syrie*, 105, 157–159, figs. 14, 68, 93–95; Vööbus, *Asceticism*, II, 227; Fiey, *Nisibe*, 205; Deichmann and Peschlow, *Ruinenstätten*, 24; Anschütz, "Ortschaften", 182f.
Bell negatives: M 182–195, R 191–193, 195–197, 201.

Dates: Text: monastery founded before 421 (supra); monastery attacked 1454 (p. 148), 1693 *(ibid.)*.

Changes since 1911: A cement roof, like that at Mar Gabriel, has replaced the tiled one; the fill in the narthex arcade has been mortared; the windows in the south wall have been unblocked and a construction placed at the south-west corner.

Bell considered this "monastic" church one of the two most solidly constructed buildings in the Ṭur ʻAbdin (pp. 10–13, 39), where its ornamented sanctuary door was "without rival" (pp. 11f., 41ff.). She shifted her dating of this church from ca. 397 (p. 10), to the sixth century (pp. 44, 79),, and then finally to ca. 700 (pp. 82f.). On the basis of its resemblance to the Kaishum church (AD 818–845) Guyer assigned Mar Yaʻqub to the ninth century and suggested that the ornamented pilasters (Pl. 246) were *spolia* from an earlier church. Deichmann and Peschlow consider it to be sixth century (*Ruinenstätten*, 24). Aside from the epitaphs from the tenth century onwards (see p. 10; note 116) there are no dated inscriptions published from the church. (See p. 43 and note 117 for painted inscriptions inside the nave.) In AD 1454 Ṣalaḥ was attacked and in 1693 the monastery was plundered by Rustem Bey and it "remained a ruin without inhabitants" (Bar Hebraeus, Appendix, pp. xlii, liii); the church itself betrays little sign of rebuilding, however. On the "monastic" churches in general, see p. ix above, and on the sculpture of this church see p. xi above.

SARE *(SARIKÖY?)*

From this village, which lies 3 km south-east of Ba Sebrina, Pognon, Preusser, and Bell published a stele with an Aramaic inscription and relief. Socin gives the Syriac name of the village as Gaveito (p. 259 no. 12).

Bibliography: Socin, 259; Pognon, 108–112, 115, no. 60, pl. VI above; Bell, *Amurath*, 305, fig. 192; Preusser, 29, fig. 7.

Church of Mar Malka (?)

Bibliography: Bell, UN Journal 1909; *idem, Amurath*, 305f.; Fiey, *Mossoul*, 93; *idem, Nisibe*, 141 note 48.

This church remains unnamed by Bell, but Fiey *(Nisibe)* refers to a "mignonne petite église" dedicated to Mar Malka in this village. Bell's description of the church in *Amurath* was limited to its fleas. Her Journal adds: "Two piers in nave w[ith] 2 barrel vaults running N.S. Then the sanctuary" (1909, 17 May). Fiey *(Mossoul)* states the entrance is on the west. This would seem to be another church or chapel of the "parochial" plan (cf. Fig. 33 and pp. 101, 121) on which see p. viii.

SHAʻIB SHAHR see TEKTEK MOUNTAINS

SHORISH see ḤIRBET SHORISH

SILVAN see MAYAFARQIN

TEKTEK MOUNTAINS

These low limestone hills run north to south between Urfa and Harran on the west and

Viranşehir and Resh'aina (Ras el 'Ain) on the east. Waterless, but offering good grazing in the spring, they have been inhabited from early times by semi-nomadic Arabs, the 'Arab of Syriac sources, whose territory reached from here down to the Mesopotamian plain to the south and stretched east to the Tigris; the Persian district of Beth 'Arabaye had Nisibis as its capital (see Segal, "Communities", 119f. and Dillemann, 75–78). Few modern travellers have explored these hills and the precise location of the few reported sites is questionable. This problem arises with respect to two monuments which Bell recorded in her Journal (see below). Aside from inscriptions, the only monuments hitherto published of the Tektek Dağ are those at Sumatar which Segal has examined and interpreted as Sabian cult buildings linked with similar structures known to have been at Harran (J.B. Segal, "Pagan Syrian Monuments in the Vilayet of Urfa", *Anatolian Studies*, 3 [1953], 97–120). A survey of the Tektek mountains in 1956 under the direction of Rice and Segal included work done on "monasteries, a castle (mainly Islamic), other buildings, inscriptions, sculpture and architectural remains": *ibid.*, 7 (1957), 7.

Qaṣr Antar and Qaṣr el Banat (?)

These are apparently two adjacent monuments in the Tektek Mountains. Bell's description of them states: "At 8 we reached the two ruins known as Kasr el Benat and Kasr Antar, the first to the S, a square stone fortress, the latter apparently a tower partly round exterior, inside something like this [Fig. 57 below] traces of Corinthian capitals. I should think the two are part of Justinian's fortification. It is this place Opp. calls Tell Sahal" (Bell, UN Journal 1911, 16 May).

A number of problems arise from this account. It is clear that this site is not the same as the Qaṣr el Banat visited by Oppenheim and Moritz from which were published a number of Syriac inscriptions (Moritz, 1899, 168–171, nos. 4–7) said to derive from a monastery (of Mar Lazarus?, *ibid.*, 168f., no. 4; see also p. 111 above) and one Greek (Oppenheim and Lucas, 61, no. 97), and where a tower tomb like that at Fafi (above p.109) is also reported to stand (Pognon, 16 note 1, 105 note 1; Segal, *Edessa*, 29). According to Oppenheim's map (Oppenheim and Lucas, *BZ*, 1905) Qaṣr el Banat lies 30 km north-east of Sha'ib Shahr. As Bell arrived at Qaṣr el Banat and Qaṣr Antar at 8:00, stopped to take photographs (Pls. 249–252), and then arrived at her next destination, Sha'ib Shahr (see below p. 151), at 9:30, it is unlikely that she travelled 30 km; furthermore, she was travelling from the east (Ras el 'Ain), not the north-east. Hinrichs (*PM*, 257) also stopped at Sha'ib Shahr from which he took over five hours to travel north ca. 10 km to Sumatar. Before arriving at Sha'ib Shahr, coming from Ras el 'Ain, Hinrichs notes: "... gegen 10 Uhr gelangten wir an die merkwürdige Ruine eines sechseckigen Gebäudes, bei der wir längere Zeit verweilten, und nach etwa 45 Minuten (arrived) zu ... Shaib Shahr". Hinrichs' map shows two sites marked "Ru. el Glea" and "R. Chan" both about 3 km south-east of Sha'ib Shahr and less than 1 km apart. The *Handbook of Mesopotamia* gives as the sources for its route 129a (p. 363) Hinrichs' report and that of an anonymous traveller. Sha'ib Shahr is given at 22 miles from Harran (i.e. the west) and at 24¼ the unnamed "Ruins of a hexagonal building possibly the Qasr el Bint of another authority". The latter may well have been Bell herself, a plausible suggestion in view of the fact that her (unacknowledged) photographs illustrate the

Handbook. It would seem that the Qaṣr el Banat (Pl. 252), her monument "to the S[outh]", may correspond to both "Ru. Chan" of Hinrichs' map and the unnamed "sechseckige Gebäude" of his report, if Bell's building is not a "square stone fortress", as her Journal states, but a hexagonal one (see below). The Qaṣr Antar (Pls. 249–251) of Bell would then be the "Ru. el Glea" of the map, as it is said to be the northernmost of the two monuments and is round on the exterior. By "Opp. calls Tell Sahal" *supra*, Bell may refer to R. Kiepert's map (1893) used by Oppenheim in *Mittelmeer*, where Tell Sahal, however, is indicated west rather than east (as one would expect of Bell's itinerary) of Sha'ib Shahr. By "Justinian's fortification" she must mean Sahal, mentioned in the Peutinger Table between Harran and Resh'aina (Ras el 'Ain; Dillemann, 165 note 2).

Bibliography: Oppenheim, *Mittelmeer*, map; Oppenheim and Lucas, 9, 61 and map; Moritz, 1899, 168–172, nos. 4–7; Hinrichs, *PM*, 257, pl. 34; *Handbook,* 363f., Bell, UN Journal 1911; Dillemann, 165; Segal, *Edessa*, 29.

Qaṣr el Banat Pl. 252

Bibliography: see above. Bell negative: T 146.

Changes since 1911: not known.

In the absence of further notes and photographs it is not possible to comment on this monument beyond noting a general similarity between the masonry and that at Qaṣr Antar and Sha'ib Shahr. Unfortunately Bell did not plan this building and merely says that it is "a square stone fortress" (see above p. 149). It is not symmetrical, however, as the tower (?) on the left is larger than that on the right, and it is difficult to be sure if the curtain wall on the left runs in a straight line to that still standing on the right. As mentioned above, this may be a hexagonal building.

Qaṣr Antar Fig. 57; Pls. 249–251

Bibliography: see above. Bell negatives: T 149–152.

Changes since 1911: not known.

Unfortunately, Bell's hurried, unmeasured sketch (Fig. 57) is inadequate. Pl. 249 shows the curved exterior wall of one side but the projecting area in the centre, which has a half-arched entrance (?) four courses high, is not indicated on this plan (Fig. 57 directly below). Inside it would seem there are remains of at least three

Fig. 57. Qaṣr Antar, sketch plan in Bell, UN Journal 1911

niches (Fig. 57; Pls. 250–251) with profiled archivolts resting on Corinthian capitals. What appears to be another Corinthian capital is visible on the ground in the centre of Pl. 251. The walls are massive and the structure may have been a tower tomb. Round towers used for cultic practises have been studied at Sumatar (Soğmatar) just north of Qaṣr Antar in the Tektek Mountains, by Segal ("Pagan Syrian Monuments" cited above p. 149).

Sha'ib Shahr Pls. 253–256

This site is in the Tektek Mountains (on which see p.148f.) ca. 30 km east of Harran, ca. 62 km west of Ras el 'Ain, and, apparently, ca. 3 km north-west of the two preceding monuments (see above p. 149).

Bibliography: Oppenheim and Lucas, 9, 62, no. 98; Pognon, 23 note 1; Bell, UN Journal 1911; Hinrichs, *PM*, 257; *Handbook*, 363; Deichmann and Peschlow, *Ruinenstätten*, 16. Bell negatives: T 155–159.

Changes since 1911: not known.

In her Journal Bell describes the site thus: "We got to Sha'ib Shahr at 9:30; a very large ruined town, stone built with lots of caves (inhabited by banu) some tombs, some houses. There was a building that looked like a church with aisles but no apse at the E end, though it was oriented. Stone dwelling houses in storeys, like the N. Syrian building. It was all full of sheep ..." (UN Journal 1911, 16 May). According to Oppenheim, the ruins were well preserved: one saw houses with gables, streets, small houses in courtyards, which had entrances to large subterranean rock-cut dwellings. To the south he found an Arab cemetery from which he published a number of Kufic inscriptions (M. van Berchem, "Arabische Inschriften", in M. von Oppenheim, *Inschriften aus Syrien, Mesopotamien und Kleinasien* [Leipzig, 1909–13], 64–66, nos. 87–97). Hinrichs also described the subterranean buildings.
The general view of the site (Pl. 253) shows the same type of ashlar masonry as the two other sites in the Tektek Mountains mentioned above. The window construction of a flat lintel on two monolithic uprights is found in northern Syria, especially in fourth-century churches, e.g. Fafertin (AD 372), Batuta and Simkhar (Butler, *Architecture* II, B, 330, 334f., ills. 370, 375, 382) and at the east end of Mar Ya'qub at Nisībis (AD 359; Pls. 70, 78), see above p. 143.

Domestic Building (?) Pls. 254–256

This building resembles in several respects the small one at Ḥaḥ (p. 113; Fig. 52; Pls. 129–130); in the proportions, ashlar masonry, the cyma cornice at the top of the wall and gable, and the small arcuated window. Here, however, there is an open arcade on the nearest side (the far wall is destroyed) rather than internal arcades as at Hah. It appears that the building at Sha'ib Shahr may have been roofed with pitched stone slabs (rather than with wooden beams as seems likely at Ḥaḥ) judging by: the large slabs visible in the rubble in Pl. 256; the rebate along the pitched gable cornice (Pl. 255); what looks like longitudinal grooves in the wall cornice (rather than the notches for wooden beams); and the two buttresses flanking the surviving arch (the buttress on the right is partially destroyed). Such stone roofs are known in Syria, e.g. that of the chapel (?) of a *pandocheion* (?) at Qaṣr el Banat in the Jebel Riḥa of northern Syria, which is composed of well-fitted slabs (Butler, *Architecture* II, B, 140–142, ill. 164). The function of the building at Sha'ib Shahr remains uncertain, but it would seem to be one of the houses leading to the subterranean chambers mentioned by Bell, Oppenheim, and Hinrichs, or some other domestic structure, rather than the "church with aisles" (Bell). A similar small buiding with an open arcade in Cappadocia is to be published by S. Hill in a forthcoming volume of *Anatolian Studies.*

TELLA DE MAUZELAT see VIRANŞEHIR

ṬUR 'ABDIN

See the Introduction and p. 146 above. In addition to the cities on its periphery listed above (p. iii), the following sites included in this book are within it: 1) the villages of Arnas, Ba Sebrina, Fafi, Ḥabsenas, Ḥaḥ, Harabeh 'Aleh, Heshterek, Ḥirbet Shorish, Kefr Beh, Kefr Zeh, Kermati, Kersifan, Midyat, Ṣalaḥ, and Sare; 2) the monasteries of Deir Ṣaliba, Deir Za'faran, Mar Awgen, Mar Gabriel, Mar Ibrahim, Mar Malka, Mar Shim'un, and Mar Yoḥannan; and 3) the forts of Qal'at Ḥatem Ṭay and Qal'at el Jedid. Cf. the Administrative List p. 159 below.

URFA **('URHAY; EDESSA; ANTIOCH ON THE CALLIRHOE)** pp. iii, v–vii, ix–xi, 28, 58

Urfa is believed to have been an ancient city refounded by Seleucus I. From BC 132 until AD 240 it was an independent kingdom under an Arab dynasty, alternately allied with Parthians and Romans; from 240 it was Roman. The city was the capital and became the metropolitan bishopric of the province of Osrhoene. A church is mentioned there ca. 200. The Abgar legend held that the city was from the first century under special protection afforded by Christ's mandylion and His letter to King Abgar. For a while Edessa possessed a famous academy, the School of the Persians, founded by refugees from Nisibis, which, however, was expelled from the Empire in 487 for being a centre of Nestorianism. Justinian restored the city after the flood of 525. Among the numerous churches known at Edessa, that of St. Sophia was especially renowned and is described as having a masonry dome on squinches and gold mosaic after being rebuilt ca. 525 (A. Grabar, "Le Témoinage d'une hymne syriaque sur l'architecture de la cathédrale d'Edesse au VIe siècle et sur la symbolique de l'édifice chrétien", *Cahiers Archéologiques*, 2 [1947], 41–67). It may have been built on a plan similar to that of Deir Za'faran (see above p. 134), cf. Kirsten, "Edessa" (cited below), 167–171, fig. 26; it was destroyed in the twelfth century. Edessa passed to the Arabs in 639. In 944 it surrendered Christ's mandylion to the Byzantines under whose rule the city passed in 1031. After 1086 it was governed by the Seljuks and Armenians until becoming in 1098 the capital of a Frankish principality. In 1144 it fell to Zengi, Atabeg of Mosul. In addition to the monuments mentioned below, there survived at Urfa a number of figural mosaic pavements (third century; these have disappeared since being published by Segal), found in the rock-cut tombs ornamented with sculpture, which surround the city; the monastery of Deir Ya'qub (or Naphshatha = tower tomb), south of the city, has recently been studied by Deichmann and Peschlow.

Bibliography: For history and monuments see Segal, *Edessa*, and art. "Orfa" by E. Honigmann in *EI* (1928–36). For monuments see also Preusser, 63–67, fig. 25, pls. 78–80; Gabriel, 276–286, pls. XCIX–CII; Guyer, "Amida", 207–209, figs. 7–8; E. Kirsten, "Edessa. Eine römische Grenzstadt des 4. bis 6. Jahrhunderts im Orient", *Jahrbuch für Antike und Christentum*, 6 (1963), 144–172; Krautheimer, 160, 173, 215; Deichmann and Peschlow, *Ruinenstätten*, 41–63, pls. 16–24; Mundell, "Deir Za'faran", fig. 4.

East Gate of City p. vii; Pl. 84

This gate is variously known as the Great Gate, the Kisas Gate, Bab el Amir, and Bey Kapısı.

Bibliography: Gabriel, 279 and note 4, pl. XCIX, 2; C. Dowsett, "A Twelfth-Century Armenian Inscription at Edessa", in *Iran and Islam in Memory of the Late Vladimir Minorsky*, ed. C. Bosworth (Edinburgh, 1971), 197–227, pls. 1–2; Segal, *Edessa*, 185, 190, 236 note 1, plan 1, pl. 5b.
Bell negative: T 206.

Dates: Inscription: tower (re)built 1122/3 (infra); Text: walls rebuilt ca. 525 *(ibid.)*.

Changes since 1911: Apparently none, see Segal, *Edessa*, pl. 5b.

Procopius claims that after the severe flood of 525, Justinian rebuilt the "main wall of Edessa and its outworks *(proteichisma)*" *(Buildings* II.vii.11). The round tower (height ca. 60 ft.) in the foreground of Pl. 84 was the south tower flanking the east gate and is probably built on early foundations as visible at its base and that of the rectangular tower behind to the left. Two other periods of building are distinguishable: one on the left and one on the right side of the tower. On the upper left side of the tower as seen here is an Armenian inscription of AD 1122/3 which reads in part: "... this fortified stronghold was completed ...". Dowsett points out that the inscribed blocks differ in size from those surrounding them and he suggests that the inscription may have been reused or that the discrepancy may be explained by haste in building. In the foreground of Pl.84 there is what appears to be an arched drain of old masonry. Little is left of the early circuit walls of the city and parts of them are illustrated in Segal, *Edessa*, pls. 4–6. There is on the Harran gate an eleventh century Byzantine inscription which is alleged to have mentioned the Emperor Alexius Comnenus (*ibid.*, 224, note 2, pl. 5a).

Bridge p. vii, Pl. 85

Bibliography: Segal, *Edessa*, 187f., pl. 5b. Bell negative: T 207.

Dates: Text: river diverted east of city ca. 525 (p. 154).

Changes since 1911: The bridge still stands, see Segal, *Edessa*, pl. 5b.

This bridge spans the Kara Koyun (Daisan, Scirtus) River, just outside the east gate

(Pl. 84). Procopius describes (*Buildings*, II.vii.6–10) how, following the flood of 525, Justinian diverted the course of the River Daisan to flow east round the city. One could conclude that a bridge was first built then outside the east gate (Segal, *Edessa*, plan II, p. 187f.). As the present bridge (Pl. 85) greatly resembles the Roman-type bridges at Nisibis (Pl. 69) and Dara (Pl. 2), it may date from ca. 525. It has been rebuilt at the top and its two arches differ in curve and also, to some extent, in masonry.

Capital at the Saray pp. 64–65; Pl. 86

Bibliography: Strzygowski, *Kleinasien*, 118, fig. 89; Sarre and Herzfeld, *Reise* II, 101f.; IV, pl. CXXXIII, 1, 3. Bell negative: T 194.

Changes since 1911: Whereabouts unknown.

A similar capital was found at 'Aqrquf in Iraq *(ibid.)*. Opinions about the date of these capitals (i.e. at Urfa, Mayafarqin and 'Aqrquf) vary from the sixth (Buchwald, *Sige*, 60f.) to the eighth century (Sarre and Herzfeld, *Reise* II, 101f.). Fragments of architectural sculpture like that at Deir Za'faran etc. (see p. 134) have been found in the citadel at Urfa (Guyer, "Amida", 207–209, figs. 7–8; Mundell, "Deir Za'faran", fig. 4), which is where remains of St. Sophia were carried after it was destroyed in the twelfth century (Segal, *Edessa*, 256).

VIRANŞEHIR (CONSTANTINA; TELLA DE MAUZELAT) pp. iii, v, vii

Known by a variety of names in antiquity–Nicephorium, Antoninopolis, Maximianopolis–it has been suggested that this city is also the Seleucid Antiochia Arabis of Pliny (Dillemann, 78). Following an earthquake it was rebuilt and fortified by Constantius (337–363) and although it was the headquarters of the Dux of Mesopotamia (381–527, 532–540), it was a bishopric of Osrhoëne under the metropolitan of Edessa (Urfa), (*ibid.,* 107f.). The refortification of the city by Justinian is described by Procopius who mentions that the walls had been composed of both basalt and limestone (*Buildings*, II. v. 2–8). Of the monasteries known round the city, that of Phesiltha (= the quarry) was the most famous (Vööbus, *Asceticism*, II, 237), on which see below. The city fell to the Arabs in 639.
Parts of the circuit walls remain standing (Preusser, 57, pl. 71, 1; Gabriel, 175 note 1) including part of a niche which decorated the east gate and a statue which adorned it (Preusser, 57, pl. 71, 2). In addition to the *tetrapylon* (see below) which marked the crossing of the *cardo* and *decumanus*, a number of other remains have been recorded. From within the city there have been published a number of Greek inscriptions, four of which record constructions by bishops and others of various buildings (a church of St. Stephen [?], a mausoleum, a *pandocheion*, and a *horreum*) during the fifth and sixth centuries (AD 456, 513, and 543; Oppenheim and Lucas, 60f., nos. 92–96; Humann and Puchstein, *Reisen*, 404–406, nos. 4–6). The *horreum* of 543 still stands. A Syriac inscription on a basalt sarcophagus has also been published (Moritz, 1899, 171, no. 8) and Preusser (p. 57) reported seeing two further ones on two beams (l. 2.40 each), one basalt and one limestone, as well as loose pieces of sculpture (*ibid.*, and fig. 18, pl. 71, 3). Fragments of mosaic pavement have been noted (*ibid.,* 58). Outside the city lies a necropolis like that at Dara (*ibid.*, 57f.) and to the west the remains of the "octagon" (see below).

Tetrapylon Pls. 87–88

Bibliography: Humann and Puchstein, *Reisen*, 403. Bell negatives: T 141–142.

Changes since 1911: Destroyed.

Bell's Journals and Notes lack any information about Viranşehir beyond recording her arrival and departure (UN Journal 1911, 12–13 May). It is possible that the two unidentified sections of wall shown in Pls. 87–88 are parts of a *tetrapylon* described by Humann and Puchstein. They explain (*Reisen*, 403) that two main streets connected the four main city gates and that at their crossing point they led through "vier mächtige Pfeiler ... an deren des Durchgängen abgewandten Seiten je eine korinthische Halbsäule haftete ...". Remains of niches with conch-shell decorations, which probably came from the piers, were lying nearby. It is possible that the masonry shown here belongs to two of the four piers of the *tetrapylon*. These two may, in fact, stand next to each other and be joined by the modern building visible in the right half of Pl. 87 and the left half of Pl. 88. Whether "korinthische Halbsäule" indicates that the columns then had Corinthian capitals is unclear. Presumably there were eight columns distributed on four sides originally.

"Octagon" p. vii; Fig. 58, Pls. 89–96

This building stands west of the city.

Bibliography: Humann and Puchstein, *Reisen*, 405; Strzygowski, *Kleinasien*, 96–100, figs. 68–70; *Amida*, 219f., 333, figs. 135–136, 283; Guyer in Sarre and Herzfeld, *Reise*, II, 32, fig. 149. Bell negatives: T 133–139.

Changes since 1911: Only piers nos. 2 and 4 of the octagon are still standing and these have lost a certain amount of masonry.

Puchstein, whose plan is used below (Fig. 58), described this building as having a circular main room (diam. 32 m) enclosing eight piers which supported a dome. On the east was a long apsed choir and on the west an antechamber with a staircase on its south leading up to a gallery and down to a crypt. Smaller antechambers stood before the north and south entrances. Strzygowski, who never visited the site, combined Puchstein's plan and description with photographs taken by Oppenheim to produce the following analysis. He agreed with Puchstein about the certainty of a dome because of the strength of the piers, but he said the building was oval-shaped, not circular, with an east-west diameter of 32 m and a north-south one of 34.50 m. He pointed out the series of vault and arch springings remaining on the piers in order to reconstruct a barrel-vaulted ambulatory supporting a barrel-vaulted gallery. He compared the cross-shaped aspect of the plan, composed of the chambers lying at the outer cardinal points, with the cross-shaped church of Gregory of Nyssa, and he suggested a fourth-century date for the Viranşehir building (*Kleinasien*, 96–100).

The masonry is double-faced basalt with a rubble core. Remains of brickwork are visible at the top of the south pier of the west porch (Pl. 93; no. 9 on Fig. 58). A keystone (?) decorated with a Maltese cross in medallion, in very low relief

(Pl. 96), photographed by Bell, may have been among the ruins of the "octagon". The "octagon" has been largely neglected by scholars as has been pointed out, for instance, by Deichmann (*BZ*, 121), in spite of its impressive scale and the fact that

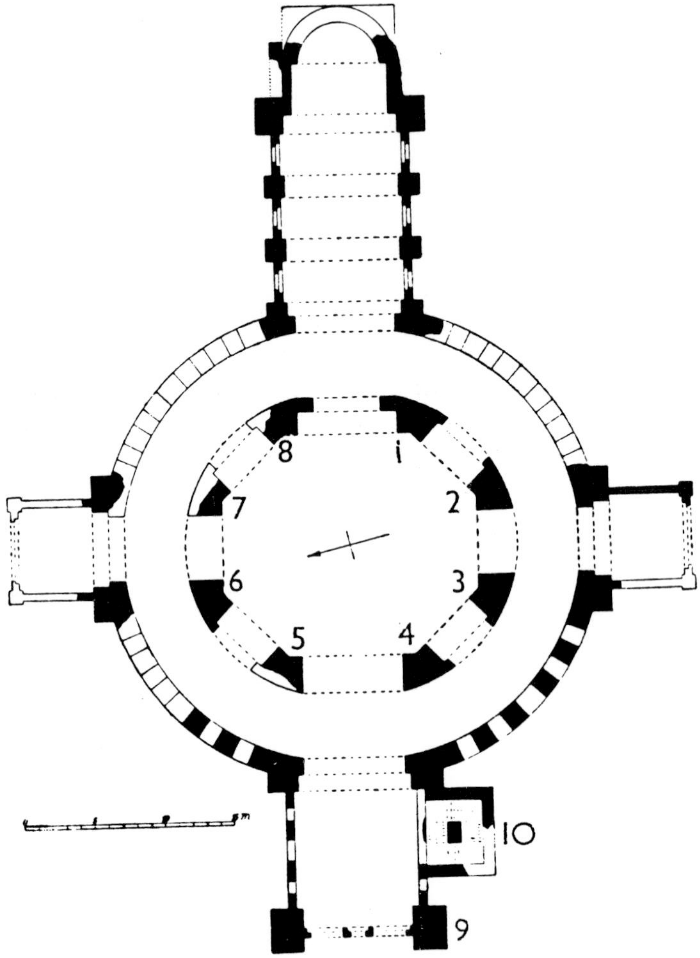

Fig. 58. Viranşehir, "octagon" W of city, plan by Puchstein in Strzygowski, *Kleinasien*, fig. 69

it was probably domed. It was undoubtedly a church, although the situation of such a large church outside the city walls–particularly if it was constructed in the dangerous circumstances of the sixth century–is difficult to explain. While too large for a monastery church, it may, as Strzygowski suggested, have been a pilgrimage church, which might explain the presence of the crypt reported by Puchstein. Three candidates known from written sources may present themselves as patron saints for such a shrine. The first is Theodore Stratelates, the name by which

the monastery of Phesiltha (= the quarry) at Tella is also known. This monastery, outside the city, may have eventually assumed the name of a famous local shrine. It would have been particularly appropriate to commemorate a noted military saint at the city which was from 381 onwards the seat of the Dux of Mesopotamia.
In the sixth century two prominent Monophysites are associated with Tella/Constantina: John bar Kursus (+ 538), bishop of Tella, who was an energetic missionary during persecutions and who died in captivity, and Jacob Baradaeus (+ 578), a native of Tella, who revived what was to become known as the Jacobite church (see p. iv above). He died abroad and in 622 his remains were brought back to Tella, to his monastery, that of Phesiltha, where he had already built a "temple" (i.e. a church) for his burial. See M.A. Kugener, "Récit de Mar Cyriaque", *Revue de l'Orient Chrétien*, 7 (1902), 196–213; on Jacob see also D.D. Bundy, "Jacob Baradaeus", *Le Muséon*, 91 (1978), 45–86. While it is unlikely that the church Jacob built is to be identified with the "octagon", it is possible that someone also built a larger shrine in his honour around 622. One can speculate further upon a possible role played by Chosroes II in such a project, since Mesopotamia was then under Persian control, and his promotion of the Jacobites (up until 622) is specifically mentioned in the account of the translation of Jacob's relics (Kugener, "Récit", 203f.). (Chosroes had himself sat at Tella in 591 while awaiting help from the Emperor Maurice to regain the throne of Persia.) One might draw attention, therefore, to the architectural features the "octagon" shares with the church of Narses III at Vagharshapat, built 641/2–661/2 (on which see Kleinbauer, "Zvartnotz" cited p. 126 above): e.g. the round exterior, the three projecting porches and an almost identical diameter.

BYZANTIUM: ECCLESIASTICAL ADMINISTRATIVE LIST

According to the *NOTITIA ANTIOCHENA* of 570 [1]

PROVINCES	*METROPOLITAN BISHOPRICS*	*BISHOPRICS*	*[VILLAGES, MONASTERIES, ETC.]*
MESOPOTAMIA	Amida (Diyarbakır)†	Martyropolis, Maipherqaṭ, (Mayafarqin)†	
		Ingila (Eğil)	
		Belabitene	
		Arsamosata (Arşamişat)	
		Sophene, Beth Ṣofanaye	
		Citharizon (Kotariç)	
		Cepha (Hasan Keyf)	
		Zeugma	
SOUTH MESOPOTAMIA	Dara Anastasiopolis †	Theodosiopolis	[Arnas†]
		Resh'aina (Ras el 'Ain)	[Deir Ṣaliba†]
		Turabdion, Ṭur 'Abdin	[Deir Za'faran†]
		(Qal'at Ḥatem Ṭay ?)†	[Fafi†]
		Mnasoubion/Banasymeon	[Ḥaḥ†]
		(Mar Gabriel ?)†	[Ḥabsenas†]
			[Heshterek†]
			[Ḥirbet Shorish†]
			[Kartmin†]
			[Kefr Beh†]
			[Kefr Zeh†]
			[Kermati†]
			[Kersifan†]
			[Midyat†]
			[Mardin†]
			[Ṣalaḥ†]
OSRHOËNE	Edessa, 'Urhay, (Urfa)†	Birtha (Birecik)	[Tektek Mountains:
		Maratha, Ma'rata	Sha'ib Shahr†
		Carrhae, Ḥarran	Qaṣr Antar–Qaṣr el Banat†]
		Constantina, Tella (Viranşehir)†	
		Markoupolis, Hikla d-Sida	
		Batnae, Sarug (Seruç)	
		Thelmarra, Telmahre (Tell el Mera ?)	
		Hemeria, 'Amrin	
		Circesium	
		Dausara (Qal'at Jabar)	
		Callinicum (Raqqah)	
		Nea Valentia	

PERSIA: ECCLESIASTICAL ADMINISTRATION [2]

PROVINCES	*METROPOLITAN BISHOPRICS*	*BISHOPRICS*	*[VILLAGES, MONASTERIES, ETC.]*
BETH ʻARABAYE	Nisibis†	for bishoprics see: Fiey, *Nisibe*, 160–193	[Mar Awgen†] [Mar Ibrahim†] [Mar Malka†] [Mar Shimʻun†] [Mar Yoḥannan†] [Ba Sebrina†] [Ḥarabeh ʻAleh†] [Qalʻat el Jedid†] [Sare†]
BETH GARMAI	Karka d-Beth Slokh (Kerkuk)	for bishoprics see: Fiey, *Assyrie*, III, 54–145	

1. Honigmann, *BZ*, 25 (1925), 60–88; idem, *Traditio*, 5 (1947), 135–161
2. Fiey, *Nisibe*, 16–193; idem, *Assyrie*, III, 11–145

† Monuments included in this book

PRELIMINARY LIST [1] OF DATED MONUMENTS BUILT BY CHRISTIANS IN NORTHERN MESOPOTAMIA [2], A.D. 200 - 1500

A.D.	before 201	Edessa, "Church of the Christians" built	o
	313-20	Nisibis, cathedral built	o
	313-23	Edessa, cathedral built	o
	327 /328	Edessa, cathedral extended	o
	after 345	Edessa, Confessors church built	o
	349/350	Constantina/Tella, city rebuilt	† o
		Amida, city fortified	† o
		Rhabdios (Qal'at Ḥatem Ṭay), fort built	† o
	359	Nisibis, cathedral baptistery built	† x
	369/370	Edessa, cathedral (?) baptistery built	o
	378	Edessa, St. Daniel/Dometius church built	o
	394	Edessa, St. Thomas church built	o
	397	Qarṭamin (Mar Gabriel) monastery founded	† o
	before 400	Amida, John 'Urtaya monastery founded	o
	408	Edessa, St. Barlaha church built	o
	410-20	Martyropolis, city founded, cathedral (?) and SS. Peter and Paul monastery built	† o
	412	Edessa, St. Stephan church built; cathedral repaired	o
	before 421	Ṣalaḥ, Mar Ya'qub monastery founded	† o
	435	Edessa, Twelve Apostles church built	o
	before 448	Edessa, St. Sergius church built	o
	456	Constantina/Tella, mausoleum built	x
	after 457	Edessa, St. John the Baptist and SS. Cosmas and Damian churches, and monasteries, towers, bridges and leper infirmary built	o
	484	Amida, cathedral and Tigris bridge built	o
	493	Edessa, tomb built	x
	496/497	Edessa, public portico built	o

4- -	Amida, *xenodochion* at Harput Gate built	x
ca. 500(?)	Mar Yoḥannan monastery built	† o
504/505	Edessa, baths built; city walls and praetorium restored	o
after 504	Edessa, Theotokos church built	o
505-507	Dara, circuit walls, St. Bartholomew church (?) and cathedral (?), *horreum*, cisterns, etc. built	† o
512	Qarṭamin (Mar Gabriel) monastery, church built and decorated	† o
513	Constantina/Tella, *pandochion* built	x
ca. 525	Edessa, circuit walls, cathedral (St. Sophia), public buildings rebuilt, east bridge built	† o
ca. 530	walls etc. restored at Dara, Martyropolis, Amida, Constantina/Tella, Harran, Rhabdios, Banasymeon (Mar Gabriel), etc.	† o
543	Constantina/Tella, *horreum* built	† x
550	Singar Mountains, St. Sergius church built	† o
ca. 550	Nisibis, School of the Martyrium church built	o
before 556	Deir Ṣaliba and Mar Aḥa monasteries founded	† o
ca. 571	Mar Ibrahim monastery founded	† o
582-602	Edessa, martyrium, bishop's palace, public buildings built	o
600-650	Nisibis, church at Mosul Gate built	o
ca. 629	Amida, St. Thomas church built	o
635	Magdal, Qarqaphta monastery built	o
ca. 640	St. Sergius monastery built, " between Tigris and Euphrates"	o
	Theotokos (Beth 'Ebre) convent built (?)	o
643-664	Mar Awgen monastery, cells built	† o
679	Edessa, "Old Church" repaired	o
691	Ḥaḥ, SS. Sergius and Bacchus monastery church built	† x
699	Harran, Jacobite church built	o
700	Edessa, Theotokos church and baptistery built	o
ca. 700	Dara, (?) monastery built	o
	Qaluq, Theotokos monastery built	o
	Nisibis, Nestorian church built	o
707-709	Nisibis, 5 Jacobite churches and monasteries and *xenodochion* built or restored	o

700-734	Ḥabsenas, St. Symeon church built or renovated	† o
	Ḥabsenas, Mar Lazarus monastery tower built	† o
	Tell 'Ubad, church and 2 mills built	o
	Deir Da'il, monastery built	o
	Mezr'eh, near Serwan, church built	o
713-758	Nisibis, cathedral, (Mar Ya'qub), north church built	† o
740	Ḥaḥ, Theotokos church built	† x
748	Büyük Kaçiçluk, monastery built	† x
ca. 750	Amida, St. Thomas church renovated	o
	Tell Beshmai, Athanasius monastery built	o
751	Mar Musa monastery, *beth qadisha,* built	† x
752	Martyropolis, Jacobite church built	o
766/7	Uç Kilise (nr. Edessa), church built	† x
770	Amida, St. Thomas church restored	o
772	Heshterek, Mar Addai, church and/or *beth ṣlotha* built	† x
793-811	Deir Za'faran, monastery refounded	† o
after 793	Edessa, several churches built (destroyed 825)	o
ca. 813	Harran, 5 churches destroyed and rebuilt	o
848	Amida, St. Thomas church rebuilt	o
934/935	Kefr Zeh, Mar 'Azaziel, *beth ṣlotha* built	† x
961	Mardin, Mar Michael, column (*esṭona*) made	x
1014	Arnas, Mar Cyriacus church restored	† x
ca. 1031	Edessa, Theotokos and St. Theodore churches destroyed and rebuilt	o
1089	Arnas, *beth qadisha* renovated	x
ca. 1099	Edessa, SS. Sergius and Bacchus monastery built	o
1122/1123	Edessa, tower built	† x
1125-66	Mardin and vicinity, *ca.* 50 churches and monasteries built and rebuilt	† o
1171	Amida, Theotokos church restored	o
1177	Amida, Holy Spirit church built	o
1199	Ba Sebrina, Mar Dodo church rebuilt	† x
1201	Resh'aina, church restored	o
1209	Mar Awgen monastery, chamber built	† x
1250	Deir Za'faran, monastery restored	† x
1250-56	Killith, Mar Abhai monastery, church, walls and towers restored	† x
1271	Mar Awgen monastery, church rebuilt	† x
1465	Kefr Beh, Mar Stephan and Mar Yoḥannan church built (?)	† x

1474	Ba Sebrina, Mar Dodo church rebuilt	† o
1481	Mar Cyriacus monastery, near Zargel, renovated	† o
1482-89	Nisibis, Mar Batala church rebuilt	o
1496	Deir Za'faran monastery restored	† o

† Monument survives
x Inscription
o Text

1 This list has been compiled from works cited in the Bibliography and will be expanded and documented in a future article.

2 The territory covered here is most of those areas belonging to the two provinces of Mesopotamia and those of Osrhoëne and Beth 'Arabaye as listed on pp. 159–160.

GLOSSARY

bema, bim	in the Ṭur 'Abdin, an ambo in the centre of the nave of the church (Pl. 158 and n. 122)
beth qadisha	"house of saints" : funerary chapel
beth ṣlotha	"house of prayer" : in the Ṭur 'Abdin, an exterior oratory in the form of a free-standing exedra often with a cross carved in relief on its conch (Introduction, p. x)
bît hilani	in ancient north Syrian and Assyrian architecture a palace entrance portico (pp. 56-57 and n. 153 above)
deir (Arabic), *daira* (Syriac)	"monastery"
guda	"choir": a pulpit in the form of a stone lectern which stands outside the sanctuary and also beside the *beth ṣlotha* (Pognon, 42f., 93)
Karshuni, Garshuni	Arabic written in Syriac characters
ḥarabeh (Arabic), *ḥarba* (Syriac)	"ruins"
'idta	"church"
'idta rabtha	"great church": cathedral (*megale ekklesia*)
Jacobite	the name of the Syrian Orthodox church as reorganized in the mid-sixth century; also called Monophysite and West Syrian
Kefr, Kaphar	"village"
korsi	"throne"
Mar	"my lord"
Mariamana = Meryem Ana (Turkish)	"Mary the mother"
Melkite church	"belonging to the king, royal": Byzantine Orthodox church
"monastic" church	type of church found in the Ṭur 'Abdin; term devised by Pognon (p. 91 n. 2) to designate the church with a transverse barrel vault, three sanctuary rooms and a western narthex; usually a monastery church (see above, p. ix)
Nestorian church	also called East Syrian; the Uniate branch is called Chaldean
"parochial" church	type of church found in the Ṭur 'Abdin; term devised by Pognon (p. 91 n. 2) to designate the barrel vaulted hall church with open eastern apse and a southern narthex; often has a *beth ṣlotha* outside; usually a parish church (see above, p. viii)
qal'ah, qal'at	fort
qaṣr	fortress, walled village
qaṣtra	*castrum*, walled village

BIBLIOGRAPHICAL SURVEY

The following summary of archaeological and historical work published on northern Mesopotamia does not claim to be complete, but offers the earliest contributions to the subject, with an emphasis on archaeology. The earliest exploration of northern Mesopotamia and the Ṭur 'Abdin was carried out by European travellers. A list of these is given in the article "Ṭur 'Abdin" by Streck in the *Encyclopedia of Islam* and is annotated by Leroy (*CRAI* 1967) as to which of them penetrated the Ṭur 'Abdin proper. Inscriptions have been gathered and published by the following (the dates given here refer to publication as listed in the Bibliography, and not to travel): the Greek and Latin notably by Humann and Puchstein (1890), Oppenheim and Lucas (1905), and Gabriel (1940); and the Syriac by Moritz (1898, 1913), Pognon (1908, 1910), Jarry (1972) and Brock (1980). Further pioneer work cited below includes that by Taylor (1865, 1968), Socin (a topographical survey of the Ṭur 'Abdin, 1881), Sachau (1883), and Parry, whose interests included liturgy (1895), I. Armalet ("Voyage au Ṭur 'Abdin" [in Arabic], *Machriq*, 16 [1913]), and Hinrichs (1914). The recording, photography and study of individual monuments started at the beginning of this century with the work of Strzygowski (1903, 1910), Chapot (a study of the frontier, 1907), van Berchem (1910), Preusser (1911), Bell (1910, 1911, 1913), Guyer (1912, 1916, 1925) and Sarre and Herzfeld (1911-20). Much interest at this period was focused on the enigmatic Ulu Cami of Diyarbakır, a subject Gertrude Bell dealt with only briefly. After the end of the First World War, some of Mesopotamia, including the Ṭur 'Abdin, was designated a military zone and remained as such until after the Second World War. This, of course, had a serious effect on exploration, which has only been resumed since 1950. In spite of this handicap, studies of varying quality were produced between the wars, on the basis of earlier investigations, notably by Guyer (1933), Strzygowski (1936), Reuther (1938) and Monneret de Villard (1940). Only Guyer and Reuther (the latter had directed investigations at Ctesiphon) had actually been in Mesopotamia. Gabriel, however, did travel in parts of northern Mesopotamia during the inter-war years, after which he published the standard work on the medieval Islamic architecture of the area (1940), which includes studies on the walls of Diyarbakır and Mayafarqin.

After the Second World War the University of Michigan conducted an expedition to the Ṭur 'Abdin in 1956, which was under the direction of Prof. G. Forsyth and included Fr. J.M. Fiey and Professor O. Grabar. Several hundred photographs were taken during this trip and are due to be published by Professor Forsyth. Abbé J. Leroy also travelled there in the 1950's when his mission included the photographing of local material for his corpus of illuminated Syriac manuscripts (1964) and he conducted in 1967 and 1968 an architectural survey of which preliminary reports, articles (1967, 1968, 1976, 1978) and inscriptions (Jarry, 1972) have been published. A final publication is expected. Monuments of Edessa, Harran and the Tektek Mountains have been the subject of study by Prof. J.B. Segal (e.g. 1953, 1970) and Dr. G. Fehervari (e.g. *EI* 1971). Harran is one of the few sites in our area to have been surveyed (by Lloyd and Brice, 1951) and excavated (by Rice, 1952). Other regional studies include those by Prof. D. Oates on the Singar Mountains (1965). Recently (1977) Prof. F.W. Deichmann and Dr. U. Peschlow surveyed the sites of Kale-i Zerzevan near Diyarbakır, and Deir Ya'qub near Urfa. In 1962 Dillemann published his topographical study of the Roman *limes* in northern Mesopotamia which reappraised the position of the Ṭur 'Abdin with respect to the frontier. The following surveys and studies of individual monuments have also appeared: on the walls of Diyarbakır (D. van Berchem, 1954); Mar Gabriel (Leroy, 1956; A. Grabar, 1956; Hawkins and Mundell, 1973; Leroy, 1976); Deir Za'faran (Leroy, 1978; Mundell, forthcoming); and Dara (Mundell, 1975). My own knowledge of the area was first gained during a trip to northern Mesopotamia in the summer of 1972 in the company of Prof. I. Sevcenko and my husband, Prof. C. Mango, who were collecting inscriptions for their corpus of dated Greek inscriptions; about 300 photographs were taken, some of which illustrate C. Mango, *Byzantine Architecture*, (1976) as well as some of the articles referred to above. In 1972, in the course of studying the mosaics at Mar Gabriel, Mr. E.J.W. Hawkins took further photographs of that monastery, which appear in Hawkins and Mundell, 1973.

The history of northern Mesopotamian cities can be found in the general works of Stein and Jones for the Seleucid, Roman and early Byzantine periods and in the *Encyclopedia of Islam* for the medieval, as well as in the books on Amida (van Berchem and Strzygowski, 1910), Edessa (Segal, 1972) and Nisibis (Fiey, 1977). Bibliographies of relevant primary sources can be found in the latter two. Much work remains to be done on the history of the Ṭur 'Abdin, of which the earliest western compilations are to be found in J.S. Assemani, *Bibliotheca Orientalis*, II (Rome, 1721) and M. Le Quien, *Oriens Christianus*, II (Paris, 1740). One monastery whose continuous history (A.D. 397 until modern times) has been published is that of Mar Gabriel (Nau, "Notice" and Krüger, *Mönchtum* I). Because of the importance of this monastery, its history embraces that of the Ṭur 'Abdin and thereby sheds light on the whole region. Krüger's work also includes a briefer historical survey of the other monasteries of the Ṭur 'Abdin ("Mönchtum" II). While Nau and Krüger drew on sources available in western libraries, it is known among orientalists that many manuscripts remain in the east (the collection at Deir Za'faran was, until its removal in this century to Mardin and Homs, one of the largest) which contain local histories and saints' lives. While Abbé Leroy has made known the illuminated manuscripts among them (*Manuscrits*, 1964), Professor A. Vööbus (1963, 1965, 1969, 1978) and Dr. S. Brock (1979, 1980) have begun the work of textual and historical evaluation of this material which has yet to be fully exploited for the composition of the history of the Ṭur 'Abdin. This task was attempted by the late Syrian Orthodox Patriarch, Ephrem Barṣaum, whose posthumously published *History of the Ṭur 'Abdin* (in Arabic and Syriac, Jounieh, Lebanon, 1963) is considered to be in need of some revision (Fiey, *Nisibe*, 21 note 32). Publications in Syriac, Arabic and Turkish have been produced locally by the late Metropolitan M.H. Dolapönü on, for example, Mar Gabriel, Deir Za'faran, Mar Ya'qub at Ṣalaḥ and Mardin. Reports on the present-day Christian communities and the villages of the Ṭur 'Abdin have been produced by Dr. C. Dauphin (1972) and Mrs. H. Anschütz (1977). Broader church history studies relevant to the Ṭur 'Abdin include those of the Early Christian Patriarchate of Antioch (Devreesse, 1945, and Honigmann, 1925, 1947, 1951), early monasticism in Mesopotamia (Vööbus, 1960), the Jacobite church under the Arabs (Hage, 1966, and Honigmann, 1954) and the later medieval Jacobite church (*ibid.*, and Kawerau, 1960). For the southern strip of the Ṭur 'Abdin and adjacent areas, namely the East Syrian (i.e. Nestorian) church of Persia in Iraq and at Nisibis (Beth 'Arabaye), the thorough studies of J.M. Fiey combine church history, topography, and archaeological material (1959, 1963, 1964,1965-69, 1970, 1976, 1977).

BIBLIOGRAPHY

AB = *Analecta Bollandiana*

Amida = M. van Berchem and J. Strzygowski, *Amida* (Heidelberg, 1910)

Anschütz, "Ortschaften" = H. Anschütz, "Einige Ortschaften des Ṭur 'Abdin im südosten der Türkei als Beispiele gegenwärtiger und historischer Bedeutung", *Zeitschrift der Deutschen Morgenländischen Gesellschaft*, Supplement III, 1 (1977), 179-193

Antioch-on-the-Orontes = *Antioch-on-the-Orontes Excavations* (Princeton, 1934-41)

Bar Hebraeus, Appendix = Chronography of Bar Hebraeus, trans. E.W. Budge (Oxford 1932), vol. II, Appendix

Baumstark, "Alterskriterium" = A. Baumstark, " Ein Alterskriterium der nordmesopotamische Kirchenbauten", *Oriens Christianus*, n.s. 5 (1915), 111-131

Bell, *Amurath* = G.L. Bell, *Amurath to Amurath* (London, 1911)

Bell, G.L., "The Churches and Monasteries of the Tur Abdin" in *Amida*, 224-262

Bell, G.L., "Churches and Monasteries of the Ṭûr 'Abdîn and Neighbouring Districts", *Zeitschrift für Geschichte der Architektur*, 9 (1913), 61-112

Bell negatives = numbers of Bell's negatives held by University of Newcastle upon Tyne

Bell, RGS Notes = Bell's notebooks belonging to the Royal Geographical Society, London

Bell, *Ukhaidir* = G.L. Bell, *Palace and Mosque at Ukhaidir* (Oxford, 1914)

Bell, UN Journal 1909, 1911 = Bell's journals belonging to University of Newcastle upon Tyne

Brock, "Fenqitho" = S. Brock, "The Fenqitho of the Monastery of Mar Gabriel in Ṭur 'Abdin", *Ostkirkliche Studien* (1979: forthcoming)

Brock, "Notes" = S. Brock, "Notes on Some Monasteries on Mount Izla", *Abr Nahrain* (1980: forthcoming)

Butler, *Architecture* = H.C. Butler, *Ancient Architecture in Syria*, II, B (Leiden, 1920)

Chapot, *La frontière* = V. Chapot, *La frontière de l'Euphrate de Pompée à la conquête arabe* (Paris, 1907)

Cresswell = K.A.C. Cresswell, *Early Muslim Architecture*, 2nd ed. I (Oxford, 1969), II (Oxford, 1940)

CSCO = Corpus Scriptorum Christianorum Orientalium

Dauphin = C. Dauphin, "Situation actuelle des communautés chrétiennes du Tur 'Abdin (Turquie Orientale)", *Proche-Orient Chrétien*, 22 (1972), 323-27

Deichmann, *BZ* = F.W. Deichmann, review of Krautheimer, 1st. ed. in *Byzantinische Zeitschrift*, 65 (1972), 102-125, 448-458

Deichmann and Peschlow, *Ruinenstätten* = F.W. Deichmann and U. Peschlow, *Zwei spätantike Ruinenstätten in Nordmesopotamien* (Munich, 1977)

Devlet Istatistik Enstitüsü of Turkey, *Genel Sayımı idari bölönüş* (Ankara, 1973)

Devreesse, *Patriarcat* = R. Devreesse, *Le patriarcat d'Antioche depuis la paix de l'église jusqu'à la conquête arabe* (Paris, 1945)

Dillemann = L. Dillemann, *Haute Mésopotamie orientale et pays adjacents* (Paris, 1962)

DOP = *Dumbarton Oaks Papers*

H. J. W. Drijvers, *Old Syriac (Edessean) Inscriptions* (Leiden, 1972)

EI = *Encyclopedia of Islam*, articles on Diyar Bakr, al-Djazira (1965), Ḥarran (1971), Maiyafariḳin, Mardin, Naṣara, Nisibin, Orfa (1928–36), Ṭur 'Abdin (1924–34)

A. Fattal, *Le statut légal des non-Musulmans en pays d'Islam* (Beirut, 1958)

Fiey, *Assyrie* = J.M. Fiey, *Assyrie chrétienne* (Beirut, 1965–69)

Fiey, *Jalons* = J.M. Fiey, *Jalons pour une histoire de l'Eglise en Iraq*, CSCO 310, Subsidia 36 (Louvain, 1970)

Fiey, "Martyropolis" = J.M. Fiey, "Martyropolis syriaque", *Le Muséon* 89 (1976), 5–38

Fiey, *Mossoul* = J.M. Fiey, *Mossoul chrétienne* (Beirut, 1959)

Fiey, *Nisibe* = J.M. Fiey, *Nisibe, métropole syriaque orientale et ses suffragants des origines à nos jours*, CSCO 388, Subsidia 54 (Louvain, 1977)

Fiey, "Tagrit" = J.M. Fiey, "Tagrit", *Orient Syrien*, 8 (1963), 289–342

Gabriel = A. Gabriel, *Voyages archéologiques dans la Turquie orientale* (Paris, 1940)

Grabar, "Observations" = A. Grabar, "Quelques observations sur le décor de l'église de Qartamin", *Cahiers archéologiques*, 8 (1956), 83–91

Guyer, "Amida" = S. Guyer, "Amida", *Repertorium für Kunstwissenschaft*, 38 (1916) 193–237

Guyer, *Journey* = S. Guyer, *My Journey down the Tigris*, trans. J. McCabe (London, 1925)

Guyer, "Le rôle" = S. Guyer, "Le rôle de l'art de la Syrie et de la Mésopotamie à l'époque byzantine", *Syria*, 14 (1933), 56–70

Guyer, "Surp Hagop" = S. Guyer, "Surp Hagop (Djinndeirmene), einer Klosterruine der Kommagene", *Repertorium für Kunstwissenschaft*, 35 (1912), 498–508

Hage = W. Hage, *Die Syrische-Jakobitische Kirche in frühislamischer Zeit* (Wiesbaden, 1966)

Handbook = Great Britain, Admiralty War Staff, Intelligence Division, *A Handbook of Mesopotamia*, IV (London, 1917)

Hawkins and Mundell, "Mosaics" = E.J.W. Hawkins and M.C. Mundell, "The Mosaics of the Monastery of Mâr Samuel, Mâr Simeon, and Mâr Gabriel near Kartmin" with "A Note on the

Greek Inscription" by C. Mango, *DOP*, 27 (1973), 279-296

Herzfeld, *OLZ* = E. Herzfeld, review of *Amida* in *Orientalistische Literaturzeitung*, 14 (1911), 397-435

Hinrichs, *PM* = W. Hinrichs, "Eine Karawanenreise von Mosul nach Aleppo vom 9. März bis 25. Aprill 1911", *Petermanns Mitteilungen*, 60 (1914), 189-193, 257-259

Honigmann, *Barṣauma* = E. Honigmann, *Le couvent de Barṣauma et le patriarcat jacobite d'Antioche et de Syrie*, CSCO 146, Subsidia 7 (Louvain, 1954)

Honigmann, *BZ* = E. Honigmann, "Studien zur Notitia Antiochena", *Byzantinische Zeitschrift*, 25 (1925), 60-88

Honigmann, *Evêques* = E. Honigmann, *Evêques et Evêchés monophysite d'Asie antérieur au VIe siècle*, CSCO 127, Subsidia 2 (Louvain, 1951)

Honigmann, *Traditio* = E. Honigmann, "The patriarchate of Antioch; a revision of Le Quien and the Notitia Antiochena", *Traditio*, 5 (1947), 135-161

Humann and Puchstein, *Reisen* = C. Humann and C. Puchstein, *Reisen in Kleinasien und Nordsyrien* (Berlin, 1890)

Jarry = J. Jarry, "Inscriptions syriaques et arabes inédites du Ṭur 'Abdin", *Annales Islamologiques*, 10 (1972), 207-250

Jones, *LRE* = A.H.M. Jones, *The Later Roman Empire 284-602. A Social, Economic and Administrative Survey*, I-III (Oxford, 1964)

Kautzsch, *Kapitellstudien* = R. Kautzsch, *Kapitellstudien* (Berlin/Leipzig 1936)

Kawerau, *Kirche* = P. Kawerau, *Die Jakobitische Kirche im Zeitalter der syrischen Renaissance*, (Berlin, 1960)

Kleinbauer, "Tetraconch Churches" = W.E. Kleinbauer, "The Origins and Functions of the Aisled Tetraconch Churches in Syria and Northern Mesopotamia", *DOP*, 27 (1973), 89-114

Krautheimer = R. Krautheimer, *Early Christian and Byzantine Architecture*, paperback edition (London, 1975)

Krüger, *Mönchtum* I = P. Krüger, *Das syrisch-monophysitische Mönchtum im Tur-Ab(h)din von seinen Anfängen bis zur Mitte des 12. Jahrhunderts* (Munster, 1937)

Krüger, "Mönchtum" II = P. Krüger, "Das syrisch-monophysitische Mönchtum im Tur-Ab(h)din von seinen Anfängen bis zur Mitte des 12. Jahrhunderts", *Orientalia Christiana Periodica*, 4 (1938), 5-46

Lassus, *Sanctuaires* = J. Lassus, *Sanctuaires chrétiens de Syrie* (Paris, 1947)

Leroy, "Baptistères" = J. Leroy, "Deux baptistères paléochrétiens d'Orient méconnus", *Cahiers archéologiques*, 25 (1976), 1-6

Leroy, *CRAI* 1967 = J. Leroy, "Recherches archéologiques sur les églises du Tur 'Abdin", *Comptes-rendus des séances de l'Académie des Inscriptions et Belles-Lettres* (1967), 324-333

Leroy, *CRAI* 1968 = J. Leroy, "L'état présent des monuments chrétiens du sud-est de la Turquie (Ṭur 'Abdin et environs)", *Comptes-rendus des séances de l'Académie des Inscriptions et Belles-Lettres* (1968), 478-493

Leroy, "Deir es-Zapharan" = J. Leroy, "Le Deir es-Zapharan et le 'Siège d'Antioche" in *A Tribute to Arthur Vööbus*, ed. R.H. Fischer (Chicago, 1977), 319–328
Leroy, "Le décor" = J. Leroy, "Le décor de l'église du monastère de Qartemin d'après un texte syriaque", *Cahiers archéologiques*, 8 (1956), 75–81
Leroy, *Manuscrits* = J. Leroy, *Les manuscrits syriaques à peintures* (Paris, 1964)
Lloyd and Brice, "Harran" = S. Lloyd and W. Brice, "Harran", *Anatolian Studies*, 1 (1951), 77–111
Mango = C. Mango, *Byzantine Architecture* (New York, 1976)
Mingana, *Catalogue* = A. Mingana, *Catalogue of the Mingana Collection of Manuscripts* (Cambridge, 1933)
Monneret de Villard = U. Monneret de Villard, "Le chiese della Mesopotamia", *Orientalia Christiana Analecta*, 128 (1940), 1–115
Moritz 1898 = B. Moritz, "Syrische Inschriften aus Syrien und Mesopotamien", *Mitteilungen des Seminars für Orientalische Sprachen zu Berlin. Westasiatische Studien*, i/2 (1898), 124–149
Moritz 1913 = B. Moritz, "Syrische Inschriften", in M. von Oppenheim, *Inschriften aus Syrien, Mesopotamien und Kleinasien*. Beiträge zur Assyriologie und Semitischen Sprächwissenschaft, VII, 2 (Leipzig, 1913), 157–179
Mundell, "Dara" = M.C. Mundell, "A Sixth Century Funerary Relief at Dara in Mesopotamia, *Jahrbuch der Österreichischen Byzantinistik*, 24 (1975), 209–227
Mundell, "Deir Za'faran" = M.C. Mundell, "The Sixth Century Sculpture of the Monastery of Deir Za'faran in Mesopotamia", *Actes du XVe Congrès International d'Etudes Byzantines, Athens, 1976* (forthcoming)
Mundell, "Decoration" = M.C.Mundell, "Monophysite Church Decoration", in *Iconoclasm*, ed. A. Bryer and J. Herrin (Birmingham, 1977), 59–74
Nau, "Notice" = F. Nau, "Notice historique sur le monastère de Qartamin", *Actes du XIVe Congrès des Orientalistes, Alger, 1903*, II (Paris, 1906), 38–75
Nau, "Resumé" = F. Nau, "Resumé de monographies syriaques", *Revue de l'Orient Chrétien*, 20 (1915), 3–32
Oates, *Studies* = D. Oates, *Studies in the Ancient History of Northern Iraq* (London, 1968)
Oppenheim, *Mittelmeer* = M. von Oppenheim, *Vom Mittelmeer zum Persischen Gulf* (Berlin, 1899)
Oppenheim and Lucas = M. von Oppenheim and H. Lucas, "Griech.-lat. Inschriften aus Syrien, Mesopotamien und Kleinasien", *Byzantinische Zeitschrift*, 14 (1905), 38–75
Parry = O.H. Parry, *Six Months in a Syrian Monastery* (London, 1895)
Pognon = H. Pognon, *Inscriptions sémitiques de la Syrie, de la Mésopotamie, et de la région de Mossoul* (Paris, 1908)
Pognon in *Amida* = H. Pognon, "Die Mitteilung einer Reihe von Inschriften", in *Amida*
Preusser = C. Preusser, *Nordmesopotamische Baudenkmäler altchristlicher und islamischer Zeit* (Leipzig, 1911)
Reuther = O. Reuther, "Sāsānian Architecture, History", in A.U. Pope, *Survey of Persian Art*, I (London and New York, 1938), 560–566

Rice, "Ḥarran" = D.S. Rice, "Medieval Ḥarran: Studies on its Topography and Monuments, I", *Anatolian Studies*, 2 (1952), 36–84

Sachau, *Reise* = C. Sachau, *Reise in Syrien und Mesopotamien* (Leipzig, 1883)

Sachau, *Verzeichnis* = C. Sachau, *Verzeichnis der syrischen Handschriften der königlichen Bibliothek zu Berlin* (Berlin, 1899)

Sarre and Herzfeld, *Reise* = F. Sarre and E. Herzfeld, *Archäologische Reise in Eurphrat-und-Tigris Gebiet* (Berlin, 1911–20)

Segal, "Communities" = J.B. Segal, "Mesopotamian Communities from Julian to the Rise of Islam", *Proceedings of the British Academy*, 41 (1955), 109–139

Segal, *Edessa* = J.B. Segal, *Edessa, 'the Blessed City'* (Oxford, 1970)

Socin = A. Socin, "Zur Geographie des Tur-'Ab(h)din", *Zeitschrift der deutschen morgenländischen Gesellschaft*, 35 (1881), 237–269

Stein, *Histoire* = E. Stein, *Histoire du Bas-Empire*, (Paris, Brussels, Amsterdam, 1949–59)

Strzygowski, *Kleinasien* = J. Strzygowski, *Kleinasien, ein Neuland der Kunstgeschichte* (Leipzig, 1903)

Strzygowski, *Syrie* = J. Strzygowski, *L'Ancien art chrétien de Syrie* (Paris, 1936)

J. Strzygowski, see also *Amida*

Taylor 1865 = J.G. Taylor, "Travels in Kurdistan", *Journal of the Royal Geographical Society*, 35 (1865), 21–58

Taylor 1868 = J.G. Taylor, "Journal of a Tour in Armenia, Kurdistan and Upper Mesopotamia etc.", *Journal of the Royal Geographical Society*, 38 (1868), 281–320

Tchalenko, *Villages* = G. Tchalenko, *Villages antiques de la Syrie du nord. Le massif du Bélus à l'époque romaine* (Paris, 1953–58)

Tritton = A.S. Tritton, *The Caliphs and their non-Muslim Subjects. A Critical Study of the Covenant of 'Umar* (London, 1930)

D. van Berchem, "Recherches" = D. van Berchem, "Recherches sur la chronologie des enceintes de Syrie et de Mésopotamie", *Syria* 31 (1954), 254–270

M. van Berchem, see *Amida*

Vööbus, *Asceticism* = A. Vööbus, *History of Syrian Asceticism*, CSCO 197, Subsidia 17 (Louvain, 1960)

Vööbus, *School* = A. Vööbus, *History of the School of Nisibis*, CSCO 266, Subsidia 26 (Louvain, 1965)

Wright, *Catalogue* = W. Wright, *Catalogue of the Syriac Manuscripts in the British Musuem* (London, 1870–72)

Zotenberg, *Catalogue* = H. Zotenberg, *Catalogue des manuscrits syriaques et sabéens de la Bibliothèque Nationale* (Paris, 1894)

LIST OF ILLUSTRATIONS

Figures:

Plates (arranged in alphabetical order)

ANTIQUE CITIES

VILLAGES, MONASTERIES AND FORTS

* = previously unpublished
† = previously published elsewhere

Pl. 1 Dara, S circuit wall, outer face of water gate (R 108)

Pl. 2 Dara, bridge inside town (R 107)

Pl. 3a Dara, E circuit wall, S of water gate (R 109)

Pl. 3b Dara, E circuit wall, on R: water gate where river enters city (R 110, 112)

Pl. 5 Dara, doorway of unidentified building (R 114)
Pl.4 Dara, granary (R 116)

Pl. 6 Dara, capital reused in medrese (R 122)

Pl. 7 Dara, loose pier capital (R 123)

Pl. 8 Dara, quarry reused as necropolis (R 126)

Pl. 10 Diyarbakır, Mar Cosmas, interior, capital of pier "C" below (N 99)

Pl. 9 Diyarbakır, Mar Cosmas, interior, moulding on pier "C" and capital above (N 100)

Pl. 11 Diyarbakır, Mar Cosmas, interior, N side (T 34)

Pl. 12 Diyarbakır, Mar Cosmas, exterior from W (N 101)

Pl. 13. Diyarbakır, el ‘Adhra, exterior, present narthex from W (N 104)

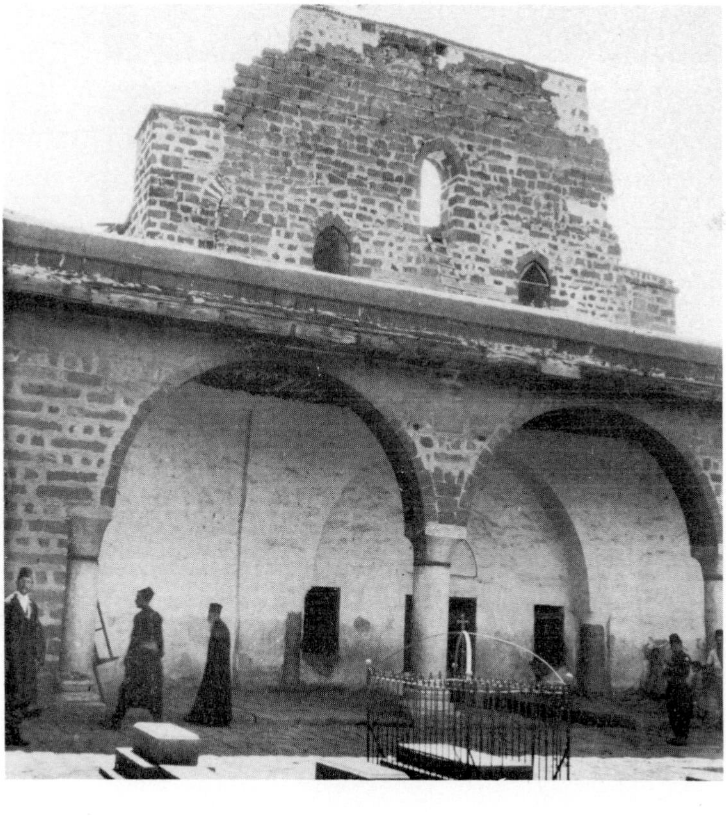

Pl. 14 Diyarbakır, el 'Adhra, exterior, N door (N 109) and profiles

Pl. 15 Diyarbakır, el 'Adhra, N exterior wall of present narthex, from NW (N 108)

Pl. 16 Diyarbakır, el ‘Adhra, exterior, apse from SE (N 102)

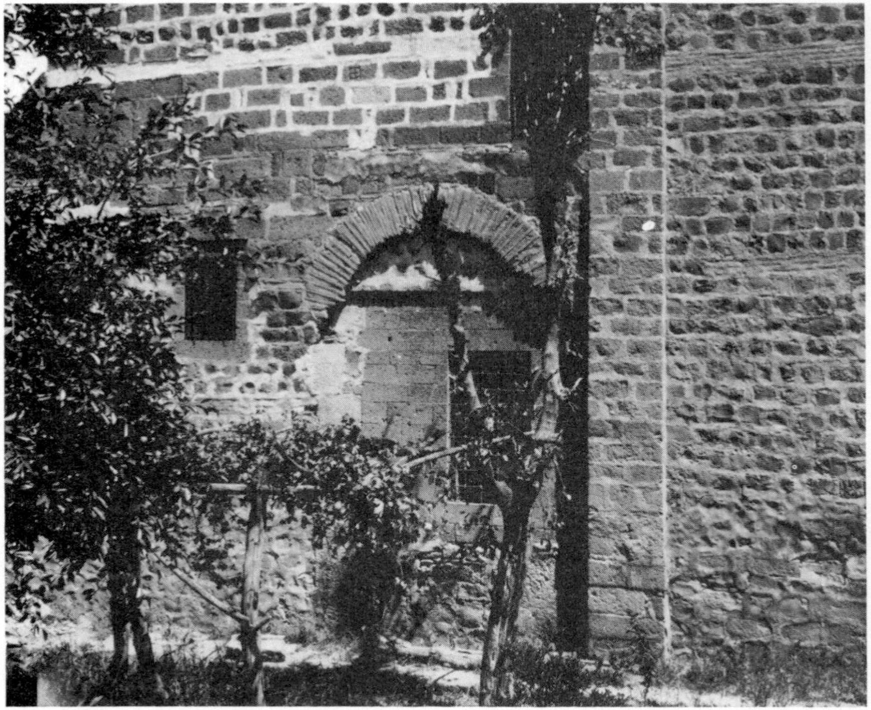

Pl. 17 Diyarbakır, el ‘Adhra, exterior, blocked S door (N 105)

Pl. 18 Diyarbakır, el ‘Adhra, S capital and archivolt of original apse (T 29)

Pl. 19 Diyarbakır, el ‘Adhra, marble window mullion reused as chancel post

Pl. 20 Diyarbakır, el ‘Adhra, detail of Pl. 18: capital
Pl. 21 Diyarbakır, el ‘Adhra, S capital of original apse (N 106)

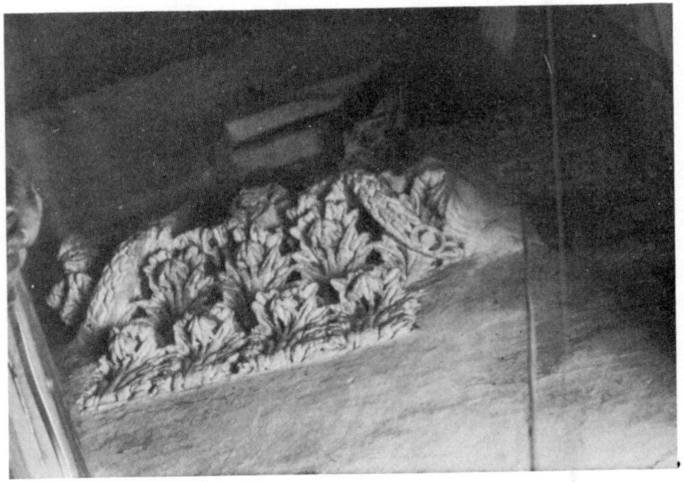

Pl. 22 Diyarbakır, el 'Adhra, marble column base reused in narthex (T 31)

Pl. 23 Diyarbakır, el 'Adhra, repoussé silver gospel book (Resurrection) (T 32)

Pl. 24 Diyarbakır, el 'Adhra, repoussé silver gospel book cover (Crucifixion) and other plaques (saints and Adoration of Magi) (T 33)

Pl. 25 Diyarbakır, citadel buildings, E end from NE (T 12a)

Pl. 26 Diyarbakır, citadel buildings, E half, exterior from N (T 15)

Pl. 27 Diyarbakır, citadel buildings, E facade (T 14)

Pl. 28 Diyarbakır, citadel buildings, E half, interior of dome looking W (T 17)

Pl. 29 Diyarbakır, citadel buildings, E half, interior semi-dome in S aisle (T 19)

Pl. 30 Diyarbakır, citadel buildings, W half, interior NW angle of dome (T 23)

Pl. 31 Kerkuk, Mar Tahmazgerd, exterior from W (Q 200–201)

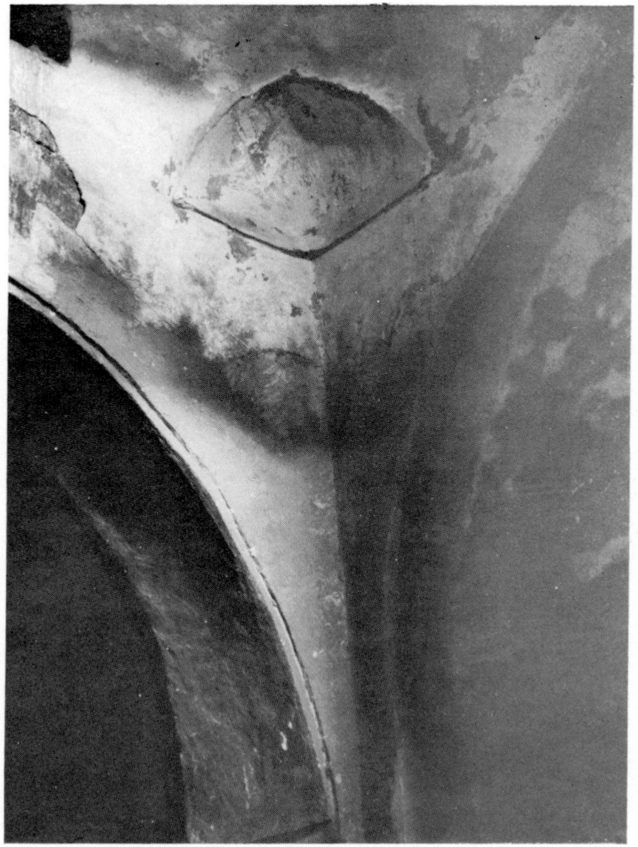

Pl. 32 Kerkuk, Mar Tahmazgerd, interior small dome of church, squinch (Q 209)

Pl. 33 Kerkuk, Mar Tahmazgerd, interior of church, looking E (Q 211)

Pl. 34 Kerkuk, Mar Tahmazgerd, interior, dome of sanctuary (Q [illegible])

Pl. 35 Kerkuk, Mar Tahmazgerd, interior, tomb chamber (Q 202)

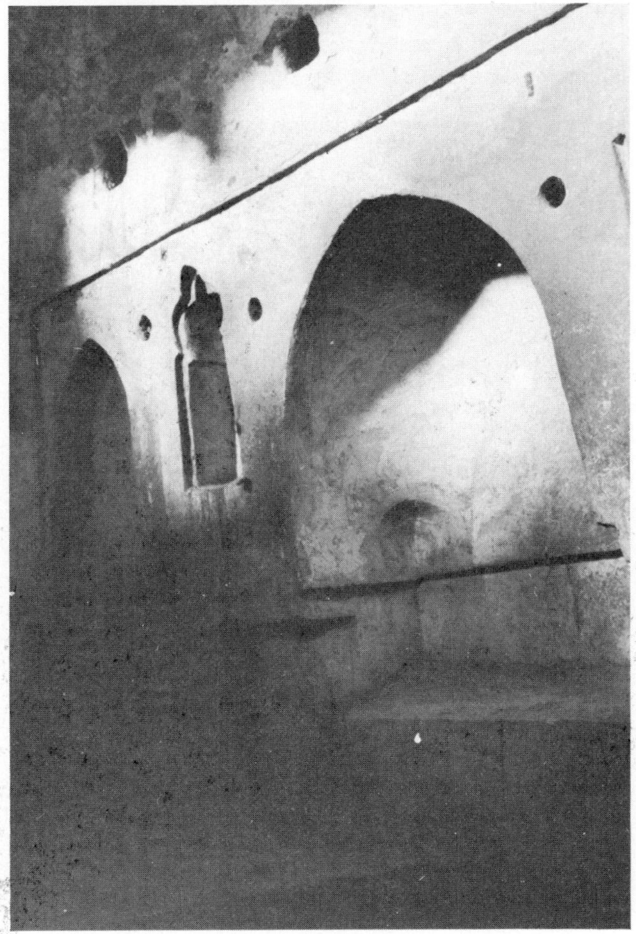

Pl. 36 Kerkuk, Mar Tahmazgerd, interior, tomb chamber, NE bays (Q 208)

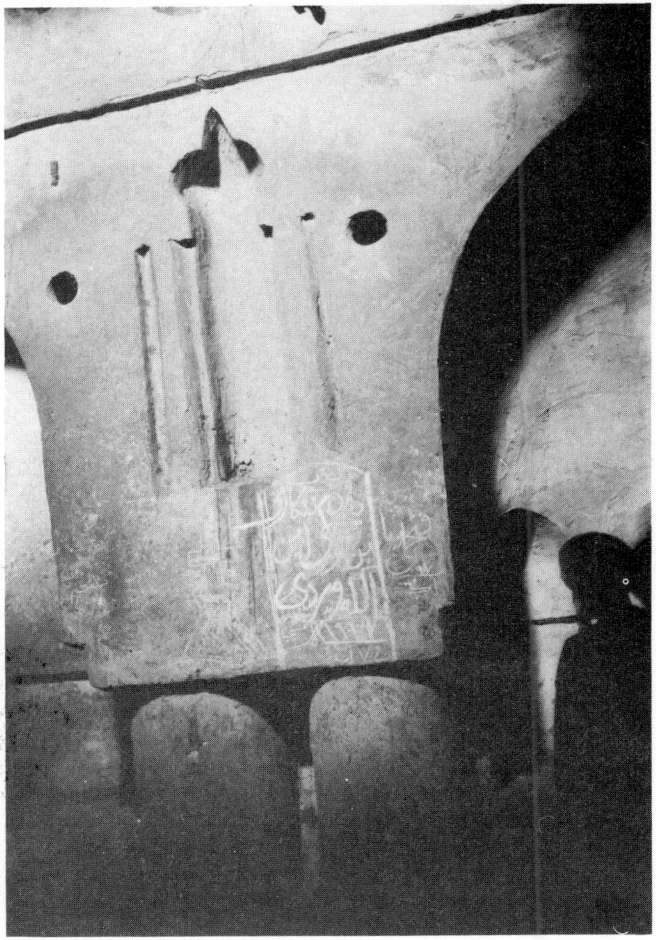

Pl. 37 Kerkuk, Mar Tahmazgerd, interior, tomb chamber, wall decoration between bays (Q 205)

Pl. 38 Mayafarqin, general view looking NW towards mosque of Salah el Din and basilica, taken from church of el ‘Adhra (S 99)

Pl. 39 Mayafarqin, basilica, S doors (S 169)

Pl. 40 Mayafarqin, basilica, exterior, E end from SE (S 168)

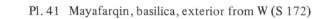

Pl. 41 Mayafarqin, basilica, exterior from W (S 172)

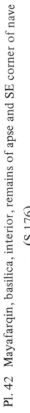

Pl. 42 Mayafarqin, basilica, interior, remains of apse and SE corner of nave (S 176)

Pl. 43 Mayafarqin, basilica, interior, S arcade, W capital, S face (S 170)

Pl. 44 Mayafarqin, basilica, interior, S arcade, W capital, N face (S 171)

Pl. 45 Mayafarqin, basilica, interior, N arcade, W capital, S face (S 175)

Pl. 46 Mayafarqin, basilica, interior N arcade, W capital N face (S 174)

Pl. 48 Mayafarqin, mosque of Salah ed Din, reused (?) column base (S 151)

Pl. 47 Mayafarqin, mosque of Salah ed Din, columns taken from basilica (?) (S 149)

Pl. 49 Mayafarqin, archway near basilica (S 178)

Pl. 50 Mayafarqin, now in Diyarbakır Museum, marble sarcophagus/reliquary found in Saray (S 199)

Pl. 51 Mayafarqin, el ‘Adhra (?), loose slab with relief of eagle (S 188)

Pl. 52 From Mayafarqin, now in British Museum, carved slab, side one (photo Beylié)

Pl. 53 From Mayafarqin, now in British Museum, carved slab, side two (photo Beylié)

Pl. 54 Mayafarqin, el ‘Adhra, exterior from E (S 178)

Pl. 55 Mayafarqin, el ‘Adhra, N facade from NE (S 177)

Pl. 56 Mayafarqin, el ‘Adhra, W façade from SW (S 180–181)

Pl. 57. Mayafarqin, el ‘Adhra, interior, N and E walls (S 184, 185, 186, 189)

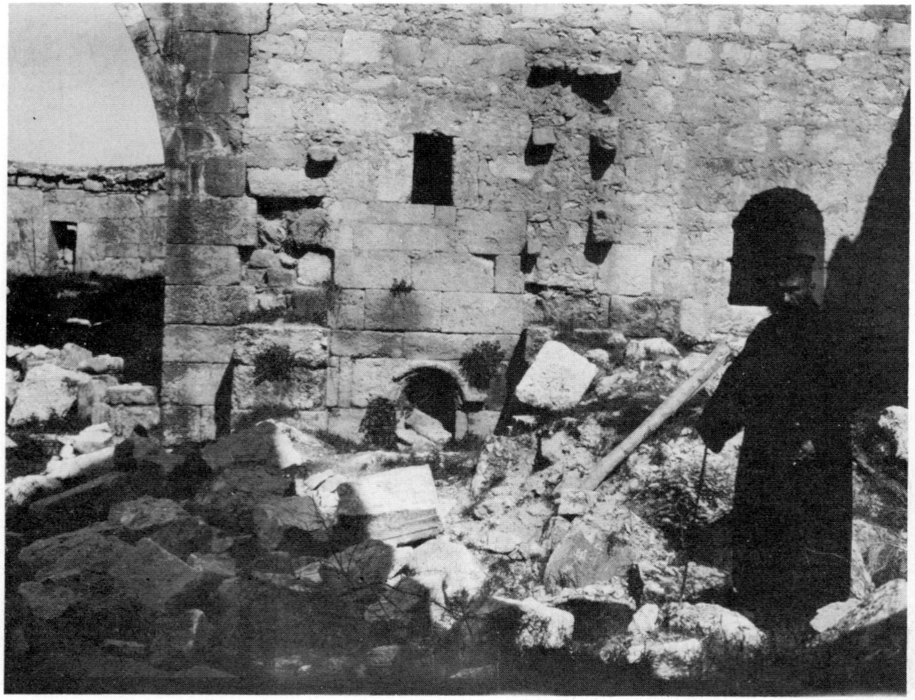

Pl. 58 Mayafarqin, el ‘Adhra, interior, SE wall (S 192)

Pl. 59 Mayafarqin, el ‘Adhra, interior, nave, SW corner looking SW (S 194)

Pl. 60 Mayafarqin, el ‘Adhra, interior, nave looking W (S 195)

Pl. 61 Mayafarqin, el 'Adhra, interior, NW pier looking E (S 182)

Pl. 62 Mayafarqin, el 'Adhra, interior, capital of W pier (S 183)

Pl. 63 Mayafarqin, el ‘Adhra, interior, second storey of NW pier, capital (S 179)

Pl. 64 Mayafarqin, el ‘Adhra, interior, capital of NE piers (S 198)

Pl. 65 Mayafarqin, el ‘Adhra, interior, capital of engaged pier N of apse (S 191)

Pl. 66 Mayafarqin, el ‘Adhra, interior, W column basket capital (S 197)

Pl. 67a Dara, basket capital (R 117)

Pl. 67b Dara, capital (R 118)

Pl. 68 Nisibin, colonnade near S gate of city (R 105)

Pl. 69 Nisibin, bridge over Djaghjagh (Mygdonius) River (R 86)

Pl. 70 Nisibin, Mar Ya'qub, exterior, E end from SE (R 89)

Pl. 71 Nisibin, Mar Ya'qub, S facade (R 91)

Pl. 72 Nisibin, Mar Ya'qub, W façade, N half (R 88)

Pl. 73 Nisibin, Mar Ya'qub, N façade (R 87)

Pl. 74 Nisibin, Mar Ya'qub, S façade, second arch from W, on R
Greek inscription of AD 359 (R 94)

Pl. 75 Nisibin, Mar Ya'qub, S façade, E arch (R 99)

Pl. 76 Nisibin, Mar Ya'qub, S façade, second arch from E (R 98)

Pl. 77 Nisibin, Mar Ya'qub, interior, N chamber, door in S wall leading into SW chamber (R 100)

Pl. 78 Nisibin, Mar Ya'qub, interior, SE chamber, looking E (R 92)

Pl. 79 Nisibin, Mar Ya'qub, interior, SE chamber, NW corner (R 96)

Pl. 80 Nisibin, Mar Ya'qub, interior SE chamber, capital on W side (R 95)

Pl. 81 Nisibin, Mar Ya'qub, interior, N chamber, jamb of door in S wall (R 97)

Pl. 82. Nisibin, Mar Ya'qub, interior, SW chamber, font (R 103)

Pl. 83 Nisibin, Mar Ya'qub, exterior, loose basket capital (R 104)

Pl. 84 Urfa, E city gate (T 206)

Pl. 85 Urfa, bridge outside E city gate (T 207)

Pl. 86 Urfa, loose capital in Saray (T 194)

Pl. 87 Viranşehir, *tetrapylon* (?), view of one pier with half column (T 141)

Pl. 88 Viranşehir, *tetrapylon* (?), view of another pier with half column (T 142)

Pl. 89 Viranşehir, "octagon" W of city, general view looking S: octagon piers nos. 1, 6, 2–4 and (on R) W porch pier, no. 9 (T 133)

Pl. 90 Viranşehir, "octagon" W of city, piers nos. 1–2 from N (T 135)

Pl. 91 Viranşehir, "octagon" W of city, general view looking SW: piers nos. 1–4, 6, 9 (T 138)

Pl. 92 Viranşehir, "octagon" W of city, piers 4–2 looking E; in foreground remains of stairwell (no. 10) of W porch (T 131)

Pl. 93 Viranşehir, "octagon" W of city, octagon piers nos. 4–3 on L; porch pier no. 9 on R (T 139)

Pl. 94 Viranşehir, "octagon" W of city, general view from SW (from L): piers nos. 6, 9, 4, 3 (T 134)

Pl. 95 Viranşehir, "octagon" W of city, octagon pier no. 6 from SW (T 137)

Pl. 96 Viranşehir, "octagon" W of city, keystone (?) with cross (T 140)

Pl. 97 Arnas, Mar Cyriacus, exterior, SE end from S (R 202b)

Pl. 98 Arnas, Mar Cyriacus, exterior, two exedras *(beth ṣlotha)* S of church (M 196)

Pl. 99 Arnas, Mar Cyriacus, interior, nave looking E (R 203)

Pl. 100 Arnas, Mar Cyriacus, interior, apse archivolt and templon screen; on far L inscription of AD 1591/2; in lower R that of ca. AD 750 (M 198)

Pl. 101 Arnas, Mar Cyriacus, apse archivolt, top (R 203)

Pl. 102 Arnas, Mar Cyriacus, apse archivolt lower R side (M 201)

Pl. 103 Arnas, Mar Cyriacus, S capital of apse (R 204)

Pl. 104 Arnas, Mar Cyriacus, apse cornice (M 200)

Pl. 105 Ba Sebrina, Mar Dodo, *beth ṣlotha* (with Syriac inscription on archivolt) S of church (M 108)

Pl. 106 Ba Sebrina, Deir Barṣauma, general view (M 104)

Pl. 107   Ba Sebrina, Deir Miriam el 'Adhra, exterior of church (M 105)

Pl. 108   Fafi, tower tomb, S façade, Greek inscription (R 174)

Pl. 109   Fafi, tower tomb, fallen cornice block (R 178)

Pl. 110 Fafi, tower tomb, from SE (R 176)

Pl. 110a Fafi, tower tomb, S façade, capital and entablature (R 174)

Pl. 111 Fafi, tower tomb, E façade (R 177)

Pl. 112 Fafi, tower tomb, E façade, capital and entablature (R 179)

Pl. 113 Fafi, circuit walls (R 181)

Pl. 114 Fafi, circuit walls (R 182)

Pl. 115   Ḥabsenas, Mar Lazarus, tower (S 6 b)

Pl. 116   Ḥaḥ, Mar Sovo, profiles and mouldings

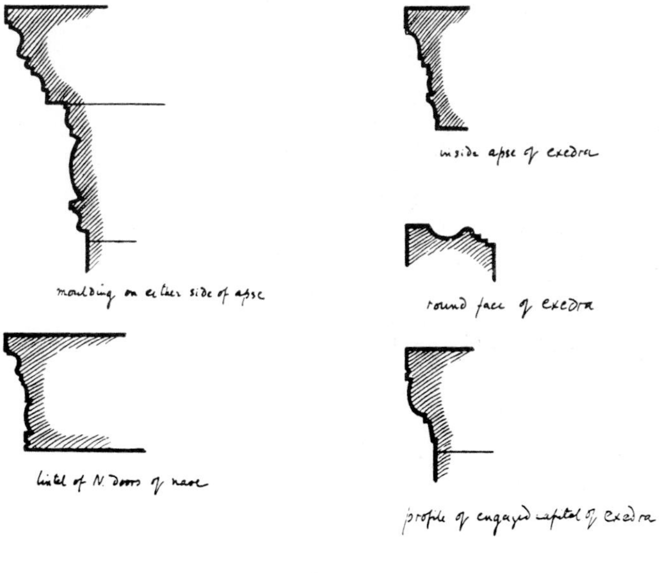

Pl. 117 Ḥaḥ, Mar Sovo, exterior from the N (N 1)

Pl. 118 Ḥaḥ, Mar Sovo, exterior SW corner from SW (N 4)

Pl. 119 Ḥaḥ, Mar Sovo, interior, N aisle looking E (N 3 a)

Pl. 120 Ḥaḥ, Mar Sovo, interior, N nave wall from SE (N 9)

Pl. 121 Ḥaḥ, Mar Sovo, interior, apse (N 12 x)

Pl. 122 Ḥaḥ, Mar Sovo, interior, N corner of apse (N 16)

Pl. 123 Ḥaḥ, Mar Sovo, vault E of apse (N 6)

Pl. 124 Ḥaḥ, Mar Sovo, door on S side, outer face N (N 17)

Pl. 125 Ḥaḥ, Mar Sovo, door on S side, inner face (N 14)

Pl. 126 Ḥaḥ, Mar Sovo, exedra (*beth ṣlotha*
S of church, with tower in background (N 1

Pl. 127 Ḥaḥ, Mar Sovo, exedra (*beth ṣlotha*
cornice (N 21)

Pl. 128 Ḥaḥ, Mar Sovo, exedra (*beth ṣlotha*)
S capital (N 19)

Pl. 129 Ḥaḥ, unidentified building, W façade (N 23)

Pl. 130 Ḥaḥ, unidentified building, S façade (N 24)

Pl. 131 Ḥaḥ, el 'Adhra, before restoration of 1903 (photo Parry, 1892)

Pl 132 Ḥaḥ, el 'Adhra, general view from SW (M 218)

Pl. 133 Ḥaḥ, el ‘Adhra, exterior from E (M 221)

Pl. 134 Ḥah, el ‘Adhra, W façade (M 219)

Pl. 135 Ḥaḥ, el ‘Adhra, N façade (M 220)

Pl. 136 Ḥaḥ, el ‘Adhra, N façade, pilaster at NW corner of narthex (M 253)

Pl. 137 Ḥaḥ, el ‘Adhra, detail of tambour on W side (S 4 a)

Pl. 138 Ḥaḥ, el ‘Adhra, exterior of tambour on W side (S 5)

Pl. 139 Ḥaḥ, el ʻAdhra, interior, central door from narthex into nave, N half (M 224)

Pl. 140 Ḥaḥ, el ʻAdhra, interior, S side of dome (M 226)

Pl. 141 Ḥaḥ, el ‘Adhra, interior, S half of door in Pl. 139 (M 222)

Pl. 142 Ḥaḥ, el ‘Adhra, interior, SE dome squinch (M 229)

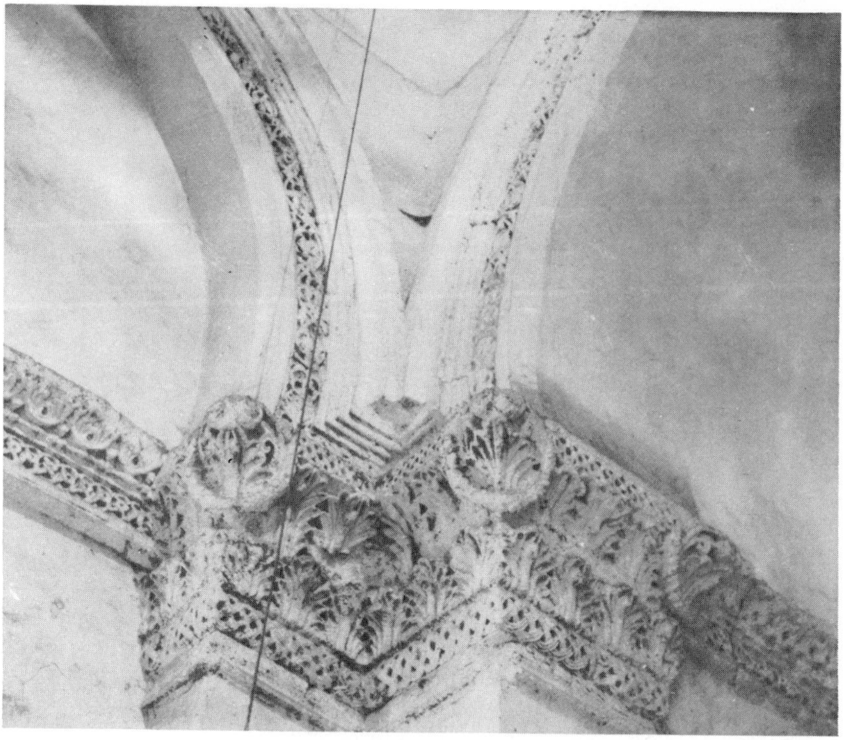

Pl. 143 Ḥaḥ, el ‘Adhra, interior, NW piers supporting dome (M 230)

Pl. 144 Ḥaḥ, el ‘Adhra, interior, N apse, cornice (M 227)

Pl. 145 Ḥaḥ, el ‘Adhra, interior, capital of apse niche (M 228)

Pl. 146 Ḥaḥ, el ‘Adhra, silver gospel book cover *Anastasis* (M 239)

Pl. 147 Ḥaḥ, Yaldath Alaha, doorway with Syriac inscription of AD 740 (N 26)

Pl. 148 Ḥaḥ, Mary Magdalen, interior, W chamber, niches and squinch (N 27)

Pl. 149 Ḥaḥ, tower N of Mary Magdalen (N 25)

Pl. 150 Harabe ‘Ale, ruins of church of Mar (Theo)doras (M 145)

Pl. 151 Heshterek, Mar Addai church and *beth ṣlotha* (AD 772) (S 9)

Pl. 152 Kefr Zeh, Mar ‘Azaziel, exterior, general view from NE (M 205)

Pl. 153 Kefr Zeh, Mar ‘Azaziel, exterior, general view from NW (M 202)

Pl. 154 Kefr Zeh, Mar ‘Azaziel, gable of W façade (M 203)

Pl. 155   Kefr Zeh, Mar ‘Azaziel, S façade with narthex (M 207)

Pl. 156 Kefr Zeh, Mar ‘Azaziel, exedra (*beth ṣlotha*) S of church (AD 934/5) (M 204)

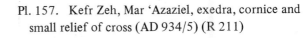

Pl. 157. Kefr Zeh, Mar ‘Azaziel, exedra, cornice and small relief of cross (AD 934/5) (R 211)

Pl. 158 Kefr Zeh, Mar ‘Azaziel, interior, nave looking E (R 208)

Pl. 159 Kefr Zeh, Mar ‘Azaziel, interior, N capital of apse (M 210)

Pl. 160 Kefr Zeḥ, Mar ‘Azaziel, interior, apse cornice (M 211)

Pl. 161 Kefr Zeh, Mar ‘Azaziel, interior, apse with templon screen (M 209)

Pl. 162 Kefr Zeh, Mar ‘Azaziel, interior, templon screen, N side (R 212)

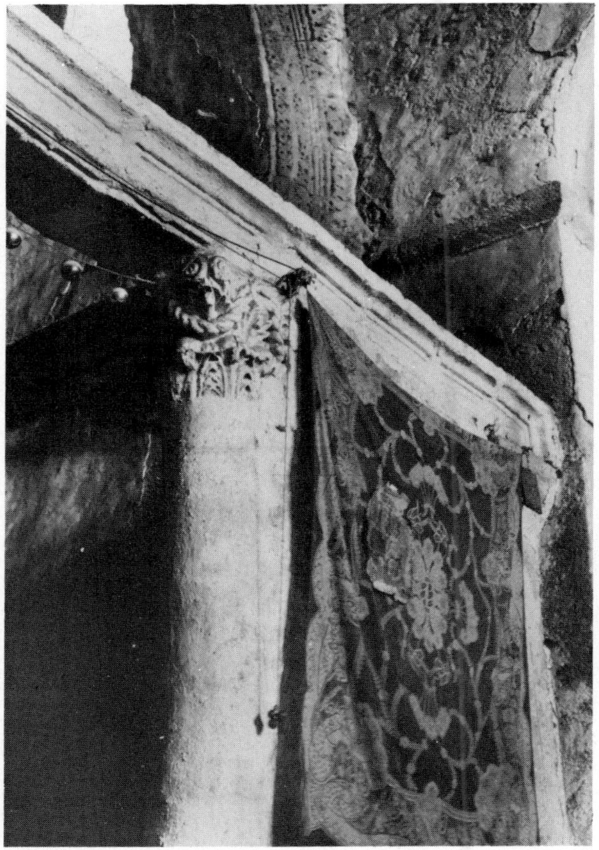

Pl. 163 Kefr Zeh, Mar ‘Azaziel, interior, templon screen, S side (R 213)

Pl. 164 Kefr Zeh, Mar ‘Azaziel, interior, nave vault (R 214)

Pl. 165 Kefr Zeh, Mar 'Azaziel, interior, nave, N arcade and vault (M 212)

Pl. 166 Kefr Zeh, Mar Yoḥannan, exterior from W (R 205)

Pl. 167. Kersifan, shrine, from S court (R 185)

Pl. 168. Kersifan, shrine, N court looking S (R 184)

Pl. 169. Midyat, Mar Philoxenus, exterior, E end from E (R 190)

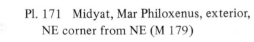

Pl. 170 Midyat, Mar Philoxenus, exterior, E end, apse conch from above (M 181)

Pl. 171 Midyat, Mar Philoxenus, exterior, NE corner from NE (M 179)

Pl. 172 Midyat, Mạr Philoxenus, capital (M 177)

Pl. 173 Midyat, Mar Philoxenus, exterior from S (M 173)

Pl. 174 Midyat, Mar Philoxenus, interior, apse and S wall (M 178)

Pl. 175 Midyat, Mar Philoxenus, interior, S arcade (M 175)

Pl. 176 Midyat, Mar Ibrahim and Mar Ubil, W façade of N church, with unidentified monastic buildings on L (M 163)

Pl. 177 Midyat, Mar Ibrahim and Mar Ubil, corner between N and central churches, looking SE (M 164)

Pl. 178 Midyat, Mar Ibrahim and Mar Ubil, W façade of central church (M 165)

Pl. 179 Midyat, Mar Ibrahim and Mar Ubil, W door of central church (M 168)

Pl. 180 Midyat, Mar Ibrahim and Mar Ubil, E façade (M 161)

Pl. 181 Midyat, Mar Ibrahim and Mar Ubil, N church, interior, door (M 167)

Pl. 182 Midyat, Mar Ibrahim and Mar Ubil, main gate, door lintel with Syriac inscription (M 160)

Pl. 183 Midyat, Mar Ibrahim and Mar Ubil, main gate, door jamb with Syriac inscription (M 162)

Pl. 184 (Monastery of) Deir Ṣaliba, general view (N 29)

Pl. 185 (Monastery of) Deir Ṣaliba, exedra *(beth ṣlotha)* (N 30)

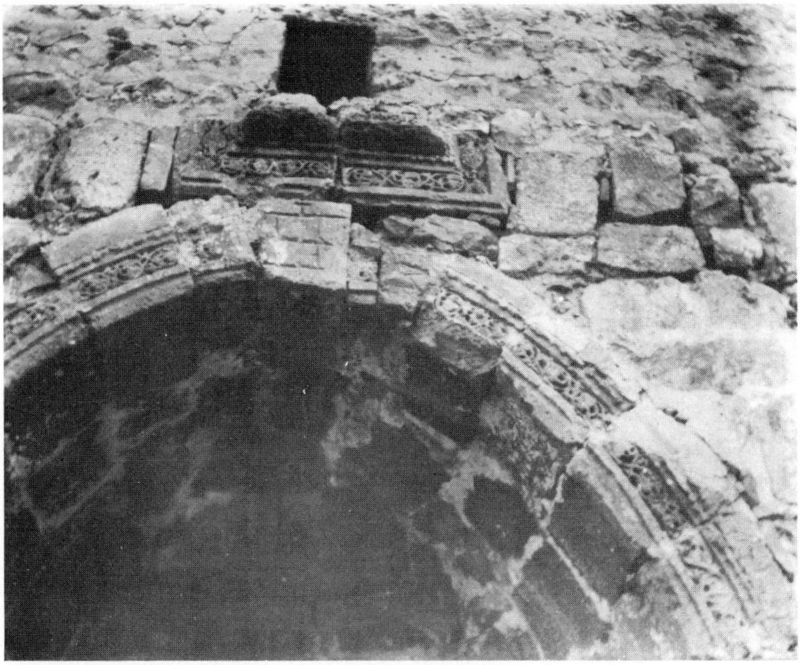

Pl. 186 (Monastery of) Deir Ṣaliba,
exedra, archivolt and window with Syriac inscription (N 33)

Pl. 187 (Monastery of) Deir Ṣaliba, exedra, capitals and bracket (N 32)

Pl. 188 (Monastery of) Deir Za'faran,
courtyard looking E to main church and S chapel (R 162)

Pl. 189 (Monastery of) Deir Za‘faran, main church, exterior, cornice (R 161 b)

Pl. 190 (Monastery of) Deir Za'faran, main church, entrance,

Pl. 191 (Monastery of) Deir Za'faran, main church, entrance,

Pl. 192 (Monastery of) Deir Za‘faran, S chapel, entrance, exterior L niche (R 163)

Pl. 193 (Monastery of) Deir Za‘faran, S chapel, entrance, exterior R niche (R 164)

Pl. 194 (Monastery of) Deir Za‘faran, main church, interior, NW corner (R 168)

Pl. 195 (Monastery of) Deir Za'faran, main church, interior, N apse (R 171)

Pl. 196 (Monastery of) Deir Za'faran, main church, interior, NE corner (R 172)

Pl. 197 (Monastery of) Deir Za'faran, main church, interior, E apse (R 173)

Pl. 198 (Monastery of) Deir Za'faran, main church, interior, niche in NW corner (R 167)

Pl. 199 Monastery of Mar Awgen, general view from W (M 122)

Pl. 200 Monastery of Mar Awgen, olive press (M 121)

Pl. 201 Monastery of Mar Awgen, cloister, NE corner (M 126)

Pl. 202 Monastery of Mar Awgen, cloister, SW corner, column capital (M 132)

Pl. 203 Monastery of Mar Awgen, cloister, SW corner (M 125)

Pl. 204 Monastery of Mar Awgen, church,
interior looking E to NE corner of nave (M 129)

Pl. 205 Monastery of Mar Awgen, open court looking E (M 131)

Pl. 206 Monastery of Mar Awgen,
square chamber E of open court, setting of dome (M 130)

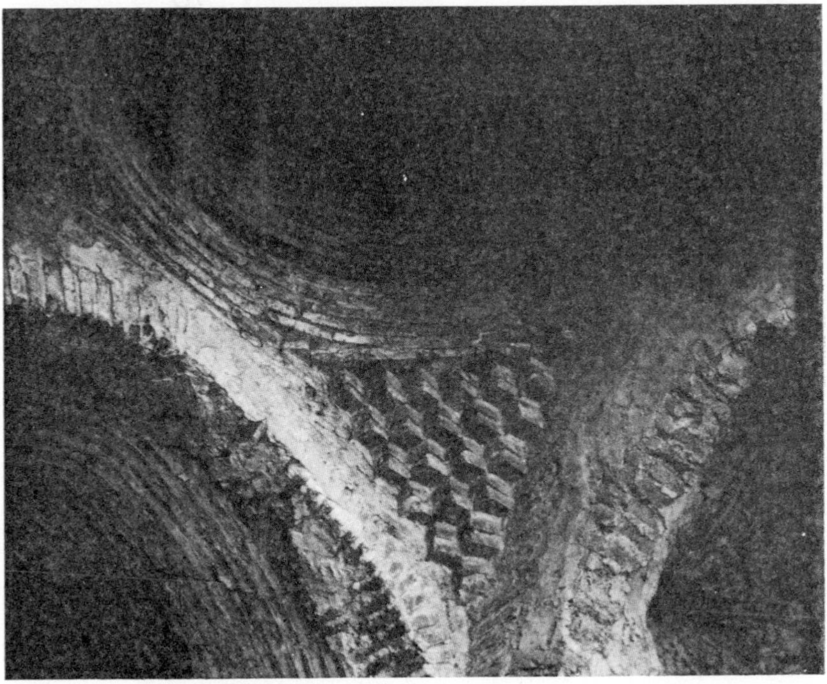

Pl. 207 Monastery of Mar Gabriel, general view from SW (M 147)

Pl. 208 Monastery of Mar Gabriel, tomb of Egyptian Monks (M 146)

Pl. 209 Monastery of Mar Gabriel, church of Mar Shim'un: example of brick masonry in Ṭur 'Abdin (M 150)

Pl. 210 Monastery of Mar Gabriel, exterior N wall (M 153)

Pl. 211 Monastery of Mar Gabriel,
courtyard looking SE to roof of main church (M 156)

Pl. 212 Monastery of Mar Gabriel, courtyard looking E, in centre: exterior wall of octagon (R 194)

Pl. 213 Monastery of Mar Gabriel, courtyard looking NE, on R: main church portico (M 158)

Pl. 214 Monastery of Mar Gabriel, main church portico, looking SE (M 157)

Pl. 215 Monastery of Mar Gabriel, main church, S facade (M 152)

Pl. 216 Monastery of Mar Gabriel, main church, E façade looking SW (M 151)

Pl. 217 Monastery of Mar Gabriel, main church, interior NW corner of nave (R 198)

Pl. 218 Monastery of Mar Gabriel, main church, interior, N wall of nave (R 199)

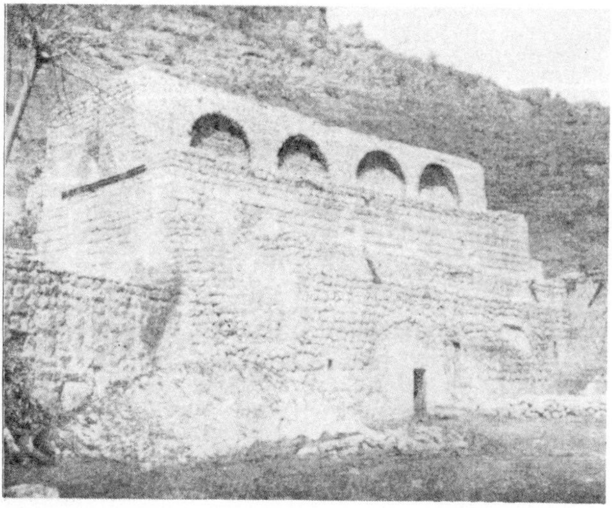

Pl. 219. Monastery of Mar Ibrahim, church, exterior from SW (photo Hinrichs)
Pl. 220. Monastery of Mar Ibrahim, church interior, capital (photo Hinrichs)

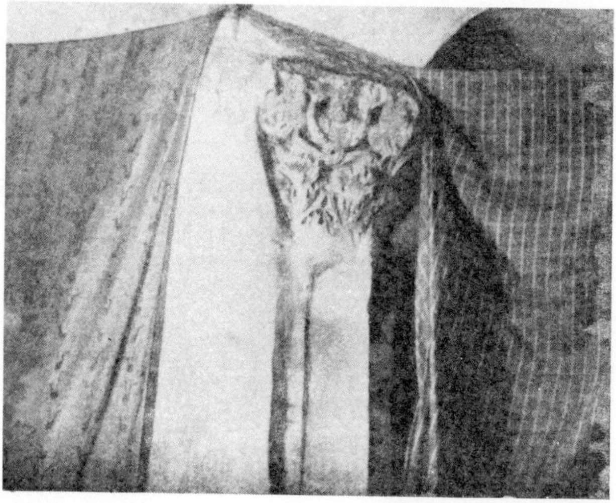

Pl. 221 Monastery of Mar Ibrahim, outside church, loose cornice block (photo Hinrichs)

Pl. 222 Monastery of Mar Malka, exterior, general view (M 140)

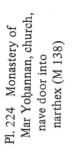

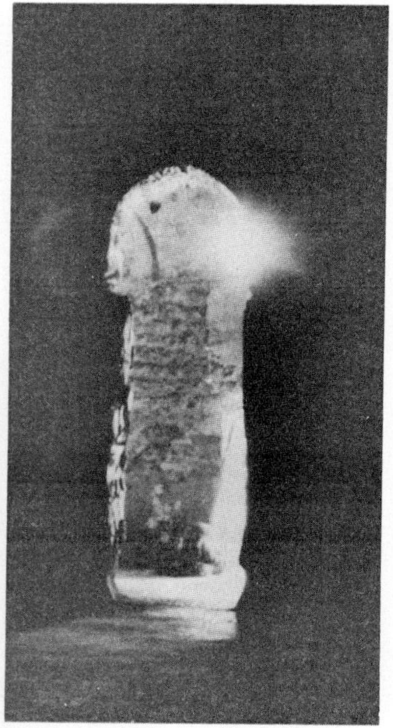

Pl. 224 Monastery of Mar Yoḥannan, church, nave door into narthex (M 138)

Pl. 223 Monastery of Mar Yoḥannan, general view from W with church in centre (M 133)

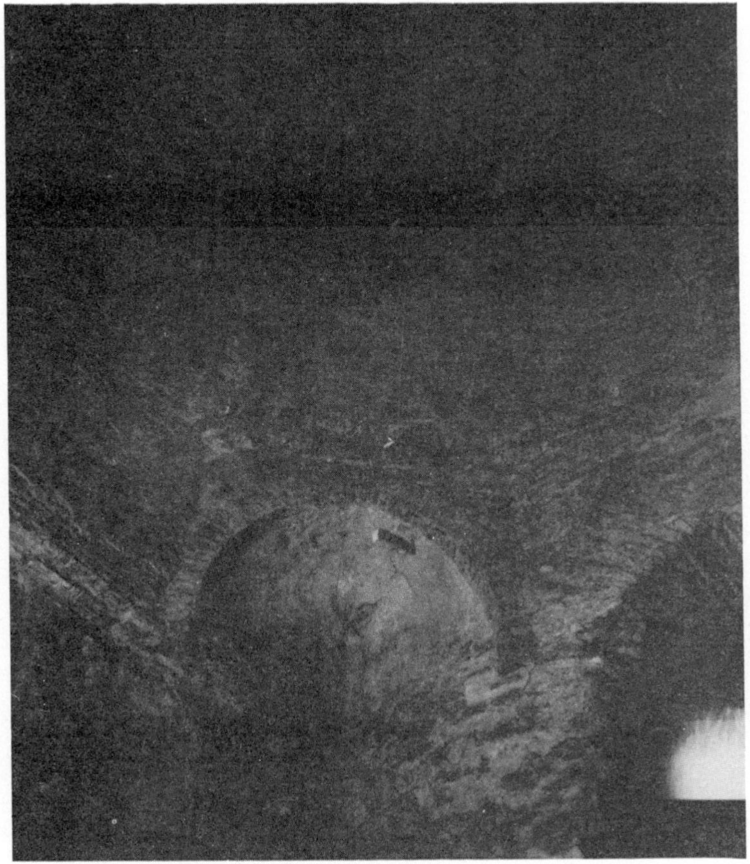

Pl. 225 Monastery of Mar Yoḥannan, church, setting of narthex dome (M 137)

Pl. 226 Monastery of Mar Yoḥannan, tower (M 136)

Pl. 227 Qal'at el Jedid, general view (M 119)

Pl. 228 Qal'at Hatem Tay, general view (M 114)

Pl. 229 Qal'at Hatem Tay, Arabic inscription of AD 1232/2 (M 117)

Pl. 230 Qal'at Hatem Tay, apse of chapel (M 118)

Pl. 231 Qal'at Hatem Tay, vault (M 116)

Pl. 232 Ṣalaḥ, Mar Ya'qub Ḥabisha, W façade pier capital (M 189)

Pl. 233 Ṣalaḥ, Mar Ya‘qub Ḥabisha, exterior from W (M 188)

Pl. 234 Ṣalaḥ, Mar Ya‘qub Ḥabisha, S façade (M 182)

Pl. 235 Ṣalaḥ, Mar Ya'qub Ḥabisha, narthex door in S façade (M 191)

Pl. 236 Ṣalaḥ, Mar Ya'qub Ḥabisha, E door in S façade (M 187)

Pl. 237 Ṣalaḥ, Mar Ya'qub Ḥabisha, N façade (M 186)

Pl. 238 Ṣalaḥ, Mar Ya‘qub Ḥabisha, view from E (M 184)

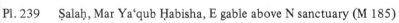

Pl. 239 Ṣalaḥ, Mar Ya‘qub Ḥabisha, E gable above N sanctuary (M 185)

Pl. 240 Ṣalaḥ, Mar Ya‘qub Ḥabisha, E wall, window into N sanctuary (M 190)

Pl. 241 Ṣalaḥ, Mar Ya‘qub Ḥabisha, ruins N of church, patriarchal palace (?) (M 183)

Pl. 242 Ṣalaḥ, Mar Ya'qub Ḥabisha, interior, narthex barrel vault (M 194)

Pl. 243 Ṣalaḥ, Mar Ya'qub Ḥabisha, interior, narthex door into nave (M 193)

Pl. 244 Ṣalaḥ, Mar Ya'qub Ḥabisha, interior, nave barrel vault, looking NW (R 197)

Pl. 245 Ṣalaḥ, Mar Ya'qub Ḥabisha, interior, nave N wall (R 195)

Pl. 246 Ṣalaḥ, Mar Ya'qub Ḥabisha, interior, nave, door into sanctuary (R 193)

Pl. 247 Ṣalaḥ, Mar Ya'qub Ḥabisha, interior, nave, pilaster of door into sanctuary (R 192)

Pl. 248 Ṣalaḥ, Mar Ya'qub Ḥabisha, interior, apse, looking SE (R 196)

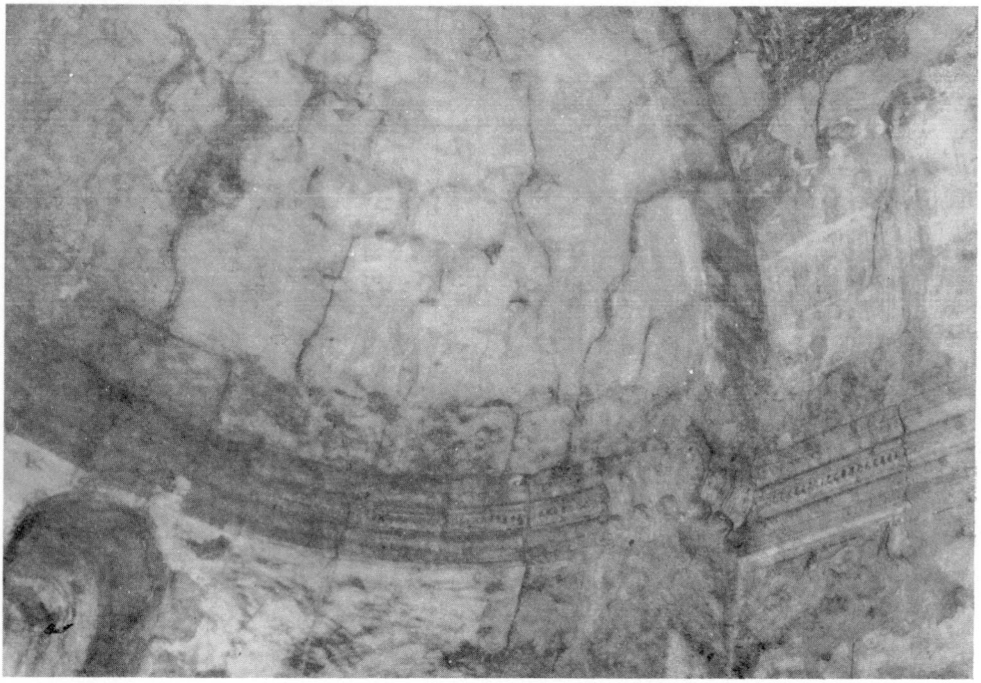

Pl. 249 Tektek Mts., Qasr Antar, exterior view of tower (T 149)

Pl. 250 Tektek Mts., Qasr Antar, interior, niche with two Corinthian capitals (T 152)

Pl. 251 Tektek Mts., Qasr Antar, interior view of tower, capital of niche (T 150)

Pl. 252 Tektek Mts., Qasr el Benat, general view (T 146)

Pl. 253 Tektek Mts., Sha'ib Shahr, general view of ruins (T 159)

Pl. 254 Tektek Mts., Sha'ib Shahr, domestic building (T 155)

Pl. 255 Tektek Mts., Sha'ib Shahr, domestic building, façade with open arcade (T 157)

Pl. 256 Tektek Mts., Sha'ib Shahr, domestic building, interior (T 156)